The Complete
Needlepoint Guide

400+ Needlepoint Stitches

Susan Sturgeon-Roberts

Published by

**krause
publications**

700 East State St., Iola, WI 54990-0001
715-445-2214
www.krause.com

Please, call or write us for our free catalog of publications.
To place an order or receive our free catalog, call 800-258-0929. For editorial comment and further information,
use our regular business telephone at (715) 445-2214

Library of Congress Catalog Number: 99-69483
ISBN: 0-87341-793-3
Printed in the United States of America

Table of Contents

Dedication

This book is dedicated to my husband, Eugene, and to Chottie Alderson. Without their support and love, this book would not have been written.

Acknowledgments

Any project such as this could never be accomplished without the generous help of many. I would like to express my gratitude to the following people for their stitches: Chottie Alderson—for Ashley, Beau Ridge, Buttonhole Flowers, Chottie's Plaid, Criss Cross Hungarian, Dana, Duck's Foot, Erin's Ridge, Framed Scotch Variation, Frosty, Ley's Trail, New Cah's Walk, Ridges, Rubato and Sandy's Slide; Anne Dyer—for Papermoon; Arte Johnson—for Arte's; Mary Lou Helgesen—for Belly Feathers and Doublet. My thanks, too, to Dot Clark for her "Unicorn in Captivity" pillow.

The following companies have graciously contributed to this project by giving permission to use their designs:

Alice Peterson Company for "Unicorn in Captivity"

Bucilla Corporation for a pre-worked motif featuring a chair seat

Ets Steiner Frères for Pinky and Blue Boy

Janlynn Corporation for Horizon's design of a boat motif.

I would also like to acknowledge the DMC Corporation for providing yarn cards.

While much care has been taken to trace and acknowledge the work of needle artists, I am surely not infallible. Any errors in acknowledgment are mine alone.

For the many hours of modeling in the photos, I thank Katie Ehresman. Without her hands, the steps would not have been illustrated. I also thank Art Browne, my computer expert. I am indebted to Phil Watkins, my photograph expert and instructor, for all his help and expertise. For help in drafting the illustrations, I thank my husband, Gene, without whose encouragement this book would not have been accomplished.

Finally, I would express my appreciation to the readers.

Happy stitching!

Introduction

It seems that for almost as long as humans have been producing textiles, we have looked for ways to embellish the work, to add beauty with color and design, and perhaps with an extra thread here and there for decoration. From this desire for the beautiful, the art of needlework has sprung. Almost every culture has its own forms of needle arts, ranging from the Blackwork in Spain, to Crewel from England, to White work, which has been adapted in almost every country, to patchwork quilting in the United States. Needlepoint is a very popular form of needlework art.

The definition of needlepoint varies from one individual to the next, as needle arts vary from culture to culture. Some people envision embroidery stitches on canvas. Others think of needlepoint as the mother of all needle crafts. Needlepoint refers to more than these simplified definitions. In many cases, the stitches differ from other embroideries, since the yarns are worked on a canvas. Because the yarns used in needlepoint are heavier than threads used in other stitched arts, a more dramatic effect can be achieved. Working the stitches and designs over squares prevents smooth, round curves.

Needlepoint, like painting or sculpting, is truly an art. Much of early history has been handed down to us on embroidery, depicting events or persons of ancient times. In earlier times, the embroiderer was also the designer. Many men devoted their lives to needle arts. The word "point" comes from the French word meaning "stitch." Needlepoint is exactly that—stitching with a needle. If one refers to the terms "canvas embroidery," "canvas work" or "tapestry," he addresses the concept of needlepoint.

The term "canvas work" refers to any stitching worked upon canvas. This includes embroidery stitches and needle weaving. Needlepoint includes many techniques, such as counted thread, abstracts, rug making and pulled work. All these can be done on canvas. This book does not cover these particular techniques, although they are accepted techniques.

Included in this book is a discussion of materials, stitches and techniques. The beginner will find a fine introduction to the subject, and the intermediate and advanced needlepointers can find new approaches, stitches, techniques and ideas for their own work.

Needlepoint can be categorized by size. The size refers to the number of stitches per inch—that is, the number of individual stitches that fit into a linear inch. The three main categories are Petit Point (16 to 100 stitches per inch), Demi Point (8 to 15 stitches per inch) and Quickpoint (3 to 7 stitches per inch). Quickpoint is also known as "Pointo Grando." This is Portuguese for "large stitches." Gros Point refers to cross stitch, but some use the name interchangeably with Quickpoint.

Earlier, tapestries were made using even, smooth Tent stitches. These magnificent pieces resemble detailed woven fabric. In fine estates, large canopy beds featured fine needlepoint hangings. Imagine sleeping in a bed with yards of needlepoint draped around you!

Today, needlepoint offers that same cozy comfort. A large pile of stitched pillows on a bed evokes warm emotions that you may have had as a child, when visiting Grandma's house.

Today, needlepoint comes in many different forms. Following along traditional lines, projects range from pillows to pictures. Other projects reflect our changing lifestyles. Of these, we have lamps, cups, clothes, shoes, mouse pads and pockets for our personal stereos. Mobiles, toys and other three-dimensional objects are created and stitched on plastic canvas. Whether our projects reflect the contemporary or the traditional, the world of needlepoint has changed from the way it was years ago.

Canvas embroidery offers the adventure of turning everyday objects into small works of individual art, while lending character to the home or office, enlightening and decorating a room. Stitching can even inspire friendships. Sitting and stitching your latest project can be truly calming to the most ragged nerves! Depression melts away as the needle travels through the canvas. Nevertheless, the most important reason to needlepoint is for the pure, solitary enjoyment it offers.

- Susan Sturgeon-Roberts

Chapter One

Tools and Materials

At first glance, the aisles of needlework shops can be daunting. The canvas choices alone seem endless—and then you have to move on to the yarns! With a little explanation, the whole collection becomes much less mysterious. That is my aim here—to take away as much of the mystery as I can, and let you worry about other things.

Canvas

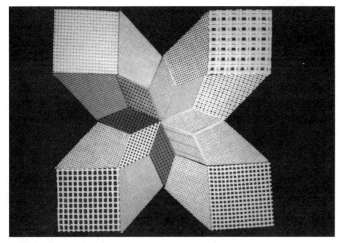

Canvas choices

Needlepoint canvas is an open-weave fabric, available in different sizes, styles, fibers and widths. Wool, cotton, silk, polyester and linen (flax) are all fibers used for canvas. Plastic is also used.

Cotton is the most commonly used fiber for canvas. Penelope and Berlin, manufactured in France and Germany, respectively, are usually made of cotton. The French canvas is firmest, clearest and most squarely set. German canvas tends to be of a lesser quality, being either too limp or too stiff. Both the French and the German canvas can be found in different widths. For projects that you might wish to wear, such as hats, cuffs and collars, polyester is a good choice for canvas. It is soft and pliable.

Raw canvas itself is strong—but add yarn, and the strength of the canvas increases greatly. With the added strength of the stitching, needlepoint is strong enough to use as upholstery, clothing and other hard-wearing items. The quality of canvas can vary greatly. Always purchase the highest quality canvas you can afford, considering the project's budget. Too many hours are spent on one project to have it last for a just few years.

If a canvas tears easily before it bears stitching, it will tear easily, too, after it is stitched. Also avoid canvases that have a dull finish. This dullness indicates either that

the canvas does not contain enough starch, or that it is made of inferior cotton threads. Sometimes the canvas is either too soft or very stiff. Some softness is imperative for the canvas. Very stiff canvas is the result of inferior threads compensated by heavy sizing. With such canvas, more effort is required to make each individual stitch, since the canvas does not allow the yarn to pass through smoothly. If the threads of a canvas are too hairy and rough, put the canvas back on the shelf and find another. Rough canvas only frays the yarn, wasting both your precious time and your expensive wool.

Good canvas features strong, polished threads and an even grid. Today's best canvas is from France or Germany. Zweigart is an example of a high quality canvas that has been available for more than 360 years.

When choosing a canvas, use your instinct. If you have doubts, pass on it.

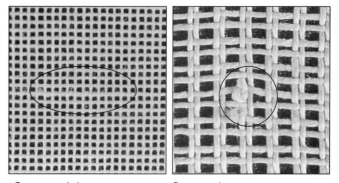

Canvas slub   Canvas knot

Inspect the canvas, looking for knots and slubs. During the blocking of the finished project, the knots could come undone. After a couple years' use, the knots could fray. This is the case with Double Mesh, Interlock and Mono canvas. When choosing break-away canvas, the fabric foundation is important—not the canvas itself.

Unravel one canvas thread. You should note four or five plies within it. The canvas should not be just a piece of string. If four or five plies are not present, you have an inferior piece of canvas. Superior canvas comes in many sizes, colors and fibers. Quality canvas is generously sized and woven in even squares.

Penelope, Mono and Interlock are your three main options, in terms of types of canvas. All are good, but one may better suit a particular purpose than another. To best determine the uses of these canvases, we need to understand the difference among them.

One of the most commonly used canvas patterns in the United States is **Mono**, "Uni" or Congress. In Mono canvas, single threads run vertically and horizontally at regular intervals, and are not bound to each other. Yellow, white and tan are the colors found most often in Mono. Mono canvas is also available in various sizes, gauged by stitches per inch. These sizes range from 10 to 24 stitches per inch.

Canvas widths range from 40" to 54". Because it has a grain, Mono is great for Continental and Basketweave stitches. Unfortunately, the weave does not allow for Half Cross—these stitches could have a tendency to disappear (see Half Cross). Quite easy on the eyes, Mono is great for counted work. In fact, Mono canvas could suit almost any project.

This canvas can become distorted after stitching, but the distortion can be corrected by blocking. When working Bargello, tan cotton and jute work best—the roughness of this canvas helps to make the stitches sharp. Cotton canvas with high polish threads allows the stitches to slip, producing unsatisfactory results.

Penelope canvas was named after Odysseus' wife. According to Greek legend, Penelope had to endure many advances by suitors claiming her husband was dead. She asked them to wait until she finished weaving a funeral pall for her father-in-law, Laertes. Every night, she would unravel what she had woven that day, thus ensuring her fidelity to her husband.

Penelope, Double Mesh and Berlin canvas are woven similarly to Mono, but these have two threads running vertically and horizontally, making figure-eights in the weave. Traditionally, these canvases are used in Europe, but they are also available on the American market. Penelope comes in both white and brown, in widths of 24" to 36".

Each pair of threads is called one mesh. This creates both wide and narrow spaces. To work with this canvas, you must train your eye to see the mesh as one intersection on the canvas. Looking at the canvas, you will notice the vertical mesh is woven closer together than the horizontal. Since the vertical mesh is always parallel to the selvage, you should always hold the canvas vertically. This enables you to see the mesh easily. If you must piece squares together for a project, the meshes will line up. Because Penelope is strong, feel free to use it for items such as upholstery, shoes, rugs or other projects that will receive much wear and tear.

Half Cross and Continental are perhaps the best used stitches with Penelope canvas, as Basketweave does not produce even stitches. Although this is true, most people stitch Penelope with Basketweave—as it is strong, and makes good upholstery.

When you examine the photographs of incorrect stitching samples, you will notice areas where the canvas was not covered correctly. This is the result when the canvas mesh is not correctly observed. To prevent problems, work areas near previously worked ones, so that your eyes can see the intersections correctly. Around the face, you will see dark brown Tent stitches on the left side. Did you notice the Tent going in the wrong direction? Do not be tempted to make this mistake. Although the Tent stitches do not touch one another, when correctly stitched, the eye sees the work as a line. Remember, needlepoint—like Impressionist art—is a series of dots on the

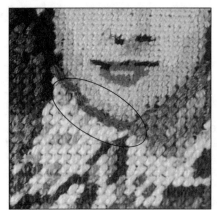

Continental running in the wrong direction

Missing stitches

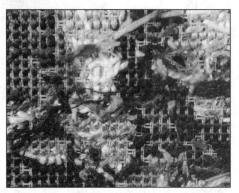

What a mess!

canvas. A short distance allows the brain to "correct" its perception, and it completes the picture.

The photograph of the arm shows Petit Point in all directions. Never use Tent Gone Wrong in a project such as this. The woman who stitched this project did not know about Tent Gone Wrong, but she worked her Tent in such a hurry, the results became a disaster. In the line of black Tent, a stitch has been missed. To avoid this, when you finish a project, hold it up to a light and check for any "holes." The holes indicate missed stitches. Filling missed areas is much easier before you have mounted the project.

Like Mono, Penelope offers a good deal of adaptability. If the needle artist wishes to add delicate detail work, she can pull the pair of threads apart and do Petit Point. One example is a motif of a lady. Using Petit Point for the head, arms and bust—and stitching Demi Point for the rest—gives detail and interest to the picture. The Petit Point area has four stitches where the

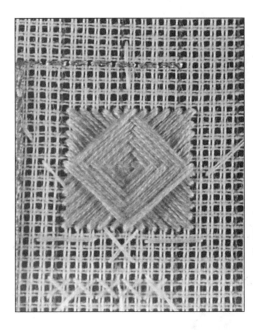

Tack down break-away canvas.

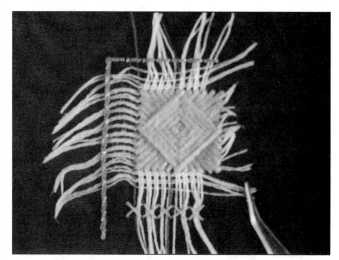

Stitch, using break-away canvas

Needlepoint on percale

Canvas removed from fabric

Demi Point has one. For projects employing Half Cross, Penelope canvas must be used to keep the stitches even and straight.

In the photo showcasing different types of canvas, you will see two that appear to have extremely thin threads. This is known as throw-away or **break-away canvas**. The purpose of break-away canvas is to create needlepoint stitches on a background of regular fabric. Woven yardage usually does not accept needlepoint stitches. Often, the weave is not correct.

To use break-away canvas, place the canvas where you would like to have the stitches, and tack it down with white sewing thread. Then, using the canvas threads as a guide, stitch through both the canvas and the fabric. When you have finished stitching your project, immerse the entire piece in water. The canvas will soften. It will want to pull apart—but do not panic! This is just what

you want. Very carefully, pull the canvas out of the stitches. This takes some time, but patience is worth the result. Years ago, I stitched an old house with black yarn on white fabric. It took me two days to remove the canvas completely. The time was well spent—I was very happy with the result. Never use break-away canvas as a foundation. Its sizing and thread weight were not made for any purpose other than disposal after the stitching has been accomplished.

Interlock canvas does not unravel as much as Penelope or Mono. The threads are similar to Penelope, but in Interlock, two threads are twisted together to make one. Interlock canvas is the least likely to distort, making it an excellent choice for a project involving a garment or household item that would get heavy wear. Although it resembles Penelope in that it features two threads running horizontally and vertically, Interlock's threads cannot be split to add

Petit Point to a project. This canvas is at its best for counted work and cross stitching. The grid is even and will not give you a false count like Penelope could. Like Penelope, Interlock is available in tan and white.

Canvas widths can vary greatly. Smaller sizes of canvas are generally available in narrower widths than the larger sizes. The range for sizes is 24" to 60", with most gauges available in 36" to 60". The term "mesh," or "gauge," refers to the number of stitches or threads in one linear inch. This can range from 3-1/2 to 70 stitches per inch. For example, number 10 canvas has 10 threads running left to right in a linear inch. Number 18 means 18 stitches per inch, 14 indicates 14 stitches per linear inch and 6 means 6 for one inch.

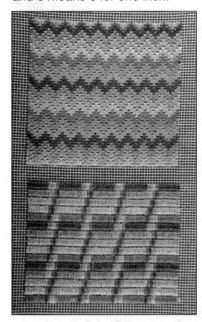

Silk canvas

Silk canvas normally has a smaller count and is well suited for delicate and fine work. It can be found in many colors including white, black, chalet and primrose. Silk canvases range in width from half an inch to a yard and a half

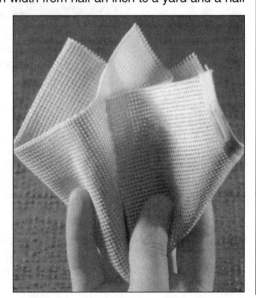

Soft canvas

wide. Silk canvas is made of silk wrapped around cotton thread. It is purchased by the square inch.

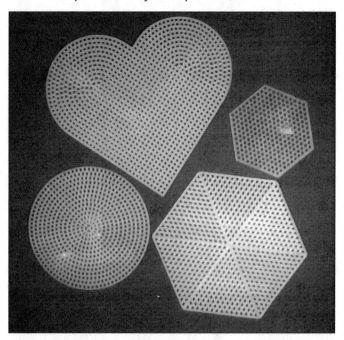

Canvas shapes

Plastic canvas usually comes in 11" by 14" sheets. With a close eye, you might find a larger sheet. Plastic canvas was developed for three-dimensional items. It is easily cut to the size needed for a project. It is also available in pre-cut sizes and shapes. Items such as purses are available already formed to inspire the needle artist. Different colors and mesh are also available. Plastic canvas can be bought by the yard in sizes 10 and 5 stitches per inch. The canvas is flexible, but at the same time, very stiff. Because it is plastic, it is not woven, but a sheet with square holes in it. Like all other plastic products, with age, the molecules break down. This means that, with age, plastic canvas items become brittle.

Plastic canvas does not need blocking after it is stitched, since it does not distort during the stitching process. Plastic can be used for book covers, belts, purses, boxes and just about any shaped, dimensional project you might imagine. A frame is never required. To finish a project, turning back non-worked canvas is never needed. A binding stitch, such as Overcast or Binding, can finish off a project very nicely.

When considering the different colors of canvas on the store shelf, think to yourself about what the project is to become. Many decorative stitches available leave part of the canvas showing. White or tan canvas may not be as striking as green or blue. If stitches will be incorporated, but will not entirely cover the canvas, as is the case with the "Scissors Charm," the color of the canvas contributes greatly to the end result. Try painting white canvas with oil-based paints, and see if that technique suits your decor. This can give a folk or formal look, depending upon how the paint is used. Experiment with scrap canvas to see different results.

When choosing canvas, consider the size of the project. Let's say your project is a bell pull. You do not want a large canvas for intricate details. That would be ridiculous. Your project would become a large wall covering, not a bell pull. The same would apply if your project were a simple abstract incorporating few details. Consider how dull it would be to spend many hours stitching a large area in one stitch, on small canvas. The canvas should fit the size and details required by the end project.

Any time you start a project, consider your canvas. No doubt, three sides of canvas will have **raw edges**. That is to say, three sides will ravel when worked. You have a choice of solutions. You can sew bias tape around the edges, use masking tape around them, or if you are ambitious, sew a binding stitch with a sewing machine or by hand. The point is to prevent the canvas from fraying when you stitch and block your work. The binding also prevents the yarn from catching on the rough edges as you stitch.

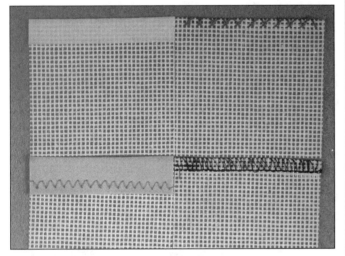

Finished edges

Penelope, Interlock and Mono canvas have definite sides. Long threads that run up vertically, parallel to the selvage, make up the warp. Threads running from left to right are called weft or woof. The selvage is the heavy woven edge running up and down on the canvas. It is impossible to successfully piece large squares together to make rugs or large tapestries without understanding this (note the first diagram).

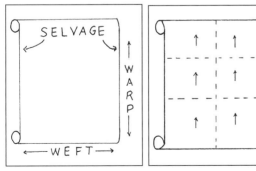

Canvas   Marked warp and weft

The warp and weft threads are not evenly spaced among each other. This can make piecing a bit of a problem. With a marker, make an arrow pointed up, showing the up/down or warp/weft pattern on the canvas (note the second diagram). Place the canvas on stretcher bars with the arrow pointing up. When all the squares are finished, match the arrows in the same direction, and then continue to stitch the squares together. See the illustration. When stitching large items such as rugs and wall hangings, handling yards of canvas at once would be chaos. Using several smaller squares prevents such nonsense. Nevertheless, the squares must be pieced together again.

To unite Interlock canvas, the following method is best:

First, leave about half an inch of bare canvas in the area that will be seamed together. Do not leave a straight line of stitches running down the canvas. This creates a visible line once the project has been completed. Of course, if you use another color as a border around the motifs, this is not an issue (see the first diagram).

Make a crease along the length of the two canvases, aligning the grids of both. With a needle and a strong, white thread, begin making cross hatches along the edges to unite both pieces. When you have finished stitching down the length, travel up the edges again to make a complete Cross stitch. Small Cross or Running stitches are only one method for combining two canvases. The following diagrams show other methods. Some of these are not appropriate, while others make a very fine and sturdy seam. The

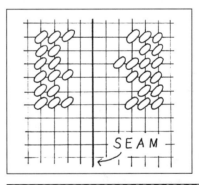

Joining canvas (1)

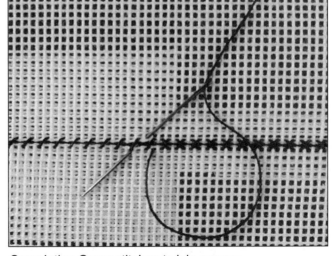

Completing Cross stitches to join canvas

first diagram below shows an inappropriate combination, while the second shows a better choice.

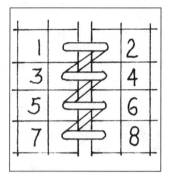

Joining canvas — not the best way

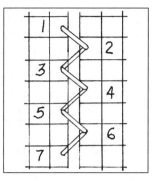

Joining canvas — a better method.

After the canvases have been joined, you are ready to fill in the empty areas with your stitches (see the diagram below).

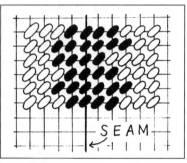

Fill in the empty areas.

Joined stitched canvas.

What about joining Penelope canvas? The method is almost the same, with the following exception. When joining the canvas pieces together, make back stitches between the threads. Again, the grid should be lined up, and you should use strong matching thread to make the union. Both methods could be stitched with a dental floss or, for finer canvas, linen thread. Also, you should steam press the seam before you stitch for a flat result. Use caution in steam pressing any needlepoint stitches. This could flatten the fibers.

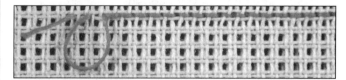

Combining Penelope canvases

Combining Interlock canvases (method 1)

Occasionally, to "erase" a mistake, yarns need to be ripped out. Let us say, in haste, **a thread on the canvas has been cut.** Now, what are you to do? First, do not panic. You are in the company of many experts, who have also cut the wrong thing at one time or another.

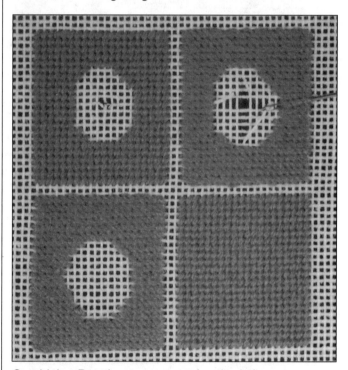

Combining Penelope canvases (method 2)

If you were using Mono canvas, this first method is best. First, fill the void area with stitches all around the cut thread, leaving half an inch of open space. Release the cut thread from the foundation and poke it toward the back of the canvas. Weave the ends in and out of your stitches. With two threads from the edge of the canvas, weave new threads in the needlepoint stitches and in the void in the canvas, making the canvas appear identical to its appearance before you snipped the hole. Finish the void area by filling it with stitches. If this is done with care and correct tension, no one will be wise to your mistake (see photo).

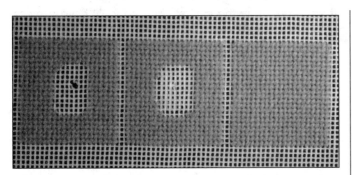

Mending Interlock canvas — three steps

If you are stitching on Interlock canvas, the method is much simpler. Remove the yarn from an area about half an inch around the hole and, instead of removing the canvas threads, lay a square of canvas on the back to cover the cut threads. With the second layer in place, stitch the area again, now working through both layers of canvas. If done with care, this procedure can save the project from destruction (see photo).

To prevent mistakes such as this from happening, cut the yarn where it is thickest. This may be on the front or back, depending upon the stitch. In cutting away a Continental stitch, cut on the back. Half Cross has very little fiber underneath, so the front is best. Decorative stitches usually have more yarn on top. After snipping the yarns, turn your canvas over and run your scissors back and forth across the fibers to loosen them. Pick out what you can and then on the other side, cut again. Continue doing so until you have removed all the unwanted stitches. The most important thing to remember is to take your time. Taking time removing yarn is better than taking much more time replacing canvas threads.

Yarn clippings

At times a larger sized canvas is desired for the whole of a project, but a certain spot requires a smaller canvas for finer detail. This can be achieved by **attaching one canvas on top of another**. An example of this is in "The Theater." Notice the two people kissing in the last row? The couple is stitched on 10/1 Mono canvas. This canvas was split to create 20/1 Mono using six-ply embroidery floss. The foundation is 14/1 interlock. To attach a Petit Point section to a Gros Point project, the following steps are required:

- Stitch your Petit Point section, making the stitched area as square as possible. Do not leave small voids (see first photo).
- On the larger project, stitch close up to the area in which the Petit Point is to be applied. You may wish to mark the exact placement on the canvas before stitching (see second photo).
- Cut the Petit Point canvas four inches from the stitched area. Unravel the canvas right up to the stitches, but use great caution to prevent the stitches' coming undone (see third photo).
- With a tapestry needle, poke the Petit Point into the Gros Point. Be sure the Petit Point lies flat without unsightly bulges. On the underside, weave the Petit Point canvas threads into the Gros Point stitches (see fourth photo).
- Finally, fill in the void area on the Gros Point. Be sure to stitch as close as possible (see fifth and sixth photos).

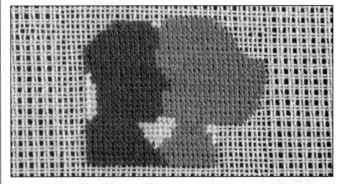

Attaching canvas (1)

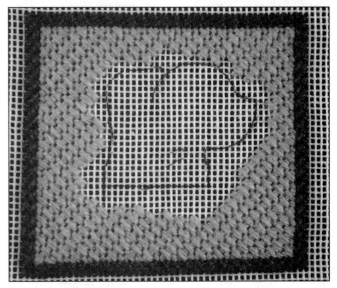

Attaching canvas (2)

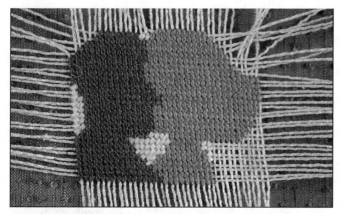

Attaching canvas (3)

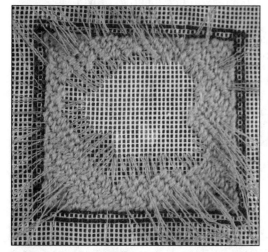

Attaching canvas (4)

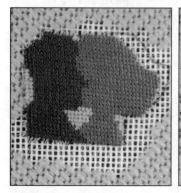

Attaching canvas (5)   Attaching canvas (6)

Before taking a **painted canvas** to the counter, take a close look at the print itself. Four different types of printed canvas are available on the market. The first is silk- or machine-screened. These are usually mass-produced, which means the price is lower. Unfortunately, the canvas is often lower quality. You need to examine for slubs and nubs in the canvas.

Depending upon the printing method, the picture may or may not be correctly squared on the canvas. If the picture includes trees, houses or other objects that require straight, upright lines, do they appear to lean to the right or the left?

If so, do not buy the canvas. You will only have a mess after putting many hours into it—you will never be satisfied with the results. Also, with screen-printed canvas, the color placement may not be as defined as you need for fine stitching. For example, you may have areas where you wonder whether the color at the intersection should be blue or green. Remember, screened canvas is quick and easy to reproduce—and therefore, much less expensive.

On the rack at the yarn shop, you can find some very expensive canvas. The pricier canvas is usually hand painted. The first of this kind is stitch painted. On stitch-painted canvas, each individual intersection has been painted to indicate the exact placement of each color. The person who has a hard time judging where a color should be stitched will have no questions with this canvas. Because the process of painting the canvas takes so long, the price is much higher than the screen-printed choices.

Other hand-painted canvases take a great deal of time to produce, but each intersection of the canvas might not be defined. These canvases may have areas that make you wonder what the color placement should be. If this is the case, examine closely whether the painting lies squarely on the grid. Again, trees, houses and other upright objects should be correctly painted. Stitch-painted and hand-painted canvases usually incorporate higher quality canvas. This also adds to the price.

Any time you stitch on printed canvas, you need to understand the color placement. Look closely at the canvas, and you will see colors painted on the intersections. This indicates where each color should be placed. Do not look at the threads but look at **intersections**, where the canvas threads cross. At times the intersection may have two colors on it. If one color has more on the intersection compared with the other, use this one. If the area has about the same amount of two different colors, the choice is yours. Stand a few feet from the needlepoint and decide which color would be best suited to the space. Perhaps the stitch would be better in one color compared with the other. This could affect the shape of an object in the painting, so take care.

Many **kits** on the market may nicely fit a home decor. In the yarn shop, you can find thousands of ideas, from pictures for children's rooms to living room pillows. Before you buy one, consider the pros and cons of kits. First, purchase the best kit you can afford. In determining what is the "best" kit, many qualities need to be examined. First, the canvas must be printed straight. Determine whether the motif lies correctly on the canvas. Any lines that should be straight should also lie straight on the grid. The canvas itself should be of good quality—poor quality will only rip when finished.

Wool yarn is the better choice, since acrylic yarn is generally poor quality and does not wear well. If fabric is included in the kit, determine for yourself whether it is of acceptable quality. Acrylic fabric is not an acceptable pillow backing. Plastic zippers are another indication of a poor quality kit. If a frame is included, is it wooden or plastic? If you still like the kit, can you upgrade the inferior parts? Zippers, fabric and frames can be replaced, but to switch the yarn often would cost more than the value of the kit.

A kit normally includes enough yarn to finish the job. Nevertheless, beware. If the instructions tell you to stitch in Half Cross, you should not be tempted to use a Continental or Basketweave stitch. The kit may not include enough yarn for stitches that require more wool. Fancy stitches "eat" a good deal more yarn than Half Cross. Most companies will give you more yarn if you should run out. You can send the company a small sample of the required yarn, and you will be soon stitching again.

Inexpensive kits make great teaching aids for the novice needle artist. It was a cheap kit with acrylic yarn that started me needlepointing, more than 35 years ago. I remember stitching the entire kit in Half Cross. I had great fun working each stitch. This is also a great idea if you have worked in other needle arts, and you'd like to decide whether needlepoint is for you. Many people who enjoy crewel, embroidery and other needle arts simply do not like needlepoint. If you do decide to purchase a kit, and many very fine designs are available, you can choose from a rainbow of motifs, ranging from traditional to contemporary projects and styles.

Upholstered items, such as dining room chairs, can be fun to stitch. Canvases with pre-worked centers are available, featuring motifs such as flowers, birds, animals, objects or musical instruments—something to fit almost any home décor! These canvases come in different sizes and shapes to fit various objects in the home, ranging from piano seats to bell pulls.

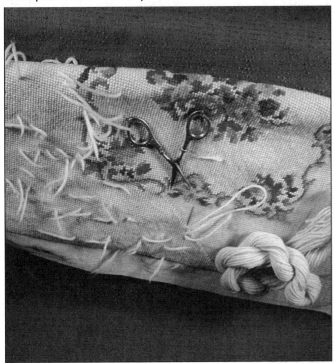

A simple project

Creating an original design. Say you know the size of the project will be 20" by 16". How much canvas should you buy? As a rule, I recommend you buy the area of the project, plus two inches on all sides. This means the canvas should measure 24" by 20".

The extra canvas serves the purposes of blocking and mounting. Measure it carefully and accurately.

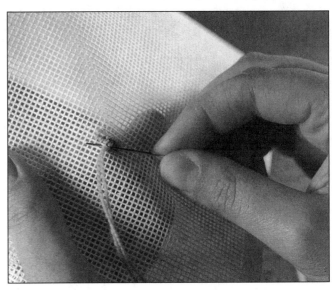

Sewing method

To ensure the project will fit the frame, another calculation is required. First, keep in mind that the frame has a lip. If you intend to stitch a border around the picture, the 1/4" lip will cover two threads on the canvas (assuming you are using 14/1 canvas). Skip the two threads on all sides when stitching the border. Otherwise, the stitches will be hidden by the lip of the frame. If the border stitch is very wide, such as the Princess stitch, the loss of the two threads is not as important as it would be if you were stitching Ribbon Cross or Shell I Variation. The latter two stitches would be a waste of time. When working pillows or upholstery items, stitch two extra rows of the Continental stitch on all sides, for the seam allowance around the machine-stitched finishing.

When you stitch from a chart, the graph is normally not the same size as your canvas. For example, the graph may show five stitches to one linear inch, and your canvas may be 14/1. You will need to calculate the finished size of the project. This is important, because the motif should fit the desired area. You might not want a chair seat with your beautifully stitched flowers running off the chair. If you stitch a bell pull, you want a bell pull—a long, thin canvas—not a tapestry. To determine the size of the finished project, count the number of squares on the chart at its largest width, and divide this by the mesh size of the canvas you plan to use. The result is the exact size of your project.

For example, the chart reads 100 by 120 squares. Your canvas size is 10/1, or ten stitches per one linear inch. The finished project will be 10" by 12". If the size is too large or small for your intended object, you can use another size canvas, depending upon the dimensions you wish to achieve. For example, if 10" by 12" is too big, use 14/1 canvas. The size of the resulting project will then be 7-1/4" by 8-1/4". If you were to stitch on 7/1 canvas, the size would turn out to be 14-1/4" by 17-1/4".

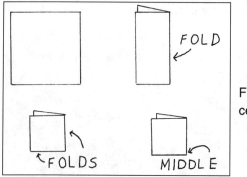

Finding the center (1)

To balance the design on the canvas, you need to find the exact center. To find the center, fold your canvas in half. Now fold it into quarters (step 1).

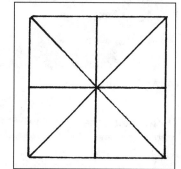

Finding the center (2)

This is like folding a napkin. The folded corner is the middle. If the grid is marked, this helps you in stitching the chart. You have two options for marking your canvas. Your first option is to make running stitches down the center and corners (step 2).

This marks the holes, and not the exact stitch placement, effectively placing your canvas off by one stitch in both directions. Another option would be, if you wish, to use a marker that disappears when wet. Remember, some disappearing markers are gone after 24 hours. Be sure that yours lasts through your project.

Place the motif so that the selvage runs vertically along the side of the picture. Keep this in mind beforehand, when you buy the canvas. Suppose you have a piece of canvas without the selvage attached on a side. How would you figure out how to place the motif? Unravel the weaving on a corner. Compare the warp and weft threads. One thread should have more kink than the other. The vertical threads, or the warp, is generally the one with more kinks. Notice that the canvas has front and back sides. In good light, carefully examine the canvas. Compare the front and back sides—you can see that the front has larger holes.

Yarn

Needlepoint, as a craft, usually requires many hours of work on a single piece. For this reason, the needle artist wants to work with a fiber that is easy to handle and yet strong wearing. For these qualities, the most commonly chosen fiber for needlepoint is wool.

Yarns

As you compare the procedures for creating various stitches, you will notice the word **ply**. Plies are the individual strands in the yarn that can be pulled apart. Persian yarn is made up of three plies, while cotton floss has six plies. Tapestry, pearl, English crewel and many metal yarns have only one ply. Some synthetic yarns have many plies, but they do not pull apart. If you do manage to pull them apart, you can forget about piecing them back together.

When you come upon a thread that is new to you, try experimenting with it using a scrap of canvas. Try stitching Tent, couching in patterns and pulling the canvas threads to learn the yarn's limitations and possibilities. Try stitching with different numbers of plies, and varied stitch combinations. A good way to learn about the variety of yarns on the market is to practice making one stitch in as many different fibers and yarns as you can find. You can learn what varied needlework you can create with each yarn.

If you decide to make a particularly special piece, or you feel a certain motif is especially beautiful, and you have determined that you will spend a good deal of time on the piece, then be sure to use only high quality canvas, yarn and other materials. Many people stitch their projects, thinking "this will never go into a museum." While this may be true, the object will be special and significant nonetheless. Each piece of needlepoint should have the consideration of becoming an heirloom. Strive to use the best yarn you can find and afford.

On the market are many varied types, fibers and sizes of yarn. Wool is available in Persian, tapestry, crewel and rug yarn. Cotton is available in pearl and floss. Silk yarn can be used in needlepoint, and it can offer a very elegant, rich look to your work. Among synthetics, the array is endless. Like synthetic yarns, some metals are strong enough to be stitched through the canvas, yet others must be couched down because of their delicacy. In addition, other yarns such as linen and fancy yarns can be used on the canvas. Knitting yarn can be used, but only on plastic canvas projects. Of course, each variety of yarn has its advantages and disadvantages to the needle artist.

Wool

Wool yarn

Wool is the product of animal hair that has been cleaned and twisted into a yarn. Sheep, goat, rabbit and llama are all animals whose fleece and fur contribute to wool yarns. Most wool yarns intended for needlepoint are made of sheep fleece.

Wool is a wonderful fiber. It is strong, and its durability ensures a long life for the stitched piece. In Siberia, a woolen rug survived by natural refrigeration in a frozen burial mound that dated 500 to 300 BC. That is not to say that you should store your needlepoint projects in the refrigerator—but I do mean to illustrate how long, with proper care, wool can last. Other than moths and other protein-eating insects, sunlight and heat are threats to wool.

One unique quality of wool is its plies' ability to blend to make one soft yarn. For an example of this, see "The Theater." The man in the white shirt, and the one in black, were stitched in English crewel five-ply wool. Another quality of wool is its great tensile strength. The tensile strength is the amount of tension required to break a fiber. Wool has more strength than most fibers—and silk is stronger still.

When stitches are sewn with uneven tension, wool has a tendency to block itself evenly. You could even think of it as a "forgiving" fiber. Silk, rayon and other yarns might not block as nicely as wool. This is why stretcher bars are not needed for wool as much as other fibers.

Wool is widely available as Persian yarn. Persian is a staple in the stitching bag. It is a fine choice for needlepoint because of its sturdy strength and excellent color range. Paternayan, Paragon and Bon Pasteur are a few manufacturers of Persian wool yarn—and Paternayan is the champagne of wool. Persian wool gets its name from its close resemblance to the yarns used in Sarouk and Kirman rugs. If you examine Persian yarn, you can see long fibers spun together. Persian wool is soft and lustrous, and comes in a three-ply yarn. Each strand is loosely twisted. You can use each ply of yarn alone, or you can use two or three together in your needle.

Because of its versatility, Persian yarn can be used on canvases ranging in size from 7/1 to 20/1. This is

also the case with crewel yarn. At the yarn shop, you may see Persian yarn in coils. This is called a hank. At times the yarn in the hank is uncut, and you will have to cut it yourself after you buy it.

Usually, the yarn is cut into strands about 60" long. A length of 30" is called a half strand. Remember, one strand equals three plies at 60". When you get the yarn home, cut the hank into lengths of about 15" to 20". This length is enough for the artist to use a good amount of yarn in the needle, without allowing the yarn to wear out before the wool is stitched into the canvas. Contact with both the canvas and the needle wears the yarn. Using longer lengths does not allow the yarn to cover the canvas as effectively. For finer mesh canvas, stitch with shorter lengths of yarn.

When you buy yarn, do not buy many small packages of wool if you are looking to work a large area, or if you need a large quantity. Smaller packages are generally pricier than buying a larger hank. Some Persian wools come in skeins totaling only a couple of yards. This is a fine choice if you only need the yarn for a few stitches, or for shading.

Appleton or English crewel yarn can be used in the same way as Persian. Use as many plies as you need to properly cover the canvas. French wool is very fine, and appears as one ply. As the work ages, the fibers blend into one ply, giving the yarn and the stitches a silky shine. The colors are wonderful, but the color range is limited.

Shades appear to be distinct, yet when they are stitched, they blend together beautifully, without ever appearing too dull or muted—which can sometimes happen when the artist attempts to shade with too many closely blended colors.

Be sure that your yarn is well suited to the size of the canvas you have chosen for your project. Crewel yarn is generally an excellent choice for Petit Point projects, and usually, one ply is all that is needed. Genuine crewel yarn is very strong. It is a two-ply twisted yarn made of long fibers, which cannot be separated. Crewels are available in a veritable rainbow of colors.

The length of the wool fibers determines the quality of the yarn. The fibers should be long for a better yarn. For Gros Point stitching, a multiple strand of crewel, two-ply Persian and one-ply tapestry yarn are all possibilities.

Another staple in the yarn bag is tapestry wool, which is available in hanks of approximately 42 yards. When you buy tapestry yarn, open the wrapper and rewind the yarn into a circle that measures 36" in circumference. Cut the yarn into 18" lengths for stitching. Some decorative stitches can be made with tapestry yarn, but it is best suited for the Tent stitch. Fancy stitches are more often made with Persian or crewel yarn. Tapestry yarn is at its best in chair cushions or other upholstery items. This yarn should be used on canvas ranging from 5/1 to 12/1, depending upon the ply of the yarn you choose to work in your needle. A larger size canvas requires more than one ply.

For projects incorporating large areas of work, such as a rug, 3.5/1 or 7/1 canvas is generally a good size. Rug yarn is the obvious choice, too. Make Tent stitches just as you would with any other yarn, but use a large tapestry needle to stitch the heavier rug yarn.

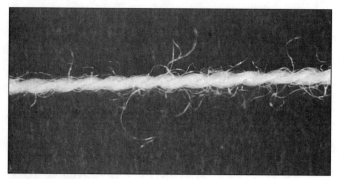

Nap of the yarn

After stitching a while on a project, you may find that some areas are filled with stitching that appears to be neat and sharp, while other areas appear fuzzy. The fuzzy areas indicate that you have not been following the grain of your yarn. When spun into a yarn, the fibers all tend to stand out in one direction compared with the other. Think of this as a right and wrong direction for using the yarn. Thread your needle with the direction of the fuzz going down. This helps to make sharper, clearer stitches.

Do not use strands of wool any longer than 15" to 18". Never double a strand to make two plies from one. Always use two plies straight through your needle. The doubled-over yarn does not cover as nicely as two single plies going in the same direction. Also, ripping out mistakes would be impossible, and you could forget about "sewing" out the stitches.

Another must for creating perfect stitches is stripping the yarn. When you strip yarn, you are pulling apart each ply, even though you have decided to stitch, for example, with three plies of Persian. For the best, neatest stitches, you must pull apart all the plies in the yarn, and then place them together again. Then, thread your needle. Stripping the yarn allows the stitches to lie more smoothly on the canvas than they would if you did not first prepare the yarn. Wool, cotton and most other fibers should be stripped. Stripping the plies lofts the fibers in wool. For cotton, pull the plies apart and untwist the lengths.

To strip yarn, cut it to the length you wish to use for stitching. Then, with the end of the yarn between the thumb and index finger of your left hand, take one ply in your right hand and pull the ply away from your left. Repeat this procedure for each ply, until you have separated each one. Then, piece back the number of plies you wish to use for your stitching on the canvas. Neither tapestry nor pearl yarn should be stripped. With these yarns, all the piecing you could muster would not bring the yarn back into a workable condition. Other exceptions include metals, braids and novelty yarns.

Because yarn has a nap, it tends to twist as you stitch. To release the twisted yarn, hold your needlepoint upside down, allowing the yarn and needle to dangle from the canvas. You will notice the bound up yarn relaxing to its correct, natural tension. To prevent the twisting, turn the needle once in a while as you stitch.

Never store wool yarns in plastic bags. While plastic bags may seem like a great way to organize your yarn stash, it is not the best home for your wool. Because wool is animal hair, it needs to breathe. Also, the plies of wool yarn can felt themselves, making them impossible to strip, and rendering the yarn worthless. Cotton, silk and other natural fibers also need to breathe, and should not be stored in plastic.

Cotton

Cotton yarns

Cotton is another wonderful fiber. For those with wool allergies or respiratory trouble, cotton is a pleasure to stitch. Cotton also eliminates the threat of insects, as most bugs prefer to eat protein, not cellulose. Aside from sunlight and harsh chemicals, cotton does not have many enemies.

Pearl yarn and embroidery floss are cotton yarns. Pearl yarn is available in various sizes, while embroidery floss exists in only one size. DMC makes a very fine cotton that can couch any fiber you might wish to use. The size of canvas determines the number of plies of cotton yarn that need to be used for stitching. Embroidery floss requires the needle artist to strip the individual plies, to allow the stitches to lie flat on the canvas. Forget about stripping cotton pearl.

Some people think that, in general, stripping floss is a waste of time. Make the determination yourself—stitch an area with stripped floss, and then stitch another area with floss straight from the package. Note the difference. You will see that the stripped plies lie flat on the canvas. For larger stitches such as the Flat stitch, this is certainly beneficial. This is also helpful when laying large flat Satin stitches where six-ply does not cover efficiently, and extra plies may need to be added to the yarn.

Like Persian wool, cotton floss has a definite nap to it. You need not worry about this, since the nap lies in the correct direction as the floss comes out of the package. To cut a length of floss, check the wrapper and see the picture of hands. This will indicates the correct direction to pull the cotton out of its papers. Pull the thread from the opposite end of the skein. Cut the floss to a length of 20", and strip the plies. Thread the needle with the freshly cut end.

Pearl cotton has a soft twist that does not separate. Take a look at pearl cotton in a store, and note the different numbers on the wrappers. This number indicates the size of the yarn. For example, #3 is the thickest. It covers 12/1 canvas quite well. Number 5 is well suited for 14/1 and 16/1 canvas, while #8 is great for 22/1 and 24/1 canvas. Note that 14/1 canvas may require two plies of #5 Pearl for sufficient coverage. The finest pearl yarn, #12, can be used in very fine canvas.

Mercerized yarn is treated under tension with a cold, concentrated sodium hydroxide solution. This process lends luster and strength to cotton yarns. Immersion in water removes the mercerized finish. Perspiration on your hands also dulls the cotton's shine.

Rayon

Rayon yarn

Imagine the yarn shop with all its many shiny yarns. You may notice that some are quite expensive, and yet others seem reasonable. What is the difference? The lower priced yarns may be rayon. Like other yarns, rayon is available in a range of thicknesses and plies. Some rayon floss appears in packaging that is very similar to the packaging for embroidery floss. This is four-ply yarn.

Some people feel rayon is a challenge to work with, while others feel it is a pleasure. Personally, I have always enjoyed stitching with it, since the fiber gives life to many projects. Use rayon as you use cotton.

When applying rayon on canvas, take time to lay the fibers flat. You may need to stroke the yarn as it passes through the holes in the canvas. Also, stop every few stitches and adjust the strands in the needle. Before stitching, strip the plies to guarantee the bright shine rayon is famous for. Some rayons in multiple strands can never be stripped. Use these yarns as they come, right off the spool.

Rayon, like any other man-made fiber, should be worked on a canvas that is stretched over bars. This holds the canvas straight and taut.

Rayon snags very easily, so protect the stitches with a piece of white fabric tacked down over the finished areas. In "The Unicorn," the first part worked was the horn. Who would not be tempted to work this feature first? To protect the horn and unicorn, a white handkerchief was tacked over the stitching. For several months, the unicorn wore the handkerchief. Keep this in mind when working any delicate fiber such as silk, rayon and metals. Many of these yarns, and more fragile stitches, need to be guarded from wear before the project is ever finished. Sometimes, it makes greater sense to save the most delicate areas for last.

Natesh rayon comes from India. Like many other Indian yarns, Natesh has the tendency to run when immersed in water. Use the standard rule, and test the yarn for colorfastness before applying stitches to canvas—or at least before immersing the work in water. Natesh is made up of very fine plies, and it is great for counted cross stitch, Blackwork and machine embroidery. The needlepoint artist could use this for such stitches as couching and surface embroidery. With a layer of Continental as a backing, French Knots, Bullion Knots and Detached Chains in fine rayon can enhance an area. Continental stitches can be worked in wool, and then a layer of rayon over the same spot can highlight a special area. One word of caution—do not be tempted to work Natesh on canvas that requires several plies for coverage, unless the canvas size is 40/1. The only result is sure to be frustration.

Silk

Silk yarn

This brings us to silk yarns, one of China's great gifts to the world. While rayon has a good deal of shine, silk has a truly unique look and feel. Silk can be found in many different yarns. Coats and Clark makes a buttonhole thread named Silk Twist. In "The Unicorn," this was used to make the French Knot flowers. Silken Detached Chain makes the flowers that lie at the animal's feet. Silk floss is available on the market in a range of sizes.

When working with silk, take a little extra time to double check, ensuring that the fibers lie straight on the canvas. Long, straight stitches going in different directions allow the light to play on the fibers. Try working Scotch and Alternating Scotch on a scrap canvas, and see the difference. The light makes the yarn appear to have been stitched in two tones. For a greater variation in the color play, stitch with lighter tones of a color. Small stitches, such as Eyelet and Tent, do not showcase the yarn's brilliance like flat stitches do.

For the finest look, strip the plies apart and then place them together again for stitching. Yes, this extra step takes time, but it helps you to create an heirloom. If you have gone to the extra expense to use silk, you may as well go to the extra trouble to give it the treatment it deserves.

Silk fibers are sensitive to water and sunlight. Take care when you stitch with them, to do all you can to prevent having to block the project when it is completed. Although silk's tensile strength is even greater than that of wool, it is sensitive, and if you must block the work, use great caution. When possible, stretch the canvas over bars before you stitch the project. Never use steam or heat on silk—they rot the fibers.

J. L. Walsh, Inc. offers 140 hand-dyed colors in twelve-ply silk floss, buttonhole twist silk cord and five-ply silk/wool blend. The silk has a slight sheen. The buttonhole twist has a thready look, similar to the appearance of cotton. Silk brings out the richness of the colors. The silk/wool combination has a soft feel, but the yarn has the look of cotton. You may ask yourself whether the difference in price is worth the investment. This is your own question to answer.

Kreinik Manufacturing Company makes several types of silk yarns. Silk Mori is a six-ply spun yarn with a lovely shine. Another is Serica, which can be found three-ply. Fifty-two shiny colors are available in Soie Platte. For a little less luster, try stitching with Soie d'Alger. More than 400 color choices virtually guarantee that no needle artist should ever have a problem coordinating a color scheme. Soie d'Alger comes is a seven-ply yarn. Also on the market are Soie Perlée, Soie Noppée and Soie Gobelin which are available in 52 colors and one-, two- and three-ply. Kreinik also makes a silk by the name of Ping Ling, which is available in six-ply in a line of 112 shiny colors.

Because the yarns may tend to run, never immerse the needlepoint in water. Kreinik recommends using the DRY dry-cleaning method. As with other silks, blocking can be a problem. When working with Kreinik silk, use stretcher bars. Protect your needlepoint when you are not stitching, with a clean, white fabric.

Splendor by Rainbow Gallery, from France, is a 100% silk thread with a large color range. Each bundle of yarn has four strands, and the twist is higher, compared with other silk yarns.

Metallics

Metallic yarns

A discussion about metals could fill volumes of books. Rainbow makes a crocheted yarn that covers 14/1 canvas very nicely in Tent or upright stitches. Clear nail polish on each end of the yarn prevents fraying; otherwise, the product is great for stitching. Talon metallic thread makes an excellent couching tool. Japanese metal cannot be sewn through canvas, but it can be couched. Use it with silk and see what great effects you can achieve. This was the procedure used around the flowers on "The Butterfly."

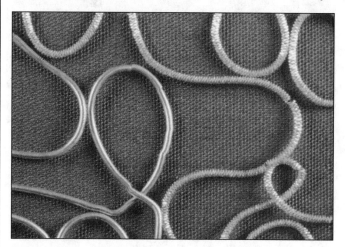

Fraze

Any time you see a new and interesting metal yarn in the store, take it home and see how you can adapt it to your own needlepoint. In shops, you can find a yarn called Fraze. These are not true yarns, but are actually very fine spirals of metal. This is the most delicate yarn I have ever used. If you use anything less than the utmost care, the yarn can pull out of shape and be rendered useless. Luckily, this yarn can be couched. Do not try to tie down the ends—simply let the metal lie on top of the canvas, and begin couching. In addition, because Fraze is a spiral, you can cut it into tiny bits, and stitch them down like beads.

This brings us back to the Kreinik Company. Blending filament can be used for couching and accenting different stitches. Metallic braids are available in 120 colors, in sizes 4, 8, 16 and 32, with the lowest numbers indicating the finest braids. The same colors can be found in metallic ribbon. The ribbons are available in two sizes, 1/8" and 1/16". Japanese threads are available in gold, silver and copper, in sizes 1, 5 and 7, along with 1/16" and 1/8" ribbon. Ombre is an eight-ply metal thread available in nine colors. Included in the Ombre yarns are gold, silver and pearl. If you wish to use an interesting yarn that looks more like something from the hardware store, try Torsades. These are twisted metallic cords, available in five sizes.

Linen

Linen is a strong yarn with a thready appearance. Square Sale offers a rainbow of colors that encourages creativity in any needlepoint project.

Novelty Yarns

Fancy or novelty yarns range from velour to slubs and nubs. Most of these should be couched on the canvas, but velour can be stitched through. The only rule for using these specialty yarns, is to always make a test sample before using the yarn on the project.

In the yarn shops, you might notice a thin strip that resembles leather. This is Ultrasuede, a suede-like yarn for needlepoint on 12/1 to 14/1 canvas, and for long stitches on 14/1 to 18/1 canvas. Ultrasuede is made of polyester polyurethane. The card holds five strands, each one yard in length. The great thing about Ultrasuede is that it can be washed. As with all other products, test it for colorfastness before immersing it in water.

A unique yarn that should be couched on the canvas is Glissen Gloss, Estaz by Madera. This is a chenille-like yarn, made of 100% nylon. Boa feathers on a woman, fur on animals, or even leaves on trees are just a few areas where Estaz can be applied to the canvas.

Another product by Glissen Gloss is Rainbow Blending Thread. Imported from Germany, this very thin, 70% nylon and 30% metallic polyester is fun to use as one or two plies for a couching tool, or as many plies as needed for stitching. The color ranges from many different natural colors to various metals, to offer just about any accent color you could want.

Sterling Blending Thread, also by Glissen Gloss, resembles very fine Japanese metal. Because it is so fine, you should not be tempted to use it in a Continental stitch. The spool holds 40 yards of thread, so you may wish to use it sparingly.

Yarn could be defined as any material that can be stitched through or on top of a needlepoint canvas. Another yarn that many forget to consider is ribbon. Ribbon can be used with a wonderful result, if it is thin enough to pass through the holes in the canvas. To stitch with ribbon, use a #20 tapestry needle. For the best results, work the ribbon area first, and then other yarns. Use a waste knot, or weave the ribbon under nearby stitches. Like all yarns, the end should be tucked under the stitches on the underside of the canvas.

Ribbon can have the tendency to twist. To prevent this, a layering tool may be needed to ensure the ribbon lies flat on the canvas. If the ribbon twists, the result is usually disaster. While you are considering ribbon, have you thought about bias tape, or other unlikely items? Experiment on a spare bit of canvas to see what you can discover.

Color

Be sure to buy enough yarn at once to finish the entire project. The rationale behind this strategy is this: when yarn is dyed, it is done in large vats of a limited quantity. Each time the dye is dumped into the tub, the color changes ever so slightly—but usually just enough for the eye to detect the difference. To determine whether yarns are from the same dye vat, check the label of the yarn for the dye lot number. The number changes each time the dye is changed in the vat. To guarantee that your yarn is all the same color, buy yarn with all the same dye lot number. If you are buying Persian yarn, ask the clerk whether the color lot numbers of your hanks match.

Suppose you bought what you thought was enough yarn and, in the middle of the project, you run out of a special color. What are you to do? First, if you are moving from one area of the project to another with the color, purchase more of the same color (different dye lots should be all right) and continue to stitch. The slight color difference should be undetectable, as long as the colors are relatively far apart on the canvas. Textured stitches show slight color changes much less than flat stitches do. If you are covering an entire area and the yarn has run out, you need to play a little trick. Before finishing the first dye lot color, strip all your remaining yarn, and separate the plies. Strip the same amount of your new yarn. Then, pair up the plies of the first yarn with the new plies. Continue to stitch the area directly adjacent to the first color, until your old/new blended strands are used up. The color change is much less detectable than it would have been had you simply switched from the old yarn to the new yarn. When the old/new plies run out, stitch with only new yarn. This method makes for a smooth transition.

Two different procedures are used to dye yarn. The first and best method is fiber dyeing. This is accomplished by submerging large quantities of fibers in an enormous vat of dye solution. After they have been dyed, the loose fibers are then carded and spun into yarn. The second, and less preferable, process is yarn dyeing. The name describes the process—after the fibers are spun, large bundles of yarn in skeins or packages are placed into the vat of dye. The reason for fiber-dyed yarn's superiority is that, with this method, the dye can better penetrate each cuticle, or horny layer of scales, in the wool. The absorbent quality that you enjoy with your 100% cotton towels is the same quality that makes fiber-dyed cotton so wonderfully color-saturated.

Not all fibers dye well. Some fibers, such as rayon and other synthetics, may have dye layered on the surface of each fiber. For this reason, colorfastness of rayon and some synthetics is questionable. Most dyes are colorfast, but a surprising number are not—and surprises of this sort are not usually pleasant! Red, blue, dark purple, dark green, bright yellow and bright orange are all of questionable colorfastness. To determine colorfastness, place a yarn sample in a cup of water. Agitate the yarns. Does the water take on a light shade of the yarn's color? If so, the dye is not colorfast. For a needle artist, this means that a finished project could run when blocked or cleaned. Always test the yarn before stitching if you doubt the colorfastness of the dye.

How Much is Enough?

To determine the amount of yarn you need for a project, sew a square-inch sample of the stitch you wish to use, and note the amount of yarn required for the sample. Then, calculate how many square inches the project should cover, and multiply this with the required number of yarns for the stitching. This will give you a general idea of the quantity of yarn required. Add 10 percent to compensate for yarn wear and ripping out mistakes. Remember, everyone ends up with some leftover yarn, from all projects. Guessing the exact amount of yarn required is almost impossible. Continental and Basketweave stitches require approximately one ounce of yarn (25 strands) to cover about forty-four square inches on 14/1 canvas. For 10/1 canvas, the same amount of yarn covers thirty-seven square inches. Decorative stitches also affect the yarn requirement.

When trying different stitches on various sizes of canvas, it can be difficult to gauge the number of plies needed for the stitching. The best solution is to experiment. Cotton floss can be used in Petit Point, but how many plies? To decide, on the side of the canvas, stitch with different numbers of plies to determine the best quantity. Your Petit Point may require one or two plies—or you may find that cotton floss is not the best choice. Keep in mind that you do not want the canvas to show when the stitches are completed—nor do you want too much yarn in the holes, which distorts the canvas shape, and makes the stitches thick and uneven. Your needle should pass through the holes with ease, but it should not drop through. Many people think samples are a waste of canvas, yarn and time—not true. A little time spent experimenting can help you to avert disaster. For a general rule, see the Canvas, Needles and Yarn chart at the end of Chapter Three.

Endless Possibilities

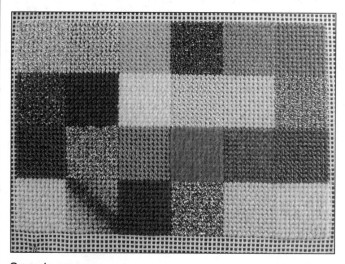

Sample squares

Here, you see a picture of squares in different yarns. This is an excellent way to see the various effects the yarns can produce. All were worked in Basketweave on 14/1 Interlock canvas.

Some yarns mentioned are not readily available on the market. Although you might not find them in craft or sewing stores, these are noted because, when looking in antique and second hand stores, you may find wonderful and unique yarns that are new to you. Do not feel threatened by their appearance. Take them home and experiment. You may discover yarns that are thirty years old, or even older. Before using them in your projects, test them to determine the correct ply and to discover the yarn's limitations. Take a good look to ensure that such yarns are clean and in good repair. Years ago, I purchased a large amount of wool, only to find the entire hank deteriorating and effectively useless. The wool was no bargain, but it did make a good lesson.

Years later, I discovered a number of old skeins of rayon. The entire cost was $4.00. To buy the quantity of yarn new in a yarn shop would have cost more than $50.00. The amount was enough to work a large portion of a picture.

Just be sure to examine the yarn, and be sure of its condition. If the fibers are soiled, can they be cleaned? Will the color run when wet? Most important, do you have enough to finish the project? When you are using a one-of-a-kind yarn, you cannot run down to the store and buy the same yarns as before—much less worry about color matching!

Needles

Needlepoint or tapestry needles have a characteristic blunt point and large eye. The blunt ensures easy stitching, as the needle can pass through wool stitches without splitting them. Sharp-pointed needles, such as a Chenille needle, tend to split the canvas. They can lead the yarn through the canvas, but the stitches are not sharp and clear. A sharp needle can only lead to constantly pricked fingers, and it is very hard to be rid of bloodstains on a painstakingly worked piece.

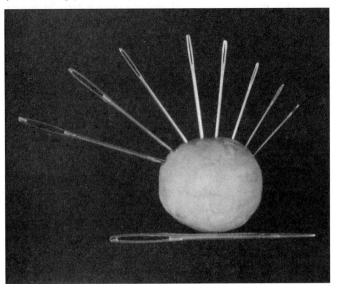

Needles

Needles range in size from 13 to 28, with higher numbers indicating smaller needles. Sizes 22 to 28 are appropriate for Petit Point; 18 to 20 for Gros Point and 13 to 16 for Quick Point.

The size of the canvas should help you to determine the size of the needle. A needle should pass through the canvas easily, without having to be pulled too hard. If the needle is too large, holes will be apparent in the work. A large needle not only causes holes, but it also easily distorts the grid. Choose too small a needle, and the yarn wears in spots and will need to be replaced. To determine the correct needle size for the mesh, drop a needle into a hole on the canvas. The needle should fall until it has reached the eye, where it stops. If it pops through with a gentle tug, the needle is the proper size for your canvas. If the needle needs to be pushed hard in order to pass through, the eye will distort the grid—and as a result, the stitches will be uneven and lumpy. Blocking will not correct these problems.

When buying needles, choose better quality ones. These should be rounded and polished. Good needles often have gold eyes and silvertone shanks. The best tapestry needles are from England. A package holds several needles; the number included in a package depends upon the needle size. Very large needles may be packaged in pairs, while smaller ones may come by the dozen.

The eye should be a bit larger than the yarn, for two reasons: the yarn can fray and wear out if the eye is too small, and yarn passes more smoothly through the canvas if the eye is a bit bigger.

Never use rusty needles. Needles should be kept in a moisture-proof container, or in wool felt. Needles can tarnish, as a result of the reaction of the metal to the acid in your skin. To remove the tarnish, use a product on the market called "acid mantle," which can be found in a local drugstore. Platinum needles do not tarnish. Needles cost relatively little to buy, and better quality tapestry needles bring pleasure to your work.

Remember, "a dull needle worketh a worried stitch." Sharp needles may be required when stitching beads, chains or other "found" items. In "The Unicorn," silk buttonhole thread was used for some flowers. Several layers of French Knots were applied to the area. A blunt needle would never have sufficed for the job. A sharp point was required to "cut" through the piles of threads.

To match the correct needle size to the mesh size, check the table at the end of Chapter Three entitled "Canvas, Needles and Yarn."

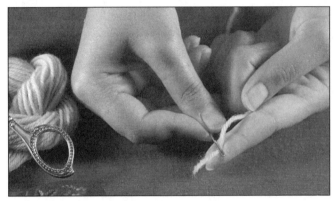

Threading the needle (1)

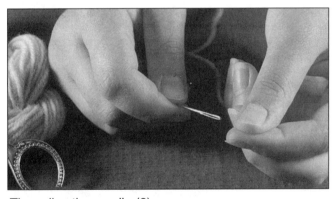

Threading the needle (2)

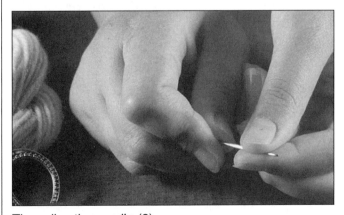

Threading the needle (3)

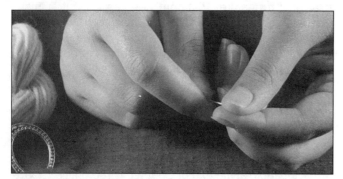

Threading the needle (4)

Threading the needle (5)

Of course, you must thread the needle before attempting to stitch a canvas with it. It is virtually impossible to accomplish this by simply licking the end of the yarn and aiming at the eye of the needle. Among your more realistic options are three quite effective methods.

The first is fast and easy, once you get the knack of it. You will need a yarn approximately 18" long. With the yarn in your left hand—if you are right handed—and the needle in your right, wrap the yarn once around the eye of the needle. Hold the crease with your thumb and index finger. Then, remove the needle from the crease while still holding the yarn tightly. The eye should slide between the thumb and index finger, and this should quite effectively lead the yarn through the eye. Continue sliding the needle until the crease is through.

When threading a needle, remember these two rules: first, do not look at the crease once it has been established. Second, while you are sliding the yarn through the eye, the needle itself should be moving, and not the yarn.

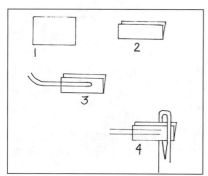

Threading a needle with paper

Another method calls for a small rectangle of paper which, folded in half, slides through the needle's eye. Lay the end of the yarn inside of the paper and fold the paper over the yarn to completely cover the end. The yarn can then pass through the eye with ease (see diagram).

You can also find a product in stores that enables you to thread your needle quickly and easily. The Muriel Yarn Threader is a metal tool with two holes in it. It can be used to thread needles ranging from very large to small sizes. Insert the hole of the appropriate size into the eye of the needle. Then, thread the yarn into the hole and pull the tool through the eye of the needle. Remove the threader, and start stitching. To keep the threader handy, place a string in the center of the tool and lace it to your embroidery scissors.

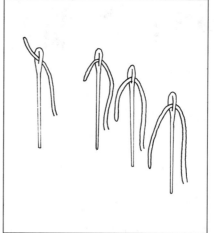

Yarn in the needle

The heavy sizing (starch) required to make the canvas stiff is hard on the fibers. Each time you pass the needle through the mesh, the yarn wears out just a little. Some people believe that folding a long length of yarn into the needle and working the needle up to the end of the yarn is the best way to stitch. This is incorrect. For work that will more likely result in heirloom-quality embroidery, fold the yarn about 1-1/2" from the end, and stitch. By using the short end method, you avoid the yarn's wearing out, ensuring that the stitches will not be thin and weak on the canvas. If you do not use this process, the result is canvas showing through the stitches.

When you want to stop stitching, you have to park your needle somewhere. Rest your needle on the edge of the canvas, in the margin area of your work. You may ask yourself, "Why?" This is to protect the canvas from the possible distortion that can result from your needle's resting too long in the canvas. Also, if you live in a humid environment, your needle could rust while parked on the canvas, causing a stain to discolor your stitching. If your needle should rust and stain your canvas, use 3% hydrogen peroxide to remove it.

Tools and Equipment

Various useful tools

Many implements are required to accomplish the jobs involved in needlepoint. Other items in the sewing basket can be thought of as "niceties," or the little extras that can make projects more enjoyable. Some of these are for vanity purposes only, while others make needlepoint tasks easier to accomplish. Of the required tools, several deserve mention:

Tape Measures and Rulers: These are necessary. Most needlepoint projects require that you determine the locations of the center and side margins of the canvas. Accurate gauging is of utmost importance when determining the center of your project. This is particularly true in working with fine canvas, such as 20/1, or finer. Plastic coated measuring tapes are better than fabric or paper, as they do not stretch or tear when used. Find one with both metric and standard measure. For cutting and blocking, a metal ruler is best. Wooden rulers are generally not as accurate, and when used with a razor blade, the edge easily accepts cuts and dents.

Thimbles: Some people cannot stitch without thimbles. I have never mastered the art of using them. Several styles and types are available, including wood, leather, plastic and metal. Depending upon your budget and preference, you might even opt for a sterling or gold thimble. If you cannot use a thimble, try a rubber finger from a stationery store, made for shuffling paper. Like thimbles, these come in different sizes.

Masking Tape: Because your canvas does not have a selvage on all four sides, it could fray. To prevent fraying, the edges must be bound in some manner. Some people whip stitch the sides, while others use bias tape. Many prefer masking tape, and for two very good reasons. First, it is much faster. Second, the tape is removed when the project is mounted—why waste so much time and trouble for something that is only useful for a short time? Place the edge of the canvas along the middle of the tape. Overlap the tape, binding the entire edge. Penelope, Interlock and Mono canvases should all have their sides bound. Plastic canvas does not require binding.

Fray Check: This product keeps fabric from fraying. It is invaluable, especially on metal yarns. After a length of metal yarn has been cut, the ends may unravel. Apply a small amount of Fray Check to the ends, and wait a few seconds.

White Penny Balloons, Rubber Disks or Rubber Fingers: When used with a large amount of yarn for upright stitches, the needle may not travel easily through the canvas. To facilitate the tug and pull required for the stitching, you may wish to have one or more of these in your sewing bag. Slip rubber fingers on your thumb and index finger, and the needle is much easier to grip and pull.

Graph Paper: As you learn more about needlepoint and discuss projects with others, you are bound to learn new stitches and discover new patterns. The most effective way to record these is on graph paper. Also, if you decide to create a pattern or stitch for yourself, the paper helps in the layout. The best graph papers have an extra-heavy line every five squares. This facilitates the counting, saving valuable time. Neatly store all your graphs in a notebook or binder.

Magnifying Glasses: Canvases measuring 20/1 or smaller can be tough on the eyes. A magnifying glass is the perfect answer, helping stitches to be more even and straight—and to keep you from missing stitches entirely. Several types of magnifiers are available. Some magnifying glasses can be suspended on a nylon cord around the neck. This is a great option, keeping the hands free to work. Other magnifying glasses can be clamped on a table. These come with or without fluorescent lights. The extra light is great for protecting your eyes. Another option would be reading glasses, which are inexpensive and available at almost any drugstore.

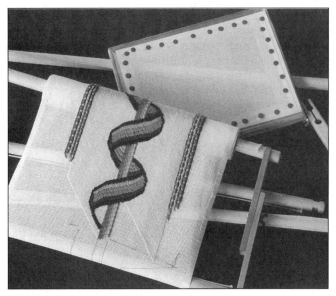

Frames for stitching

Embroidery hoop

Frames: These greatly enhance not only the appearance of the needlework, but also the experience of creating it. Beginners, right along with old pros, find their stitches are much more even. If the project is correctly placed on the frame in the first place, little blocking is required after the project's completion. At first, frames can be hard to master, but once this is accomplished, the result is worth the effort. Some people are annoyed that frames slow the stitching process—but remember, stitching is for fun. You can use frames in different ways. First, some people use clamps to attach the frame to a tabletop, while others prop the frame up on their laps. Some frames are made with a stand to be placed under the stitcher's leg, and other frames stand on the floor themselves.

If you are right-handed, place your right hand under the frame, since your dexterity is best here. If left-handed, use your right hand on top. Your better hand is generally more proficient at needlework without the help of your eyes. With a little time and practice, your needle will fly in both directions. Using the stabbing method to needlepoint helps to prevent the yarn's fraying as quickly as it does when the sewing method is used. If the project is small and can be held in the lap, canvas-stretching bars, like the ones used by painters, are great. These come in different lengths, made in whole inches, to fit your canvas. Quite inexpensive, canvas stretcher bars are enjoyable to use since you can see the entire picture at once, without having to adjust the frame.

After a quick and simple assembly, you may want to square up your homemade frame by using a 90-degree angle. Attach the canvas to the boards with thumbtacks. Start in the middle of an edge, pushing one tack into the board. When all four edges have a thumbtack in their middles, the center of the canvas should be taut. Then, place tacks on either side of each of the first ones. Repeat this on all four sides. Continue tacking until you have reached the four corners, which will be your last four tacks.

Remember to keep the canvas straight while you tack it. If it is not straight, remove the canvas from the stretcher bars and start over. This will be a blessing later when you move on to the blocking step. The only area on the canvas where the stretcher bars should actually touch canvas is in the margins. Never allow "to be worked" areas to rest on top of the stretcher boards.

Another type of frame is the scroll bar frame. Large pictures can be easily transported, since the worked area is rolled around two posts. In the photograph of the stretcher bars, note the pole and ribbon project. This is a bell pull that measures three feet in length. The size of the project would make it otherwise next to impossible to hold in two hands. Keeping the project rolled makes it easier to stitch. Scroll frames are available in a variety of sizes. The sides are adjustable for a custom-fit tension. These do not slip when used. To attach the canvas, simply stitch it onto the twill tape attached to the roller bar. Be sure to center the canvas on the roller bars on both ends, to prevent the canvas from pulling on the bias and distorting the grid.

A floor stand

If you can manage it, a floor frame is great to have. It frees both hands for stitching, plus it allows you to view your project from several feet without having to prop it up on something.

Rayons, silks and various other yarns need extra help to ensure the fibers lie flat on the canvas. Keep both hands on top of the frame, and use one to smooth the yarns, while the other places the needle. As you lead the yarn through the canvas, stroke the yarn with your other hand to position the plies smoothly.

Marking Pens: Many different brands of marking pens are available on the market. Find an indelible one. Your marks must resist bleeding when wet. Pilot SC-UF and Marvy permanent black are good markers.

If you are not sure whether your marker is indelible, test it. On a scrap of canvas, make a few marks and then immerse the canvas in water. If the color runs, do not use the pen on your project. If your project is composed of pastels or all white, a yellow marker is a wise choice, since the light tone does not show through the stitches.

There are also felt pens whose inks disappear when wet. Search the notion department of your favorite fabric and needlework shops. Please note, some pens dissolve with water—but there are also pens whose inks disappear in 48 hours or less, water or no water. Unless your project is small, you should find another pen.

Never use pencil or ballpoint pen for marking canvas. The graphite in the lead and ink can deteriorate the fibers. They also bleed through the fibers when immersed in water.

Scissors: I recommend three types—paper scissors, sewing shears and embroidery scissors. Paper scissors are good for cutting canvas, tape and paper. Large dressmaker's shears are perfect for easily cutting large quantities of yarn, fabric and cording. Embroidery scissors are fine for cutting thread, yarn and ribbon. When you have to rip out areas of stitches, the embroidery scissors is best. Never use your dressmaker's or embroidery shears for canvas or paper, and always cut canvas through a row of holes.

T-square or Triangle: This is an excellent tool for blocking and drawing designs. A good T-square is fine in either metal or plastic.

Blocking Board: This is another must for the needlepoint artist. To make a board, look in Chapter Four under "Blocking and Finishing."

T Pins: These are required when blocking the finished needlepoint. Wig pins are not usually strong enough for this job.

Pliers and Screwdrivers: Although these are not essential, they save your good scissors. When removing thumbtacks from stretcher boards, sometimes one is tempted to pry the tacks out of the boards with the blade of the scissors. One slip or miss could break the tip off the scissors, or create nicks in the blade that cannot be removed. Save your shears and have a small set of pliers or a screwdriver to pry tacks from boards.

Thumbtacks: These are for mounting blank canvas on stretcher boards. Do not use rusty or bent tacks.

Additional Equipment

Stitch Counter: If you look with care, you may find one in a yarn shop, but do not be misled. This is not a ruler, but rather, a device that has gauges for 6/12, 7/14, 9/18 and 10/20 canvases. It saves time in counting and placing your motif on the canvas. It can also be helpful when you decide what size canvas is best for your project.

Needle Holder: This accessory is not imperative, but it is great for organizing. The photo on page 25 shows a wooden needle holder. Plastic pillboxes and metal tins also make good needle holders.

Wing Nut Tool: This wooden device helps tighten or loosen the nuts on your scroll frame's roller bars. The one in the picture was given to me many years ago. If you cannot find one in the local yarn shop, have a woodworker or handy friend devise one. A simple stick with a long groove and a hole in the middle does the job. This saves your fingertips each time you tighten the wing nuts on the stretcher bars.

Makeup Brush: At times, you might want to brush mohair or other yarns to get a fuzzy look. In "The Theater," a lady's white sweater was brushed after it had been stitched in mohair yarn. You want a brush that fuzzes the yarns without making them worn out and frayed. Do not use brushes that could be coated with cosmetic residue.

Laying Tool: To make ribbons, rayon and other yarns lie flat on the canvas, you need a tool to keep the yarn from twisting as you stitch it. A long, flat laying tool does the job very nicely. Holding the tool in your left hand on the surface of the canvas, stitch the thread up and over the tool. When the yarn is passed back down to the underside, stroke the yarn to ensure that it lies flat. Trolley needle and Takobari Japanese stiletto-type tools are available. Again, you can find these in your yarn shop—but if you look around, knitting needles, bobbins, rug needles, plastic collar stays, cocktail stirrers, metal skewers or dental tools can all be used. Keep different sizes and shapes on hand for various jobs.

Clear Plastic Graph Sheets: For quick transfer of pictures onto graphs, try clear plastic graph paper. It comes in a package of plastic sheets with different grid sizes. I have seen grids of 11, 14, 16, 18, 22 and 25/5 squares to the inch. To use the sheets, lay the desired size on a picture, card, portrait, wallpaper or whatever, to create a needlepoint motif in minutes. You may need to use your imagination for the correct count. This is a great way to copy heirloom photographs of family members without ruining them.

Thread organizer

Palettes and Thread Organizers: There are many different palettes available to organize the yarns or threads for your current project. Some resemble an artist's palette, while others are long boards with large holes in them. I have never invested in them, since I have had old wooden embroidery hoops in my sewing basket for years. Wooden hoops are best, since metal can rust, damaging the yarn. If you are working with only a few colors, large safety pins might work to keep your yarns organized. Some people prefer to use plastic soft drink rings. Use whatever works best for you.

Stands for Frames: You may be tempted to purchase a stand for your frames in the yarn shop. This could become a pricey investment. Before taking a stand home, ask the clerk if you can try it out to see whether it works for you. With a stand, both hands are free to stitch. Some models stand on the floor while others tuck under your legs. Some better models allow you to change the angle of the stretcher boards so that the position is uniquely yours. Be sure to find one that is well balanced. Stands for frames come in both wood and metal.

Look for a sturdy stand that can hold a frame of the size you usually use. If the stand is made of wood, be sure it is durable, hard wood. You do not want to be surprised in the middle of stitching to find your stand in two or more parts. Also remember, yarns need to be started and stopped. Find a stand that allows you to conveniently flip your frame so you can see the underside of the canvas. If you like to switch from one project to another before completion, you will want to find out how easy or difficult it is to change frames. If you like to travel with a stand, determine whether the stand folds for transport. Also, is it small enough to pack into your suitcase?

Lighting: Good light is imperative. A floor lamp, whose angle you can adjust, is a good choice for adequate lighting for any project. Fluorescent lights with attached magnify glasses are an extra help to those who have a hard time seeing tiny stitches. Some attach to tables, while others stand on their own. Your lighting choices depend upon your needs and personal taste.

All of the above tools are possibilities, but the decisions are yours. Many extras in yarn shops are important, while others are frivolous toys that only clutter your sewing bag. Some turn out to be costly mistakes, while others become personal favorites. If your stitching improves when you use a particular tool, then that tool was a worthwhile investment. Examine the items in the shops, and decide carefully.

Chapter Two

Start Stitching!

Transferring Designs to Canvas

Perhaps you have found a design you would like to stitch. How do you transfer the idea onto canvas? Several options are available

Painting canvas is relatively quick and easy. To do so, you need a paintbrush, oil-based or waterproof acrylic paints, a plastic acetate sheet, turpentine and your drawing.

Do not use acrylic paint that is not waterproof, or watercolors. Watercolors dissolve quickly in water, and take care—not all acrylic paints are colorfast. Oil-based paints mixed with turpentine create a thin paint that does not clog the canvas holes. Also, after it dries, the paint does not run when the needlepoint is blocked.

Place your drawing on a table. Lay down the acetate sheet, and then place the needlepoint canvas on top. You may wish to secure the whole lot with masking tape. Paint the desired motif in the colors you wish to use. Allow the paint to dry completely. This ensures your stitches will not be discolored by wet paint. Take a little extra care to lay the design squarely on the canvas. Trees, buildings and other upright items should stand straight.

Design

If you do not wish to paint the canvas, you can **trace the pattern** with an indelible marker or India ink. Many felt-tipped markers read "permanent on most surfaces." The important word for a needle artist to define here is "most." Test the marker by drawing lines on a piece of scrap canvas. Wet the canvas with water. If it runs, it will run just as easily after the canvas has been stitched. Try other markers until you find one that is truly permanent. If using India ink, be sure it has dried completely before stitching the canvas.

The photograph shows the correct method for transferring your design onto canvas. Place the picture on the table. Secure it with masking tape. Place the canvas on top of the picture and draw the motif. For the best results, draw a thin line. In the picture, you can see a line parallel to the bottom of the canvas. This is a placement line. It ensures the grid of the canvas is running properly on the picture.

Again, do not use pencils, ballpoint ink or non-permanent felt-tipped markers. When you finish stitching and go on to the blocking step, the fibers in your yarns could become discolored. And, do not think that your needlepoint will not need to be blocked. Even if it does not need blocking, if it ever needs to be cleaned later, the colors in the markers will run. If you wish to use a disappearing marker, be sure the ink is not one that disappears within 48 hours. Unless you stitch very fast, you will need to mark your canvas again, and the second time, you may not be as accurate as the first.

When you mark your canvas, draw the design as though you were working on paper. Flower petals should have rounded curves. Do not think of the canvas as a series of dots, or squares or steps in the design. You will interpret the placement of the stitches later.

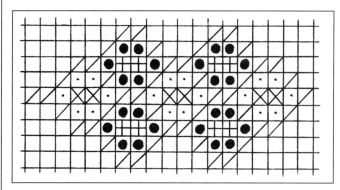

A symbol-coded diagram

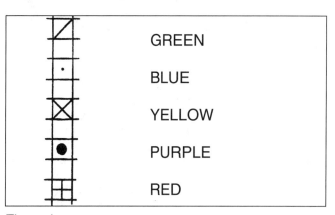

The code

Graphs are wonderful tools for assisting the artist in transferring the design to canvas. The first featured is coded with different symbols. Each symbol represents a color used for the motif. For example, in the graph, a dot is used to depict blue. A slash in a square means green.

A color-coded graph is easier for the beginner to read. Each color is the exact color used for the stitch. This also makes visualizing the end product easier. Most graphs are color blocks, rather than coded symbols. The exact colors required for each graph are usually accompanied by a legend, showing the recommended yarn brand and colors.

In the graph, each square equals one canvas intersection. If four blocks of blue are on a linear line on the graph, you stitch four blue stitches. Because the design is detailed in patterns, most graphs are stitched in Half Cross or Continental. When using a graph for transferring, it is imperative that you allow enough canvas on all sides to fit the motif. When in doubt, allow a few extra inches for the canvas. Start in the center and work outward. Your motif will then be centered on the canvas. One of the oldest methods of transferring patterns on canvas is Tramé. For this method, see Tramé in the Glossary of Stitches.

Beginning a Project

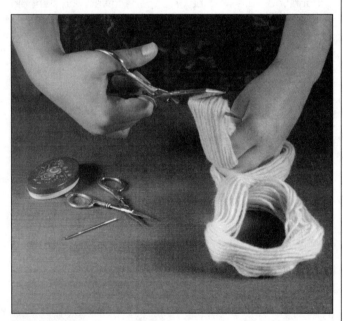

Cut yarn to start.

Now, you are relatively well-versed on the subject of the yarns themselves. So how do you begin stitching your canvas? The length of your thread should be no longer than 18" to 20". Any longer, and the yarn will wear out before you have finished stitching the entire length. Using an extremely long piece of yarn can cause the yarn, by the time you have stitched with the entire length, to wear to the point where it shows the canvas grid. When working such very large stitches as Florentine, Bargello and others, longer yarns can be used.

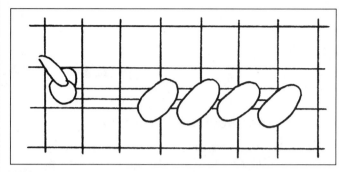

Waste knot

Anchor your yarn using a **waste knot**. Start with a threaded needle, and make a knot at the end of your yarn. Start on the canvas about 1-1/2" away from your first stitch. This will leave a trail of yarn underneath the canvas. Then make your set of stitches, traveling over the front of the canvas toward the knot. The stitches should cover the yarn under the canvas. This serves to secure the end without leaving an unsightly bump on the canvas. When you reach the knot, simply snip it off with your scissors (see diagram). This is a fine way to start stitching on an empty canvas, or in an area far from areas you have already worked.

Once your project is well underway, you will have areas in which your yarn can be anchored under previously worked spaces. Simply run your needle through the yarns underneath the canvas, and begin to stitch. To finish off your yarn, again, run the needle under the stitches, pull the yarn through and then cut off the excess.

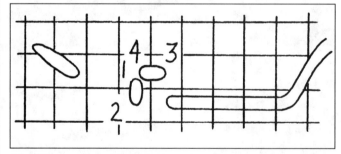

Securing "L"

Another good method for anchoring the tail is the **securing L technique**. A knot is not necessary before stitching. Thread your needle as desired. You will want to make the "L" four or five intersections away from where you wish to start stitching. Starting on the top of the canvas, insert your needle downward. Come up at one on the graph. Your next stitch goes down at two, and up at three. The "L" is formed when you insert the needle down again at four. Bring the needle up on top of the canvas a few threads away from the "L." Your yarn is anchored. This method is appropriate for many different stitches. The "L" can be completely worked over with your needlepoint stitches, without removing it. The only clipping required is the tail, which you used to start the anchoring.

When starting a project, work small areas first. Depending upon the project, you may wish to work the background along with the motif, as in a bell pull with decorative stitches and Basketweave for the background. As the motif is stitched, the background can also be filled in. A scroll frame's roller bars hold the project with even tension along the top and bottom. Working the front and background stitches simultaneously breaks up the tedious work of the Basketweave.

White should be stitched first, and then other colors. While white might not be the most exciting color to begin working, it must be done first, to prevent the darker colors from mixing into it, and making the white yarn appear dirty.

General Stitching Technique

A quick survey of various needlepoint projects—pictures, pillows, and other objects—will illustrate to you the variation in neatness and stitch quality. In the more impressive projects, you can be sure that the artist not only had an eye for design, but also had a good understanding of various techniques that work to make the project smoother.

Here, we focus on some of those techniques, looking to create clean stitches, smooth work and a neat appearance. Techniques include a broad range, from beginner steps to more advanced techniques for more experienced stitchers.

There are enough rules and tips to fill volumes. Some rules are not strict, while others are truly imperative. The best thing to keep in mind is to have self-confidence, and use your own intelligence and skills. If you discover a trick or technique improves your stitching, then by all means, use it in your projects!

The following tips are some basics I use for creating lovely stitches:

1. When creating Cross stitches, make all your cross hatches in the same direction. It does not really matter which one is on top, but consistency is key. Also, the yarns must lie flat, and not twisted, on the canvas. This makes a neater overall appearance.

2. To create sharp, clear stitches, bring the needle up from a hole that does not yet hold any yarn, and then insert it back down into the one that does already contain yarn.

3. Always count the threads on the canvas, and not the holes. You cannot enumerate something that is not there. Run your needle along the threads while counting to improve your accuracy.

4. If you must rip out stitches, never sew out the mistake. Remove the needle from the yarn, and pull the yarn out of the canvas. If you have a large area, cut out the stitches. Never reuse the yarn. The used yarn is tired, and will look bad and wear poorly.

5. When a project includes white yarn, do the stitching in white first, if possible, and then the other colors. If the white is worked after colors, the colored yarns infuse fibers into the white, making the white appear dirty. It is a time-consuming process to try to remove the colored fibers from the white yarn.

6. Sometimes, when counting Bargello, you may make a stitch that is one thread less than needed. You do not want to rip out the mistake, since much work has been done. Do not panic. With the same color in the needle, create the correct stitch over the incorrect one, right on top. With a little more tension than usual, anchor the end of the yarn. The idea is to make the correction without piling up too much yarn on top of the canvas. This hides the problem without hours of extra work.

7. When embellishing a background in Basketweave, make the rows as long as possible. Work the indentations into the motif along with the rest of the background. You never want to break up the Basketweave pattern on the back. This would result in lines on the front that can never be blocked out.

8. To center Bargello on the canvas, find the middle, where you want the first row of stitches to be. Decide what kind of stitch needs to be placed in the middle, and make the stitch on the canvas. Then work outward in both directions, right and left, to the end of the row.

9. For chair seats or other items with symmetrical motifs, first locate the middle of the design, and work out from there.

10. Large stitches usually do not belong in small areas. Always keep in mind that the project should have balance. If you try to place large stitches in a small area, the area will only be overwhelmed, and the design might not be highlighted as well as it should be.

11. Small stitches in a large area can be busy, but this depends on the motif and design. Small stitches in larger areas can also be great.

12. If you make a mistake in the middle of your stitches, cut the mistake out with fine embroidery scissors, being careful not to cut the canvas. If you do cut canvas, the hole must be patched. When the error has been removed, pull out some stitches around it to create ends to weave on the underside.

13. In crewel point, stitch with Tent as close to the Satin stitches as possible. No canvas should be showing when the project is finished.

14. To prevent void canvas from showing, compensate when needed (see page 33).

15. If the underside of the stitched project is flat, with little yarn for anchoring a new yarn, start with a waste knot. If you anchor a new yarn in too little yarn, this creates a bumpy canvas. For example, Half Cross leaves little anchoring for a new section. The new yarn should be started as though Half Cross stitches were not already stitched into the canvas.

16. If the canvas is printed and the intersection is not distinctly marked with the color that should be used, work freely with your needle. Look at the curve, and work on your own. Using your own color judgment creates a more natural curve, and a more convincing picture. No large "steps" should appear in the motif.

17. Do all you can to keep your tension consistent throughout the work. If your tension is too loose, the look will be lumpy. Too much tension distorts the canvas, and sometimes this does not block out.

18. If you will be joining two canvases for a rug and you will be using Tent stitches, never stop the yarn at a row and go directly under the previous one. The rows of stitches should be staggered.

19. When you are not stitching your project, never park the needle in the canvas. If you must do so, place it on the edge of the canvas that will be cut away later. If your needle rusts, the rust may never come out of the yarns. Also, the needle distorts the canvas and may weaken the thread.

20. When working stitches, pull the thread in one complete movement. Do not pull, stop and then finish pulling. An incomplete movement makes uneven stitches.

21. Be sure to use waste knots and cut them off when the project is finished.

22. When working Basketweave, always start and finish yarns by weaving on the underside in a perpendicular or parallel direction. Never weave yarns in a diagonal direction.

23. Trim extra yarn on the underside for a smoother finish.

24. When you must begin working with a second thread before you have finished with the one you are working, pull the yarn to the top of your project. This prevents your grabbing the yarn by mistake while stitching.

25. While stitching, take the time to check that you keep your yarn properly twisted. If you do not, you will end up with knots or weak spots.

26. If you find stitches that are not pulled to the proper tension, turn the project over and pull the yarn a little until it is tight enough. If you have not stitched very far from the improper one, pull all the stitches until you get to where you left off.

27. When working Basketweave, if you cannot decide whether the next row should move up or down, remember that the needle should point vertically for down rows, and horizontally for up rows.

28. If your project has a large background and you have decided what colors and stitches to use to fill it, work on the background along with the foreground.

Buttons

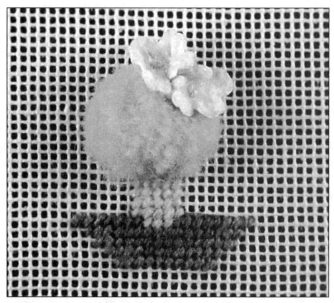

Silk flowers

29. Add fun objects to the work. Rhinestones, beads, chains and other items can be stitched on for added color, texture, and interest.

30. Always work with the correct size needle to fit your canvas and yarn.

31. When traveling with your needlepoint, carry only the yarn you need while you are traveling, and not the entire amount for the project. This keeps the yarn clean and fresh. It also guarantees that you cannot possibly lose a large amount of valuable yarn.

32. If the project is stitched on separate pieces of canvas, make sure the stitches travel in the same direction.

33. A magnet bar attached to a frame or stretcher bars makes an excellent needle park, and serves as a caddie for extra needles.

In terms of canvas, keep the following tips in mind:

1. The back of your canvas is just as important as the front. Avoid building mounds and voids on the underside of the canvas. Otherwise, when the project is mounted in a frame, the texture of the back makes the front appear lumpy and unsightly.

2. Use stretcher bars from the beginning to lessen your efforts in blocking later.

3. Block your work, whether or not it appears to be straight. The blocking process truly enhances the overall appearance. The only exception to this rule is that you should first test silk, rayon and metals. Kreinik silk, along with many others, bleeds when immersed in water.

4. If the canvas has void areas, try painting the area, to link the background with the motif. Or, consider ahead whether the motif will produce void areas, and try colored canvas.

5. Never fold canvas for storage. Rather, roll it to ensure that it lies flat on the frame and does not distort when you use it in a project.

6. Use dissection pins or silk pins to block areas in the motif on your canvas that need correction.

7. Rather than having to buy new stretcher bars to fit projects, you can sew fabric on the sides of the canvas to fit bars you already own.

8. Be sure to allow enough blank canvas around the motif for blocking.

The following tips are helpful concerning yarn:

1. When constructing a tapestry in Tent stitches, do not mix yarns. When working with tapestry yarn, do not incorporate Persian. If you were to use the two together, one would appear fuzzy and the other smooth. Another not-so-terrific combination is pearl cotton and embroidery floss. Pearl is shiny and embroidery floss has a thready look.

2. Always purchase the entire amount of yarn required to complete a project, plus extra for surprises.

3. When you buy yarn, always be sure to check the dye lot numbers. If you must change lot numbers, see the instructions on page 21 for a gradual transformation.

Shiny cotton

4. After finishing an area that includes stitches with such yarns as metals, silks, rayons or other delicate materials, protect the area by basting white fabric over the area. The cloth prevents abrasion and soil from ruining your creation, and using white ensures that color will not bleed into your yarns.

5. When using Persian yarn, be sure to strip the plies apart and then replace them, whether you are using one, two, three, or more plies in the needle. Embroidery floss should also be stripped.

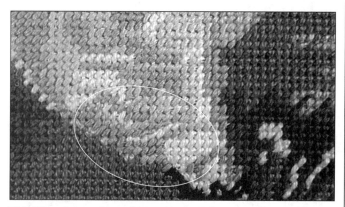

This Continental has been worked incorrectly.

6. When you begin a stitch, always double check to make sure that you are stitching in the correct direction.

7. When buying or storing wool, never wrap the yarn around cardboard. This pulls on the wool, wearing it out before it is even stitched into a project.

8. If you need two plies in the needle for a small area, never double over the yarn. Thread two individual plies of yarn into the needle's eye. This ensures that the yarn lies smoothly. Also, you cannot rip out stitches if the needle cannot be removed.

9. Use waste knots to start your yarn. To tie off, make the last stitch, weave the needle under the back side of the previous stitches and pull through. The yarn is anchored.

Yarn thicknesses.

10. Never use worn or used yarn.

11. Avoid working with yarn with slubs as imperfections. Some specialty yarns have slubs for added texture. But, if the yarn is supposed to be smooth, be sure that it is.

12. Never use long strands of yarn. Depending upon the fiber, the strand should not be longer than 18" to 20".

Compensation

Compensation can be defined as the art of making a stitch appear to be a whole unit when it is really only a partial stitch. As you develop a repertoire of stitches and incorporate them into motifs, you will find that there are sometimes spaces in the design where the stitches do not fit perfectly. Square stitches in round areas leave void areas. Some areas need to be filled, but perhaps the stitch cannot be finished before you reach the end of the canvas. In this case, the area can be finished with a partial stitch, rather than switching to an entirely different stitch. The use of this partial stitch is called compensation, and to achieve it, you have several different options.

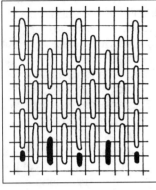

Upright compensation
(in black)

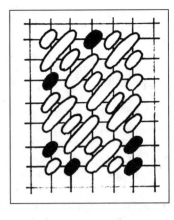

Small compensation
(in black)

Continental compensation
(in black)

You might use either a partial stitch or a Continental stitch to finish off an area. For example, when working an area with Bargello stitches, you could fill the voids with Gobelin. For very small upright stitches, you may need to thicken the yarn with another ply, to ensure a completely covered canvas. Notice the black upright stitches at the bottom of the graph. These help to create the illusion that the pattern travels up the canvas.

Interlock and Penelope canvas generally do not pose any problem for the artist who uses small, upright compensation stitches. Mono canvas, though, tends to hide some stitches. With Mono, your best choice may be to use Continental for compensation. Note the graph. Continental stitches are used anywhere the canvas shows through the stitches. This may require that small stitches be tucked under long upright or diagonal ones. Remember, you want the entire canvas covered. If stitching Four-Way Bargello, do not use Continental to fill the void canvas. Always use Upright Gobelin in a thicker ply than you used on the rest of the canvas.

In the diagram above, dark stitches in the illustration represent the compensation required to make a square. In this example, think of it in diagonal long and short stitches. You may need to use this technique when working Small Checker, Scotch or Arrowheads.

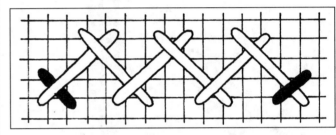

Cross compensation (in black)

Cross stitches may require small cross hatches to fill voids. Herringbone and other never-ending stitches require small stitches, which trick the eye into seeing an unbroken pattern. Other examples of this are Long Armed Cross, Ley's Trail, Fishbone I and Montenegrin.

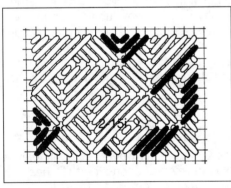

Oriental
compensation
(in black)

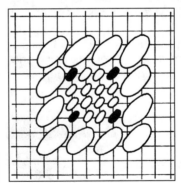

Petit Point compensation
(in black)

Large-patterned stitches, such as Oriental IV, travel in all directions on the canvas, without definite starting and stopping points. Work the area with your desired stitch, and then fill in the voids. The diagram shows Oriental IV stitches in a square. Notice how the arrowheads are only partially worked on the edges. Half stitches are required to compensate for Moorish, Byzantine and other patterned stitches.

When working a project on Penelope canvas, stitching Petit Point and Demi Point in the same picture, compensation is required to finish the smaller stitches. A stitch in Demi Point uses four intersections on the canvas, compared with one intersection for a Petit Point stitch. For this reason, if three stitches are required to make a curve, you need to have one compensation stitch to fill the void.

In the sample graph on page 34 are large, white stitches. This represents one color. The small, lighter ones refer to another color. Compare the lighter with the darker stitches. Note the four small black stitches in Petit Point. These are compensation stitches, needed to fill the smaller stitched area. On the actual project, these would be the same color as the larger white stitches. If you were making a picture of a woman and wished to stitch the face in Petit Point and the hair in Demi Point, a change in stitch size would be required. The face would be a flesh tone and the hair in, say, brown. Petit Point requires one-ply Persian yarn, compared with Demi Point, which calls for two-ply Persian yarn. To finish the Petit Point around the face line, one-ply brown yarn is correct. Never try to use more plies than needed for Petit Point.

Sometimes, the decision of how to compensate a stitch is a difficult one. Sometimes it can be helpful to view a partial stitch to get an idea, and make a better decision. Cover part of the stitching diagram, to see how many and which stitches require compensation.

Throughout Chapter Three, you may see many interesting stitches that you would like to use in your projects. Some stitches cannot be compensated, such as Square Herringbone, Double Knot, Sprat, Shell III and Brazilian. To use them, you need to increase or decrease the area. At times, a smaller version of the stitch can be made to fit the area. Sprat and Brazilian cannot change in size, but Double Knot and Shell III can be made smaller or larger depending upon your needs.

Chapter Three

The Stitches

Overview

Many people think of needlepoint as having only one stitch, and as being useful for making only pictures, pillows and seat cushions. Hundreds of stitches are known today and more are constantly being created. There are, of course, many benefits to having the great variety of stitches A three-dimensional effect, either smooth or chunky, can be created. Texture and relief can be added to everyday projects. The enjoyment of exploring and experimenting with different stitches makes your project more fascinating to create. Imagine working a large project with many areas where several different stitches could be applied—for example, a large tapestry worked in different colors. Instead of using Tent as your single, solitary stitch, you might use bold stitches such as David, Gloria and Raymond. In smaller areas, you might use Crosses, Rice, Eyelets and the underside of Basketweave. In areas where you would like to attract attention, try using Jus, Edge or Suzie's Garden. Less of an "eye popper" would be Diana or Emily.

Stitches can be grouped into five distinct categories. These include vertical stitches, such as Hungarian; horizontal stitches, like Rep; angle stitches, such as Tent; diagonal stitches, like Cross; and such upright stitches as Gobelin Tramé. Choosing from these five categories, you can create thousands of stitches and stitch combinations (see diagram).

As you read this book, try to create as many of the stitches as possible. Experiment and make changes to create variations on your own. Use different yarns, fibers and textures to explore the possibilities. Some stitches will become favorites, while others will be best forgotten. Many are very useful for many different projects, while others are good for embellishing belts, purses or other items where you want only one stitch. The Eugene stitch is a great example of this. When first created many years ago, it was used as a belt. However, as of late, Eugene has been used on a multitude of stitched projects.

Most of the photos show Persian wool on 14/1 Interlock canvas. Follow this example to make your stitches, unless directions are listed differently. Note, too, that the yarn is generally two-ply Persian wool. The yarn is never overlapped in the needle. For further explanation, see the discussion of yarn beginning on page 16.

The stitches are arranged in alphabetical order, to assist you in quickly finding the correct stitch for your projects. The individual stitches can be great fun to learn, and even more fun to create with afterward. Most importantly, do not be afraid of making mistakes! Better to make them while paging through the book, in the name of learning, than to make them with a limited quantity of special yarn for a prized project. Have a great time exploring and discovering these stitches!

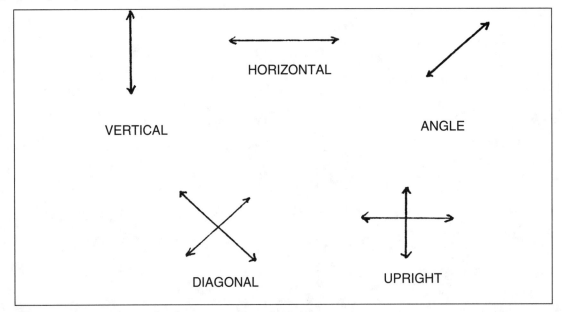

Stitch angles represent the five catergories of stitches

A Glossary of Stitches

Algerian Eye I

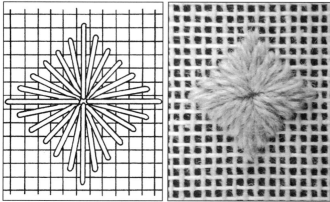

This is a very hard-wearing stitch, even though the points of the star are long. By using two-ply yarn in the needle, you stuff quite a lot of wool into the canvas. First make a hole for the middle. This hole allows the yarn to pass through without making a messy pile. Use a large knitting needle to make the hole. Do not cut the canvas! When stitching, be sure to draw the thread taut but not too tight. Try not to overlap the threads, but keep them straight. When drawing the needle through the middle, rotate it as you travel down. This forces the hole to remain open, ensuring even stitches. The graph shows Algerian Eye I over six threads on the canvas. It is better to have it between four and eight. Any longer, and you end up with too much yarn in the middle—and a very delicate stitch. To create Algerian Eye I, work the corners first, then the next two at each point, working until you have reached the middle.

This stitch would make a fun background using different colors, or only one. You might consider Algerian Eye I for a quilt. Clothing for a child is another idea. In a more abstract project, you could use this stitch as flowers. Always work from the outside of the eye toward the middle.

Algerian Eye II

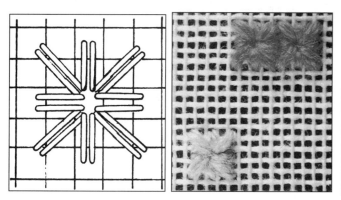

This small, delicate stitch traverses two intersections. When I ponder its pattern, I think of individual flowers, or wallpaper in a little room. Use Algerian Eye II as an isolated stitch or in a group. Try a rainbow of colors for a plaid. Metallic threads could make twinkling stars in a midnight sky. A row of Algerian Eye II would make a beautiful border around a motif. Stagger the stitch to create yet another effect. Again, this is a hard-wearing stitch, so do not be afraid to use it on pillows or other functional items. Work one stitch at each point, then the sides. Then, repeat the process all around the eye. This creates a neat, straight eye. Again, you may choose to enlarge the hole in the center with a knitting needle before stitching. Use two plies on 14/1 canvas.

Algerian Eye Variation

This stitch has a pleasant, clean appeal. If you work this stitch in a background, be careful not to make Algerian Eye Variation too busy. One solid color, or shades in a single color family would be better. Poke a hole in the middle of each eye. As with the other Algerian Eye stitches, caution should be used to avoid cutting the canvas. Work the stitches at the north, south, east and west points then the two on each side of these. Then, work the diagonal lines to finish the eye. This hard-wearing stitch traverses three intersections in the large circles, and two in the smaller ones.

Alternating Flat

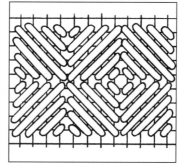

This medium-wearing stitch is exactly like the Flat I Stitch, but here, the squares move in opposite directions. At its longest point, the stitch crosses four intersections. The rules are like Flat I—work each square completely, and then continue to the next. If it is convenient, you may want to work the stitch diagonally. Use two plies in the needle. Use it any project, in a single color, or in combinations.

Alternating Scotch

Like Scotch, Alternating Scotch is a hard-wearing stitch, good for almost any project. It traverses three intersections at its longest point. To create the stitch, complete each square before continuing on to the next. Use two plies in the needle.

Alternating Scotch Variation

This medium-hard wearing stitch is at its best in samplers. Begin this stitch by working the white lines, in two plies, to create the foundation. Then, insert the black lines on the graph using a darker hue. Using starkly contrasting colors creates a deep, dramatic effect on the canvas. For a less dramatic look, choose two colors that are closer together. The stitch crosses three intersections at its longest point.

Alternating Tent

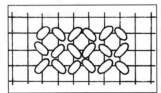 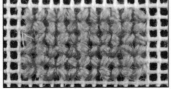

As it crosses only one intersection on the canvas, this is one of the hardest-wearing stitches you can choose. While it is slow to work, I truly believe it is well worth the effort. If at an impasse about which stitch to use in a small area, try this one. It functions equally well in a line, a background or in a small area. While you stitch it, take the time to prevent your stitches from pushing the previous row upward. Use two-ply Persian yarn, in one or two colors.

Alternating Tied Gobelin

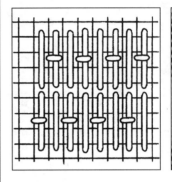 

This medium-light wearing, upright stitch allows lines of canvas to show both above and below the definite horizontal rows. If you do not want canvas to show, paint the area with an oil-based paint in a color to match the yarn. The more even you can make your stitches, the cleaner and smoother the look you can achieve. The stitch crosses four intersections on the canvas. As with all upright stitches, strip the yarn before working. Depending upon canvas size, you may need two or three plies of yarn in the needle. Most upright stitches require three.

Ant Weft Edging

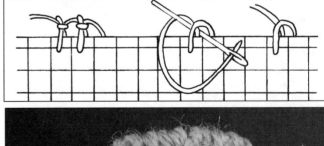

This hard-wearing edging stitch is a little different from others. While most are flat, this one makes a flap along the side. It, too, allows canvas to show through. On 14/1 canvas, use two plies in your needle. If you use more than two, the knots will be too large, creating an uneven stitch.

Arrowheads

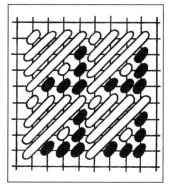 

This stitch seems to lend an amazing softness to a motif. The effect is bold in two or more colors—but for a subtle look use one color, or a combination of shades that differ only slightly. Imagine how Arrowheads might look in dark blue with white. Then, imagine the effect the same stitch would have if you were to use medium and light blue. Keep these possibilities in mind when deciding which stitches to use in your designs. Arrowhead requires two plies in the needle for the entire stitch.

Arte's *(Courtesy of Arte Johnson)*

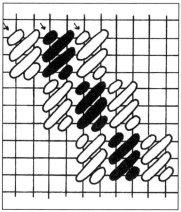 

As you begin and complete more and more projects, you will notice that your bag of yarn is growing fatter and fatter. Arte's stitch is the perfect hard-wearing stitch to put all those bits of yarn to use. The stitch was named after its creator, Arte Johnson. When you use it, keep in mind that it can become very busy. Arte's creates a tweed effect that can be a wonderful background in the right picture—and it is a great way to use all that spare yarn you have been saving.

Place all your yarns of the same color family into a bag, and without looking, grab two strands. Thread into your needle whatever you pull. You may have combinations of shades of blues, or browns or grays, etc. Work diagonally, stitching from top to bottom. If you run out of yarn, find two strands of the same colors, and continue. Stop at the end of each row. Change yarn for the next set of stitches.

Ashley *(Courtesy of Chottie Alderson)*

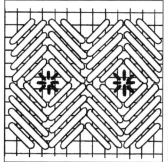 

Needlepoint is a two-dimensional medium. The challenge in many projects is to trick the viewer into seeing a three-dimensional effect. Ashley has just that effect, when you use light colors for the long stitches and dark for the small. Stitch the diagonal in two plies, and then the little eyelet in one ply. You can create a deep effect by using two rich tones of the same color. Ashley is a medium-light wearing stitch.

Astrakhan Velvet

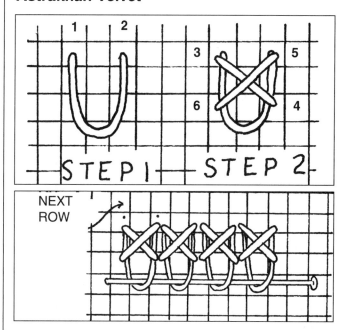

Finished Astrakhan Velvet

Does your design require the addition of a pile of loops in a certain area? Are you looking for a dramatic effect for a special spot on the motif? Astrakhan Velvet does just that. It eats a good amount of yarn, as do all pile stitches. What would be more fun than a rug made entirely of Astrakhan Velvet? A word of caution—the loops should be equal size. To create equal loops, use a needle, rod or other straight object to measure. Note the second diagram.

Aubusson

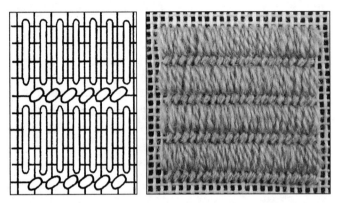

The soft, horizontal lines are distinctive of Aubusson. This is a quick stitch to work, but it is only medium-light wearing. The upright stitches should be in three-ply yarn and the Continental in two-ply. The upright stitches traverse four threads on the canvas. Use Aubusson where you want a horizontal line to appear.

Back

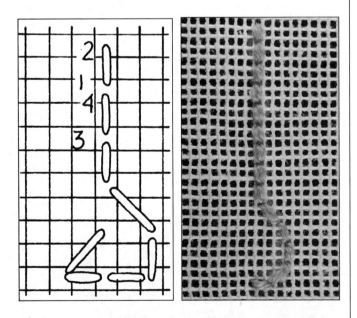

Often, an area needs a little extra definition. Sometimes, a simple line is required. Whatever the case, the hard-wearing Back stitch might be the answer. You can use this simple stitch over one, two or more threads in any direction. Add it to other stitches for a finished look or use it in a straight line for a border. Any way you stitch, a smooth line appears, compared to others that create squared edges. Use one ply or more, depending upon the effect you wish to create.

Banded Cross Weave

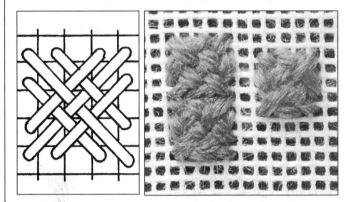

Banded Cross Weave is another versatile, hard-wearing stitch. The long stitches are laid in one direction. After the long stitches are finished, the others are woven in and out of the first set. Banded Cross Weave can be adapted to any area, big or small, quite nicely. Two-ply Persian works well on 14/1 canvas. Use it where compensation is not required.

Bargello

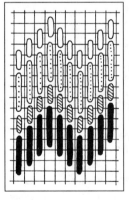

Volumes have been dedicated to this stitch. Bargello is a family of stitches that use strong up and down movements on the canvas. Florentine, Flame, Hungarian Point and Irish work are all included in this family. Patterns and color combinations are endless. Bargello stitches are distinguished .by their flat and smooth stitches that lie either perpendicular or parallel to the canvas threads. You would never see diagonal stitches in a true Bargello. The number of canvas threads over which the yarn travels is determined by the motif, and can range from two to eight. Color combinations are also up to the artist. A family or group of matched tones can create a striking pattern. Do not choose too many dark colors for stitching Bargello. Varied values from dark to light better balance the motif.

Think of Bargello as an accent stitch for a background. If the other stitches are in Tent, Bargello can transform the project from everyday to special. Try a motif in Bargello with a background in Tent.

The stitch in the diagram is just one example of the Bargello family. Stitches range from threads that run up and down in repeats of four to large ribbons that lap down the length of the canvas. Pillows, shoes, purses and entire chairs are covered Bargello stitches. Because the stitches are upright, three-ply Persian is required for 14/1 canvas. Tapestry yarn fits 12/1 canvas very nicely. The wear depends upon the pattern you choose.

Basketweave

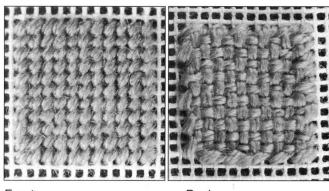

Front   Back

Basketweave is a truly historical, universal stitch. In the 1920s and 30s, Basketweave was used for Berlin work. One example is a counted motif of birds and flowers. The needle artist would buy the "pre-worked" canvas and finish the work in one solid color. Usually, it was stitched in black or another dark color. Today, motifs are commonly available in yarn shops. Dozens of motifs and designs can be bought for projects ranging from bell pulls to seat cushions. The stitching technique for Basketweave creates a very hard-wearing stitch that does not distort the canvas as much as Continental and Half Cross can.

Basketweave's reverse side resembles an even-weave wicker basket. It is this back that ensures the hard-wearing quality of the stitch, which is why dining room chairs and other functional items are worked in Basketweave. In large areas, you can create very even stitches, and rows that are free from tension changes, ridges and other unsightly errors.

Another plus for Basketweave is its tendency to reinforce the canvas. Because you create the stitch by pulling yarn through an empty hole and inserting it into an occupied one, you produce clear, defined stitches. Another great attribute is that you do not need to reverse the canvas when you reach the bottom of a row. Once you master this stitch, you will be tempted to use it in any area that calls for a Tent stitch.

On a down row, the needle always points downward. On an up row, the needle points horizontally. Never work two adjoining rows in the same direction. Doing so creates a diagonal line that can never be blocked out. Another sure way to create a diagonal line is to have your waste knot lying in the direction of your row. Always place the waste knot either horizontally or vertically. Once you understand that Basketweave is identical to Continental at the end of the rows, working a corner will be easy. Never pull your yarn too tight—this distorts the canvas, and blocking will never remove the distortion. The rows are parallel to the edges of the canvas, except at the ends.

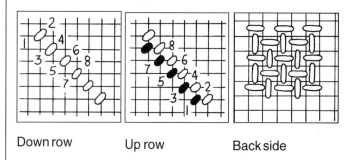

Down row   Up row   Back side

Begin by working at the upper left-hand corner. Come out of one and enter at two, then work three and four. Continue this until you have reached the bottom right-hand corner (see diagram). Your down row is the same, except the needle is perpendicular to the bottom of the canvas. The back of the canvas should look like a woven piece of fabric.

Mono canvas has an even weave, in which the horizontal threads travel over and under in an even pattern to the vertical threads. In the graph you can see that, in a true diagonal, each thread runs over or under its mate. This is important in making the vertical rows of Basketweave. With a little time and effort to make sure the down rows cover the vertical canvas threads and the up rows cover the horizontal threads, you will create stronger stitches that do not slip to a vertical position.

Any time you start or finish a yarn, weave the end in and out of the underside weave, following the pattern made by the stitch. Clip the yarn close to the work. This secures the yarn and ensures a neat back. Sometimes, if you are working a large project, you do not want to carry your scissors to snip each time you start and end a yarn. To eliminate the need to clip each time, pull the end of the yarn to the top of your project. This keeps the yarn from catching in the others. Yarns are a bit like little children. If you do not keep an eye on them, they are sure to get into trouble!

Bath

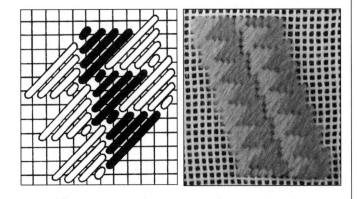

Stitch Bath in two different colors to create a dramatic effect. The long stitches traverse over four intersections on the canvas, making Bath medium-light in durability. It is best in samplers. This stitch distorts the canvas, so use stretcher bars. Also, use two plies in the needle on 14/1 canvas. Stitch the rows diagonally.

Battlement

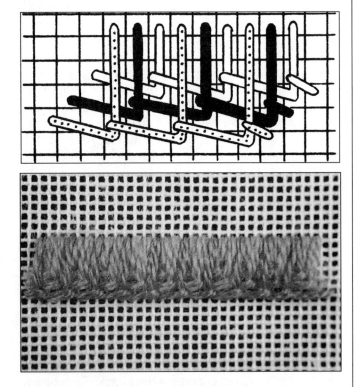

This light-wearing stitch is great fun to work. When I consider this one, I envision borders around a picture or sleeves on a dress. Try mitering the corners to make a sharp point. Think of Battlement in a rainbow of colors or a family of one, ranging from light to dark. Battlement is a simple stitch to work, but the possibilities for its application are endless. Use two plies in the needle.

Beau Ridge *(Courtesy of Chottie Alderson)*

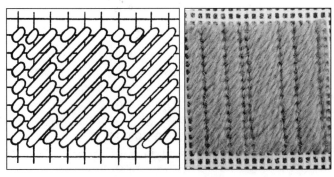

This light-wearing stitch is not restricted by fixed rules. The vertical lines can be of any count you choose, and you can use a single color or a combination. It is great for squared areas where you do not need to compensate. Consider using it as a fence post, ridges on the trunk of a tree or as an overall background pattern. Use two-ply yarn.

Belly Feathers
(Courtesy of Mary Lou Helgesen)

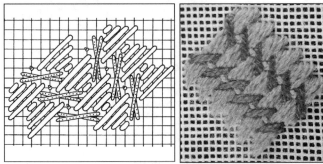

Belly Feathers, created by Mary Lou Helgesen, is an intriguing stitch, incorporating wool and pearl cotton for interest and texture. To create Belly Feathers, stitch the long diagonal lines first with two-ply wool yarn. Then, work the crosses in one-ply pearl cotton. Last, use one-ply wool for the French Knots. Belly Feathers is great in samplers.

Ben

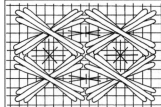 

Ben would be an excellent stitch to include in a sampler. Because it is light-wearing, it is best used in items that hang on the wall, rather than pillows or other functional projects. For a neat appearance, be sure to cross hatch in the same direction. Use two-ply yarn for the crosses and one-ply for the elongated and Smyrna crosses. Feel free to mix colors and fibers.

Binding

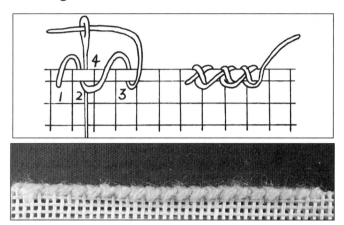

Often, a piece of needlepoint work needs finishing at its edges. This is the case with purses, eyeglass cases, key chains and other items that are not purely decorative. You could turn the edge over and use fabric or binding tape, but why not try stitching? You cannot fold over the edges of plastic canvas, so the hard-wearing Binding Stitch is the answer. Do not be afraid to use Binding for projects intended for a good deal of wear, such as a needlepoint rug.

With the wrong side of the canvas toward you, bring the needle, threaded with two-ply yarn, up at one. Go over the canvas and enter at two. Whip the needle away from you and enter at three, then at four. Do this until you have reached the end of the area you want bound. You can bind around a box without stopping the binding pattern. With a little practice, you should become quite proficient.

Bokhara Couching

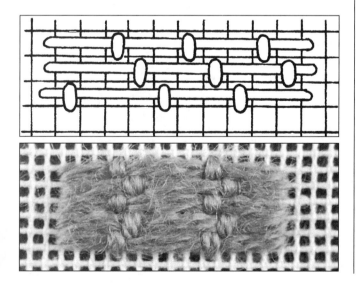

This is a soft technique that can adapt to any area, any number of plies, and any fiber. Use the same thread to lay down and couch. Lay the yarn over the desired row, and couch with the same needle. Work the couching in a random pattern. This is a light-wearing stitch.

Bow

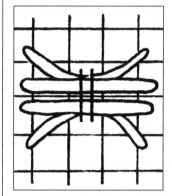 

This simple, hard-wearing stitch can be added to a project to accent a girl's hair, a tie on a man or shoes on a baby. Place the Bow in an unexpected area. For a different effect, try using this for a border, stitching the bows end to end, and filling the void areas with Continental. Use any fiber or number of plies you wish.

Boxed Stepped

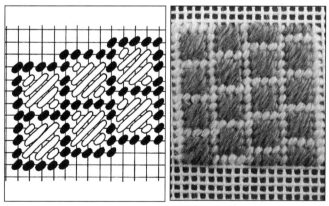

This is another great background stitch. It would be hard-wearing, if the boxes were not filled with Scotch Stitch. But, because the Scotch snags and pills, Boxed Stepped is considered medium light in its durability. I recommend working Scotch first, and then Continental. Think of the horizontal Continental as long lines going upward. This creates a clean look on the back and saves yarn. Use a single color or more colors.

Brazilian

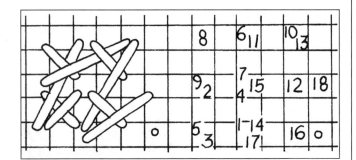

Eighteen steps and two-ply yarn make up this medium-wearing stitch. The result of Brazilian is a "bowl of raw wheat" effect. Keep this stitch in mind for grass, leaves, or textured clothing. Be careful to keep the count accurate and the yarns straight.

Breton

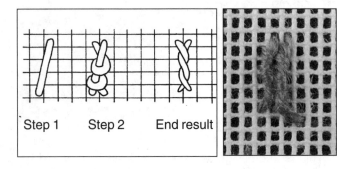

Step 1   Step 2   End result

Breton is not a true needlepoint stitch. Incorporate it in a needlepoint project by stitching over Continental or Tent. Think of Breton as an isolated accent piece. Depending upon the intensity of the effect you wish to create, one-, two- or three-ply yarn would be correct. This is a light-wearing stitch.

Brick

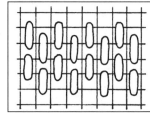

For a clean, diagonal, hard-wearing stitch, try Brick. The look is flat and can be quite attractive in small or large areas. Try more than one color. Turning the diagram on its side creates another look. Stitch Brick with two-ply yarn in the needle. Complete the first row, and then stitch the second. Brick traverses two intersections on the canvas.

Brick Cashmere

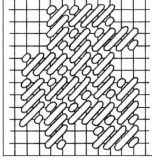

This medium-hard wearing stitch reminds me of a large, brick house. With brick red and gray in your needle, you can create a brick-and-mortar look. Many people enjoy stitching their own homes. If yours has brick siding, chimney or garden walls, try this. You might also stitch a church or a lighthouse. Other interesting uses are clothes on a boy or a blanket on a bed, or a brick path through a flower garden. Use two plies, and work the stitch in groups of blocks.

Brick Variation I

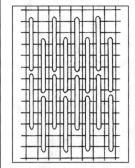

As with Brick, think of the lines in pairs. Because of the long stitches, you may need to thread three plies in the needle. Experiment on the side of your canvas. Work the first row, stitching from left to right. Then, using the same color, stitch the second line from right to left. Do not turn the canvas.

Brick Variation II

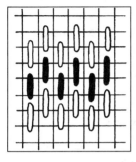 

This medium-light wearing variation allows you to create definite lines. The color combination determines whether the look of the stitch is bold or soft. The desired look should be determined by the finished project. Depending upon the yarn, use two or three plies in your needle for 14/1 canvas. The stitch crosses two canvas threads.

Brighton

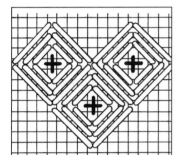 

Since it crosses four intersections at its longest point, Brighton is not a hard-wearing stitch, but it creates a dramatic effect if stitched in two different colors. Think of this as wallpaper or a large coverall pattern for a background. Metal threads in the center of the stitch would catch the eye. Work the larger straight lines first, and then stitch the crosses in the middle.

Bucky's Weaving

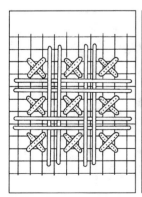 

Bucky's Weaving creates a deceptive graph. At first glance, you might think this is a flat, hard-wearing stitch. Not so! The weaving floats on the surface of the canvas. This stitch would never work on a pillow or other oft-used item. Pictures and other projects are better choices for the stitch. Use stretcher bars on the canvas when creating the stitch. Make sure the weaving is taut, but not too tight. Stitch the crosses first, and then weave. For an heirloom piece, take the time to create long, straight stitches that do not twist. Make the crosses in two plies and the long stitches in one. For tips on stitching the crosses, see Cross stitch, page 54. Have fun with this stitch, experimenting with colors and shades.

Bullion Knot

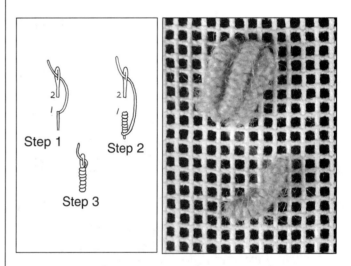

Step 1   Step 2

Step 3

A close cousin to the French Knot, the Bullion Knot can be useful for many details, such as ringlets for a little girl's hair, clumps of wheat grains, or wool on a sheep. If your project features flowers, think of Bullion for the stamen. Use a slightly larger needle than your yarn requires. The yarn must pass easily through the loops without your having to pull too much. To create the stitch:

Bring the needle and yarn out at 1 and back down at 2. Leave a loop.

Come out of 1 again, but this time do not pull the needle completely through.

Wrap the yarn around the needle several times.

With your thumb and index finger, hold the yarn around the needle. With your other hand, pull the needle out of the canvas and insert again at 1.

Pull the threads completely through, and finish with a rounded knot.

Practice this stitch to get pleasant, even, round knots. The size of the stitch is determined by the distance between points 1 and 2. Depending upon the number of times you wrap the yarn around the needle, the knot can either lie flat on the canvas, or be curved.

Butterfly

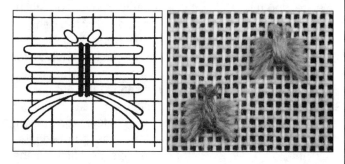

This tight, hard-wearing stitch can be used, in any fiber or number of plies, as an accent piece or as a row for a border. Cover the void canvas with Continental stitches. Work the long yarns first, and then finish by stitching the "body" of the butterfly. The last step is a Continental stitch for the antennae. For a truer butterfly look, pull the "body" stitches tightly to sharpen the form. Try using several different colors in your needle.

Butterfly Variation

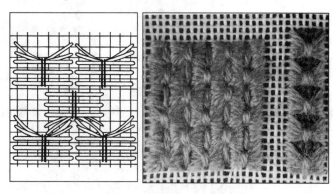

In this very hard-wearing variation, the butterflies are in two directions and the yarn is packed into the canvas. Depending upon the product, you may wish to use one or two plies in the needle. The sample shows two plies, but one ply gives a lighter feel. At the same time, one ply is not as hard-wearing as two. This stitch is best in samplers.

Button

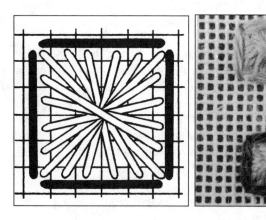

Button is a delightful, hard-wearing stitch that does not look like its diagram. Try stitching this in a series, using a range of light to dark tones in the same color family, for a dramatic look. Use it as a bold border around a picture. Use care in doing so, or the underside will be quite bulky. Do not use Button if the project will be mounted on a hard surface—as in the lacing method of finishing a picture. Consider Button for an isolated accent stitch in a special area.

Buttonhole

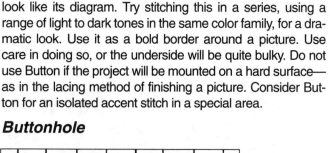

Buttonhole

Open

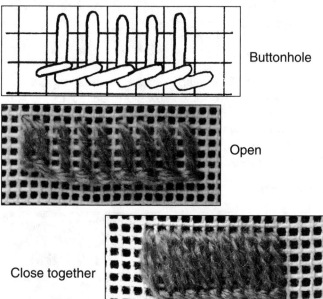

Close together

Buttonhole would make a great border or outline. Keep it in mind for shading on hills or skylines. Flowers, leaves, rainbows and sunsets would be striking in Buttonhole. When stitching Buttonhole, you can determine the effect by choosing to traverse one, two or more canvas threads. The graph shows the Buttonhole moving down two threads, then over one. Use your imagination. You might consider this medium-light wearing stitch comparable to Battlement.

Buttonhole Flowers
(Courtesy of Chottie Alderson)

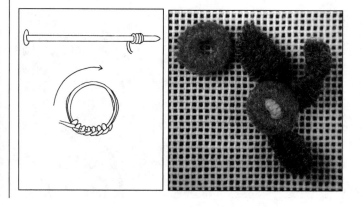

This is not a true needlepoint stitch. In projects such as a bird's eye view of a garden or three-dimensional flowers, medium-light wearing Buttonhole Flowers is a perfect stitch. It would also be a fun choice for buttons on a shirt. For a whimsical effect, use the stitch for animal eyes. Add knot stitches such as Bullion Knot or French Knot. A rhinestone in the middle adds sparkle to eyes. To make flowers, work off the canvas until the circle is completed and then attach it to the design. Use any fiber or number of plies. The directions are as follows:

First, take a #2 knitting needle and wrap the yarn around it four times.

Slide the yarn off the needle and then work buttonhole stitches around the loop.

When you have reached the complete circle, draw the yarn to the back side of the canvas by inserting the needle into the loop that makes the first Buttonhole stitch.

To attach the flower, stitch under the circle and over the top of the canvas.

Buttonhole Half Moons

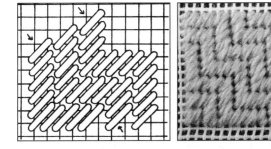

This hard-wearing stitch creates a clean edge and a smooth center. The diagram is a bit deceiving. Use two-ply yarn. The center will be quite packed with yarn, so enlarge the hole in the middle with a knitting needle. Work left to right to finish the stitch. Buttonhole Half Moons cannot be compensated. It traverses four canvas threads, and is great for samplers.

Byzantine I

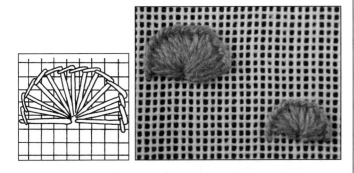

The soft zigzags of Byzantine I are a fine choice for a background. In terms of a picture, I envision clouds in the sky or grass on a rolling hill. To use this stitch for grass, try using different shades for each zigzag. This is a hard-wearing stitch, even though it traverses several threads. Some people stitch Byzantine I across two canvas threads, while others cross three. Either count is correct. Use two plies in your needle and follow the direction of the arrows in the diagram.

Byzantine II

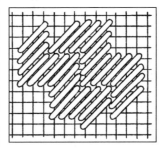 

For a bolder motif, try light-wearing Byzantine II. Like Byzantine I, two plies are required in your needle. When stitching Byzantine II, it is imperative that you keep the plies straight on the canvas. The twists and turns of the yarn would otherwise detract from the beauty of this stitch. It crosses three canvas intersections.

Byzantine III

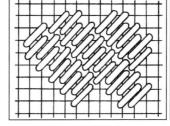 

This is the most durable stitch in the Byzantine family. For this reason, I recommend using it if you want to incorporate a Byzantine stitch on a pillow, or another functional item. Also, because it is a more compact stitch, you can employ it in smaller areas than you could the other Byzantine stitches. It is best in one color.

Byzantine IV

This extremely delicate stitch crosses four intersections on the canvas. Never use Byzantine IV on

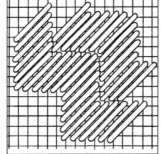 

objects you intend for functional use. When creating this stitch, remember to lay the fibers flat on the canvas, and take your time to create a true piece of heritage embroidery. Rayon floss would make Byzantine IV stand out on the canvas. It is also a possible choice for a background stitch.

Byzantine V

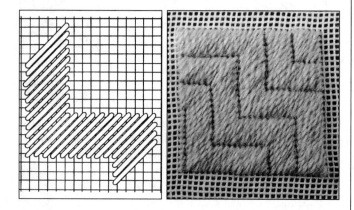

This light-wearing stitch is one of the boldest I know. The yarn traverses five intersections on the canvas and the stitches do not change direction until they have been worked eleven times. Wool creates a cushion effect on the canvas. Floss creates flat-lying stitches. Use two plies in the needle.

Byzantine Scotch

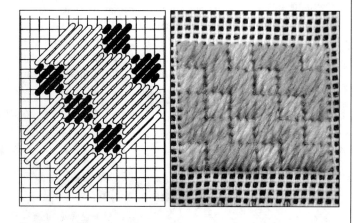

Depending upon the colors you employ, you can use Byzantine Scotch to create either a bold look or a subtle one. For more drama, stitch the Scotch in a different shade or color from the zigzag. Because it lies diagonally, two-ply yarn works best. Byzantine Scotch is best in samplers.

Carl

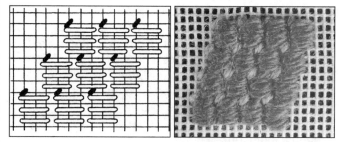

Thread your needle with three plies, and stitch the perpendicular lines first. Then, insert the small Continental stitches, using two plies in your needle. Although this is a two-toned stitch, the effect is soft. Stitch medium-wearing Carl anywhere you want a soft feel with a little texture.

Carla B.

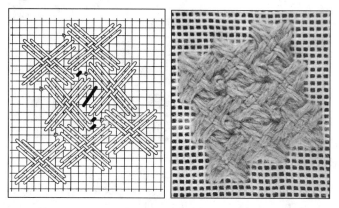

The heavy crosses are woven at the intersections. Be sure to weave in the same pattern throughout the area. The dark lines indicate fill-in stitches. Do this wherever you feel it is needed. This light-wearing stitch is great in samplers. Two-ply Persian yarn is required to cover 14/1 canvas.

Cashmere

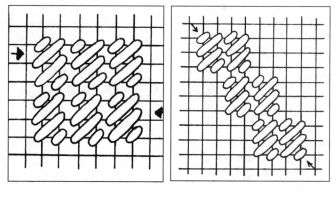

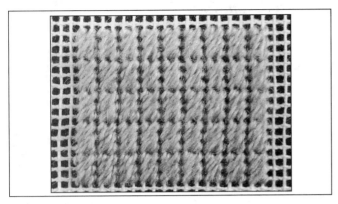

Cashmere is a universal, hard-wearing stitch with which most beginners start. It usually distorts the canvas, but can be blocked out with relative ease. If you do not want to do much blocking, use stretcher frames. There are two approaches for creating the Cashmere stitch. The first approach requires that you stitch into worked holes, while the second requires that you always stitch into holes that are not worked. In the first method, it is easier to place the stitches when compensating, while the second approach may leave you wondering what to do once in a while. Use Cashmere in almost any project.

Cashmere Checker

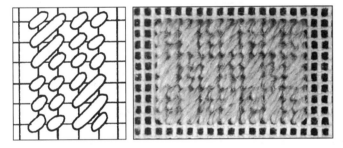

For a little texture that can hold up to any mishandling, try using Cashmere Checker. The yarn crosses two intersections on the canvas in some areas, but the majority of the steps cross only one intersection, creating a strong stitch. Work from left to right, alternating the Cashmere and Continental stitches, until you finish the row. Then repeat the process from right to left. Use two-ply Persian, in one or two colors.

Chain

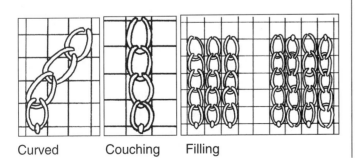

Curved   Couching   Filling

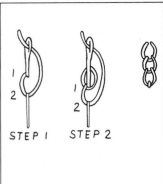

To create Chain, you must start with a waste knot. Bring the yarn up to the top at point 1. Hold the thread down with your left hand, and bring the needle down at 1 again. Then bring the needle up at 2, and pull through. Repeat this until you finish the line. The last stitch is a small anchor that holds the last loop.

Needlepoint tends to create squared-off shapes on the canvas. Sometimes, a softer curve is more attractive in a design. A curve can be created by using Chain or Out Line. In the graphs, you can see Chain as lines, and as some filling stitches. On 14/1 canvas, used to cover a solid area, Chain can be quite a hard-wearing stitch. Your choice of yarn dictates the softness and subtlety of the stitch.

Chain Couching

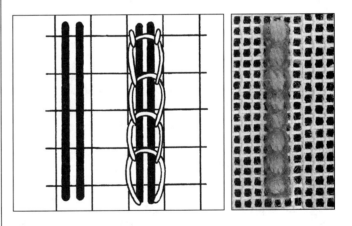

Many different yarns make terrific candidates for couching. Metals, silks, rayons and other "fancy" yarns add creative and unique looks to otherwise everyday projects. Couching protects more delicate yarns, such as silks and rayons. For the artist, the yarn palette is endless. A light, airy effect can be achieved by using one-ply silk to anchor a ribbon or fancy yarn. To create this medium-hard wearing Chain Couching, you need two sets of needles and yarns. Start by anchoring the first yarn, which is the yarn that is to be couched. Bring it to the top of the canvas.

Start a second thread the same as the first. Again, bring this to the top and start stitching Chain over the first thread.

Continue stitching the Chain stitch until you have reached the end of the line to be worked.

Bring both yarns to the underside and anchor.

Check

Check can be used to create the illusion of a meadow of daisies or a starry night sky. This stitch is fast to work, but it is not a hard-wearing stitch. Even so, it is relatively versatile—there are many possibilities where you might choose to apply it. The corners are void. Use Continental to fill the areas. Try stacking the stitches close together for a unique look. Stitch the horizontal line first, then the vertical ones. Or, if you wish, needle in the opposite order. The only rule is to be consistent in the Cross stitches. Use two plies, in one or more colors.

Chevron

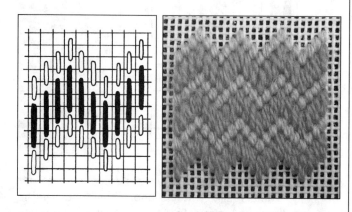

A close cousin to Bargello, medium-hard wearing Chevron is worked vertically, so use three plies of yarn in a tapestry needle on 14/1 canvas. Work one row completely from left to right and then begin the next. Once you have determined the count on the first row, your motif will be fun and easy to stitch. Use any color combination—while this pattern may be too busy for a background, it is perfect for samplers.

Chinese Loop Knot

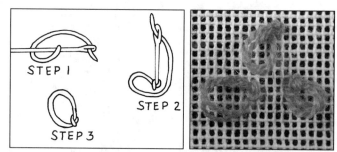

If your design uses Continental as a background, you can create wonderful effects with the light-wearing Chinese Loop Knot. This stitch creates a three-dimensional look for such features as lambs, poodles or curly hair. Use a knitting needle to gauge the size of the loop, and use any number of plies you wish. To create the stitch, bring your needle out where you want the knot. Hold the yarn with a knitting needle and take the needle back into the same hole, making a French Knot while traveling back in.

Chop Sticks

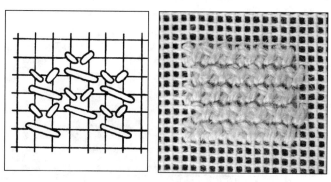

When I first made this hard-wearing stitch, it reminded me of a bowl of rice. However, the name Rice had been taken—so, I figured, what do you eat your rice with other than Chop Sticks? This very durable stitch can be used in almost any project. Because the motif is small, it can adapt to any size spot you choose. Use two-ply yarn.

Chottie's Plaid
(Courtesy of Chottie Alderson)

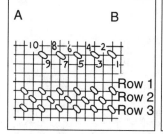

Step 1

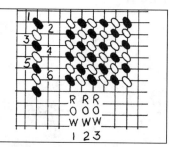

Step 2

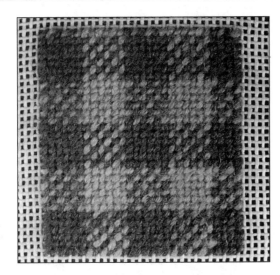

Chottie's Plaid is a unique, completely reversible, hard-wearing stitch. When finished, the front and back of the canvas resemble woven plaid fabric. Keep this stitch in mind for clothing such as vests or coats. Use two-ply yarn in your needle on 14/1 canvas. Interlock canvas is best. Mark your canvas "B" at the right side and "A" on the left. Then, turn the canvas to match the "A" and "B" of the diagram. This would turn your canvas 90 degrees to the right. Hold the canvas in this position while stitching. To create a plaid, you must change colors for each row. You can use any color and combination you choose, but remember your color choice. For an even plaid, stitch the vertical and horizontal rows with the same color layout. Stitch following the first diagram.

Using the same color combination, stitch the next set of rows following the second diagram.

Three rows of one color, two of another and one for the third makes a nice combination for plaid. The pattern to mimic houndstooth fabric requires two rows traveling in both directions. When stitching a kilt or other tartan, work the plaid in the desired colors, using Chottie's Plaid instructions. To create a kilt in a stitched picture, when the plaid is finished, make long Running stitches for the illusion of pleats. A sample of a tartan representing the Roberts clan has been worked in the "Plaid Pillow." A bell pull would be another possible project to create using a family tartan. Use your imagination!

Closed Cat

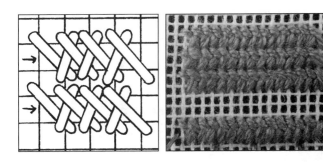

The Closed Cat stitch creates a pleasant, sharp, small braid. An absolute rule for Closed Cat: do not use it on Mono canvas. On Mono, you would lose your stitches behind the canvas. Also remember to work from left to right for each row. This stitch is not reversible. The back of the canvas is not covered as well with Closed Cat as with other stitches, but it is hard-wearing in two-ply yarn. For this reason, you should not be afraid to use it in almost any project.

Continental

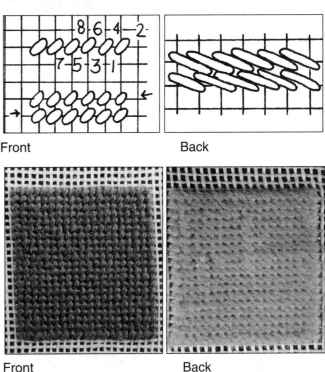

Front   Back

Continental is rather the grand daddy of all stitches. English and European tapestries are stitched in Continental. Many people know this stitch by different names, such as Diagonal Tent and Running Back. Depending upon the size, Continental is also called Petit Point (small stitches) and Gros Point (large stitches).

Continental is also appropriate for many uses, such as small areas, backgrounds, needlepoint rugs and Berlin work. It is a useful stitch for shading, compensation, or receding areas. While Continental is sometimes used to fill large areas, it is at its best as an outline or in a small area. Basketweave would be a better choice for larger spaces. Because of its compact size, Continental is very hard-wearing. Feel free to use it for tapestries, pillows, purses and shoes. Because it is so versatile, it is imperative that you learn to master this stitch.

Continental traverses only one intersection on the front of the canvas, and two intersections underneath. The only rule you must remember is, always slant the needle. Use two plies of yarn on 14/1 canvas.

Continental Gone Wrong

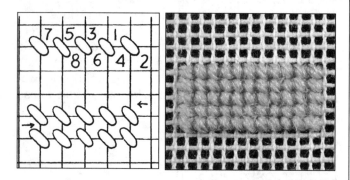

Continental Gone Wrong is stitched just like Continental, but in the opposite direction. Instead of the Tent stitches slanting right to left, Continental Gone Wrong slants left to right. Unless stitching a sampler, never mix Continental Gone Wrong with other Tent stitches in the same project. It will not have the intended effect—rather, it will only appear as though you have made a mistake. Take a look at the examples in Chapter One under "Canvas," page 8, and you will see Continental and Continental Gone Wrong used in the same project. The result is certainly not heritage embroidery, but rather a sad mess! For Continental Gone Wrong, use the same number of plies as for any other Tent stitch.

Continuous Woven Scotch

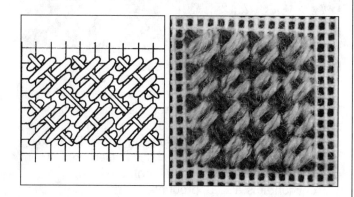

Depending upon the color combination, this stitch can offer either a dramatic or subtle effect. The light and dark hues of the stitched sample lend boldness and drama to the pattern. This medium-light wearing stitch is relatively versatile. The motif travels down in both directions, which makes the eye move around on the design. For this reason, if you decide to employ the stitch for a large area, use caution, and choose colors whose values are not too far apart. To create the stitch, lay the Scotch on the canvas. Then, weave a contrasting color under the second and fourth stitches. Use two-ply yarn for both sets of stitches. Insert the needle under the canvas at the end of the row.

Coral

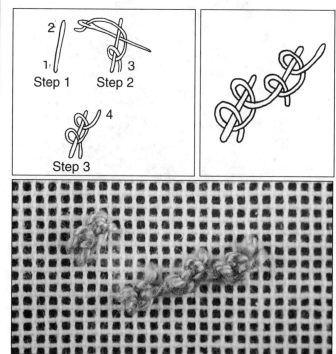

Coral is not a true needlepoint stitch, but sometimes an embroidery stitch can enhance a project. It resembles the French Knot. Embroiderers have been using Coral for years, and needlepoint artists have adapted it for use on canvas. Coral can be stitched in any fiber and any number of plies, as a border or an isolated stitch. It is medium-hard wearing.

To follow the first diagram to make an isolated stitch, work from left to right:

Make a small stitch coming out at point 1, and then back down at point 2.

Now, returning to the top of the canvas, bring your needle up at point 3 and make a loop around the first stitch.

Repeat, making another loop and then go down at 4.

If you would rather stitch Coral as a continuous line, omit going down at point 4, but make a longer anchor (see the second diagram).

Corn Field

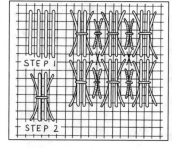

Using two-ply Persian wool, follow the count on the graph. After you have finished the first step, tie the four upright stitches with a small horizontal stitch, in one ply. Continue doing so until you have reached the end of the row. Fill in the voids with a series of upright stitches in a darker hue. Use more than one color to show off this medium-light wearing stitch.

Couching

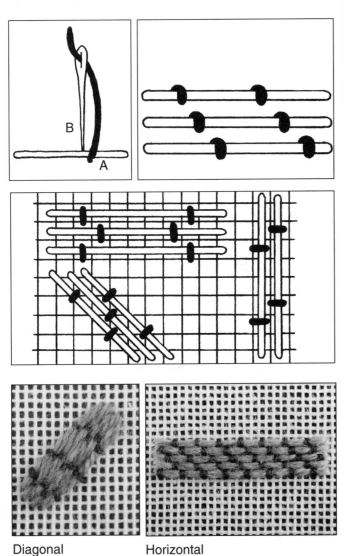

Diagonal   Horizontal

Looking around in the yarn shops, you will find an array of wonderful, interesting yarns that cannot be used in needlepoint—but perhaps you would like to incorporate them into your projects. Metal yarns, such as Japanese metal, would fray after a couple of stitches. So, how do you use these fun yarns? Try couching them.

To couch yarn, you need two yarns and two needles. You need the yarn you would like to couch, and the yarn you use for couching, or fastening the specialty yarn to the canvas. Just about any yarn you wish can be couched. If the yarn is too bulky to pass through the canvas, you may have to get a little creative with the ends.

Anchor the end onto the back of the canvas. Bring the yarn to the top of the canvas and set it aside. Do the same with the second yarn—only bring it up where you want to start couching the first yarn. Loop the second yarn over the first, and lead the second yarn back down through to the underside (see first diagram). Repeat this until you reach the end of the yarn. The first yarn can be laid on the canvas in a line, or in a shape or design (see second diagram).

The design is up to you. Couch in patterns or at random using any yarn that will pass through the canvas holes without fraying. Have fun and experiment. Keep in mind that Couching creates a light-wearing stitch.

Yarns can be couched in various directions. In the third diagram, you can see Couching done horizontally, vertically and diagonally.

Cretan

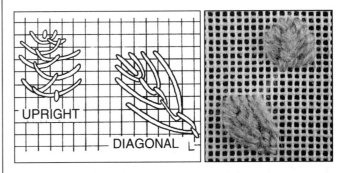

As an isolated stitch, Cretan can be useful for leaves. In clumps, it makes fine representations for trees. It could be used as a background as well. Stitch Cretan in a random order and see what happens. Use a family of shades to create a contemporary motif. A word of caution—this stitch, if used as a background in combinations of too many colors, could be busy. Cretan has two variations, upright and diagonal. Try both. Cretan should be stitched in two-ply yarn. It makes a medium-hard wearing stitch.

Criss Cross Hungarian
(Courtesy of Chottie Alderson)

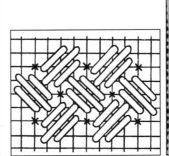

Like Bucky's Weaving and Belly Feathers, Criss Cross Hungarian creates a three-dimensional effect. Criss Cross Hungarian is surprisingly durable. For this reason, it is quite versatile—feel free to use it in any project you wish. Keep it in mind for smaller areas that call for extra texture. In a single color, this stitch is quite an eye catcher—in two colors, it is an eye popper! Stitch it in an array of colors to create the illusion of a field of flowers. First, work the long, diagonal lines in two plies and then the small crosses in one-ply wool. Create a deeper look by stitching the crosses in a shade darker than the other stitches.

Cross I

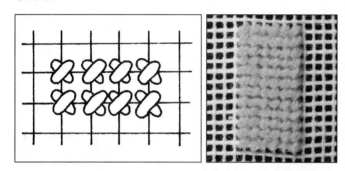

Use Cross I to make the smallest cross possible on the canvas. The stitch traverses only one intersection on the canvas, making it very versatile and hard-wearing. Because the stitch is so compact, one-ply Persian yarn is required. Like all other Cross stitches, make a row of the first cross hatches in one direction and finish by traveling back down the same row, stitching the second set of cross hatches. Rather than creating complete stitches, you should stitch Cross I in rows.

Cross II

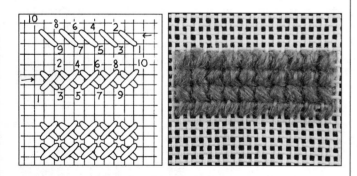

Another old ancestor of all stitches is Cross II. People have used this hard-wearing stitch on everything from everyday fabric to needlepoint canvas for years. By itself, as a row or as an entire picture, this stitch produces a simple yet dramatic effect. Cross II is quite strong. Consider it for projects ranging from rugs to pictures. The only rule you need to remember is to create the cross hatches all in the same direction, as discussed in Cross I. Use two-ply yarn on 14/1 canvas.

Cross Corners III

Another name for Cross Corners III is Three Tied Rice—and it does, indeed, resemble rice. First make the long cross and then the cross hatches. Each individual stitch should be completed before proceeding onto the next. Quite hard-wearing, Cross Corners III could be used for clothes or other functional items. For a fun variation and a deeper effect, try stitching it in two colors, one for the large crosses and another for the short ones. Use two plies for this stitch.

Cross Cushion

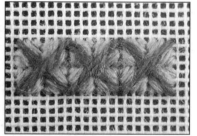

I would describe medium-light wearing Cross Cushion as one large cross with a fill-in. It draws the eye toward a particular area, so it is best in samplers. To tone down the effect of the stitch, use only one color. In two colors, you achieve a more dramatic effect. Try the stitch both ways and see which you prefer.

Cross Mosaic

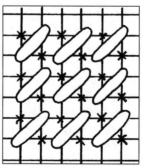

This medium-hard wearing stitch is best done in two colors, as two tones improve the effect of the crosses. In one color, the little crosses are much less noticeable, and the stitch resembles Cross stitch. You have two choices in stitching Cross Mosaic. First, you can make the little crosses and then finish with the long stitches. Conversely, you could also create the long ones first and then fill them in with crosses. Regardless of the order you choose, the stitch requires one ply for the crosses and two plies for the long, diagonal lines.

Cross Stitch Gone Wrong

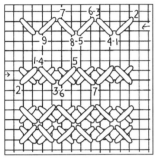

Cross Stitch and Cross Stitch Gone Wrong look very much alike. However, if you examine and closely compare the two, you can see that the tops cross in different directions. If your project presents a small spot where Cross Stitch would work, but you want more texture, work it "gone wrong." Use two plies in your needle, and use this stitch almost anywhere.

Cross Stitch Tramé

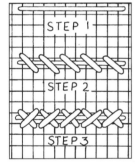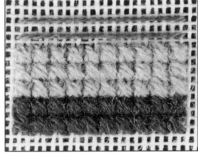

Often, a needle artist wants to work a counted motif. But, you may not want to be counting while inserting the final stitches. Cross Stitch Tramé is a convenient way to place your design's entire count on the canvas, so that you do not have to take the graph with you every time you needlepoint. Once you have threaded the long, thin yarn through the canvas, you are through with the graph, and the entire count is on the canvas.

Use the graph to count out the rows of color. Then, on the canvas, make a long, simple stitch, marking the appropriate length. For example, if the graph shows that you must make four blue stitches, pull your blue yarn to the top of the canvas, cover four intersections on the

canvas, and then return to the underside. Continue doing so with the next color until the row is finished. Check the illustration. Cross Stitch Tramé yarn should always be one-ply. It is used for counting purposes only, not coverage. After you finish counting and marking the canvas with Tramé thread, work the Crosses on the canvas. The Crosses in this stitch should be done like regular Cross stitch, for a hard-wearing stitch.

Cross Tied Gobelin

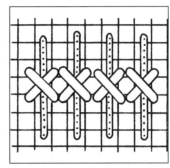

For a stitch that is made up of such long threads, Cross Tied Gobelin is quite hard-wearing. Because the crosses tie down the long threads, this is a practical stitch for items intended for wear. The boldness of the stitch, however, makes it a good choice for samplers. The crosses add a dimensional effect, leading the eye horizontally. Two colors help to show off the stitch. The canvas sometimes tends to show through the stitches. If you do not want the white of the canvas to show, first paint the area to match the yarn. To create the stitch, first work the long, parallel lines with three-ply yarn. Then insert the crosses in two plies.

Cross with French Knot

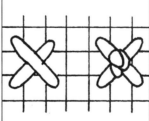

Tying the Cross stitch with a French Knot creates a very hard-wearing stitch. You may wonder where the Cross with French Knot stitch should be used. It is a fine choice anywhere you wish to have a Cross stitch, but would like a little more texture. Create the Cross stitch as you normally do, and then make a French Knot in the center of the cross. For fun, try using two different colors in the same stitch.

Crossed Scotch

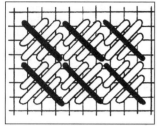 

Worked correctly, medium-wearing Crossed Scotch creates strong, diagonal lines on the canvas. If you do not want to create the strong diagonals, choose colors closely related to one another. Construct the Scotch on the foundation and place long, diagonal stitches on the top. Two tones, in two-ply yarn are required for Crossed Scotch.

Cushion I

Cushion I can serve many purposes besides the obvious background stitch. A quilt on a bed, a border on a picture or a plaid on a shirt are just some ideas for employing Cushion I in a design. This medium-wearing stitch reminds me of a man's black and red flannel shirt. Keep the longer stitches straight to ensure a lovely shine to your yarns. Keep in mind, this is a large, bold stitch.

Cut Turkey

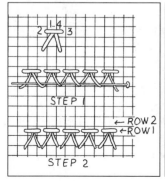 

In the sixteenth century, hard-wearing Cut Turkey was invented to mimic the wonderful rugs for which the country is famous. The upright pile of this stitch adds interest to animals, insects, flowers and the occasional English Palace guard's hat. Look at the graph and follow the number pattern. Notice the series of Back stitches, creating loops. To measure even loops, use a knitting needle or other rod. Work the rows up to the top of your canvas. When the entire area has been filled, take a pair of scissors and snip the loops. You can cut very closely to the canvas without risking the stitches coming out. Taper the edges for a clean curve. Of course, if you wish, you do not need to cut the loops at all.

Dana (Courtesy of Chottie Alderson)

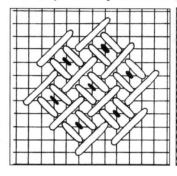 

At first glance, you might think that medium-wearing Dana is the same as Bucky's Weaving. Actually, the opposite is true! While Bucky's Weaving is laid on top, Dana is worked into the canvas for durability. Dana resembles a small wicker basket. You might stitch it in one color, but this does not preserve the drama of the stitch. For an interesting effect, use Dana for rolling hills or grassy fields. I find it best to work the diagonal stitches first and then insert small Continentals.

Darning

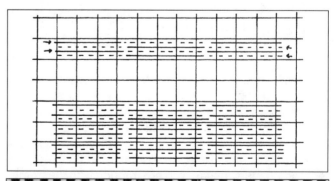

Darning offers the flattest stitch available. It is soft, shiny and smooth. Keep light-wearing Darning in mind for shading, sunsets, water. If stitched horizontally in many muted colors, this can give the appearance of a sunset over mountains or sea. The stitch does require a good deal of yarn on the canvas. It is not, however, very durable, as the long stitches can snag. It is, however, easy to stitch. Come out at "start," and weave in and out until you reach the end of the row. Go back down, and return at the hole you just finished. Repeat until you have worked four rows in one canvas line. Sometimes more than four repeats of a row may be required, depending upon the yarn thickness. In the graph, the solid lines show the upper stitches and the dotted ones are underneath the canvas. Darning is one continuous line.

Darning Variation

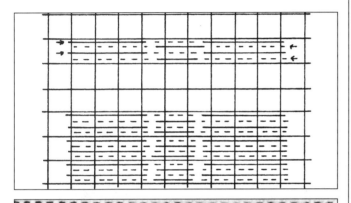

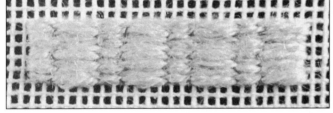

This is just like the last stitch, but with a little modification. To stitch the variation, you create equal vertical lines. When using Darning, consider using the variation in its place.

David

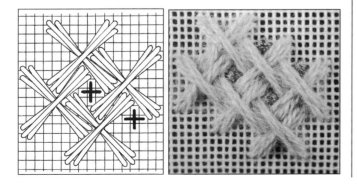

Looking at the diagram, you should see pinwheels. The motif is bold and has a lively effect on the canvas. Use two-ply Persian wool for the large pinwheels and a shiny yarn for the small crosses. Because the crosses are dominant, it is imperative that the cross hatches are made all in the same direction. This light-wearing stitch is best used in samplers.

Detached Chain

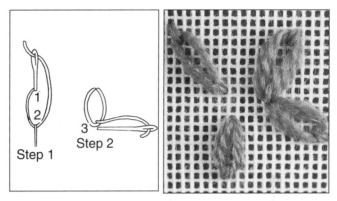

Although Detached Chain is not a true needlepoint stitch, it is included because of its many possible uses. This is another example of a stitch that does not have a true size. If you want to make Detached Chain large, go ahead and create the length you wish. The size of the stitch and number of plies effect the durability of the stitch. You can stitch in any direction or grouping. Experiment to see the different effects you can create with this stitch. To work Detached Chain, bring the yarn up to the top of the canvas at point 1. Hold the thread down with your left hand and bring the needle down at 1 again. Poke the needle up at 2, and back down at 3. This finishes the stitch.

Diagonal Butterfly

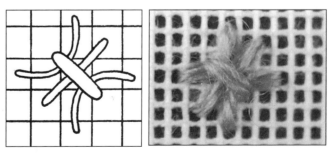

If you think an area could use a little something, why not try hard-wearing Diagonal Butterfly? A couple of interesting possibilities might be a bit of sky, or a leaf. The sample shows two-ply Persian yarn on 14/1 canvas. Depending upon the effect you wish to achieve, you might use any number of plies of any yarn.

Diagonal Cashmere

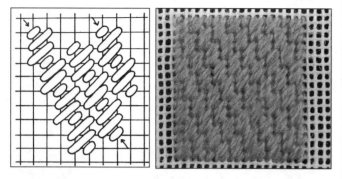

Diagonal Cashmere is a close cousin to Cashmere. Looking at the two, you might think they were identical. In fact, Diagonal Cashmere is missing a small stitch. Anywhere Cashmere can be worked, Diagonal Cashmere is a fine alternate choice. It does distort the canvas a bit, but either stretcher bars or a few minutes of blocking can solve the problem in no time. Use this hard-wearing stitch wherever you please. Use two-ply yarn.

Diagonal Cross

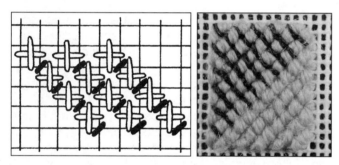

Diagonal Cross is a very hard and busy stitch. In the sample, two-ply yarn was used on 14/1 canvas. Try one ply, and see if you like the result. First work the crosses, and then the diagonal lines.

Diagonal Fishbone

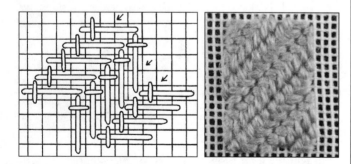

This hard-wearing stitch creates definite diagonal lines with a sharp texture. Be sure to stitch in rows from the right side toward the left. Stitch it in two-ply yarn. First, make the long stitch and then cross hatch over the top. Work a complete row if you wish to set down your needlepoint project for a break. The tension will change in the middle if you do not finish the row all at once.

Diagonal French

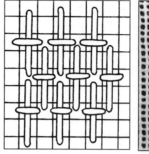

This is a very deceiving graph. Looking at Diagonal French, one would think it is made up of upright crosses without a distinct personality. However, this is not the case. The texture is tight, but it leaves an appealing motif. Because it is hard-wearing, you can use Diagonal French for any functional item. This stitch is almost child proof. Stitch the upright lines first. Then, go back up the line and work the cross on each. Use two plies for the entire stitch.

Diagonal Hungarian Ground

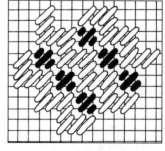

For a bold, dramatic look, and a medium-hard wearing stitch, consider Diagonal Hungarian Ground. As the name implies, this stitch is excellent for large areas such as a background. Two-ply Persian yarn is sufficient for proper coverage.

Diagonal Knit

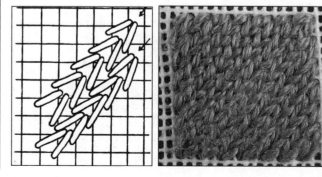

Hard-wearing Diagonal Knit can be used anywhere you choose, in large or small areas where you want a lot of a texture and small motif. Stitch entirely in one direction for a cleaner, sharper look. This stitch traverses two intersections on the canvas. It is best in one color.

Diagonal Leaf

This small, hard-wearing stitch can effectively accent special areas. Try using Diagonal Leaf for shrubs and trees, or petals on a flower. Two-ply Persian yarn is required for 14/1 canvas.

Diagonal Long Armed Cross

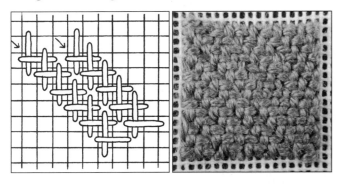

Diagonal Long Armed Cross resembles Diagonal French. But, if you look closely, you can see a distinct difference. This is another tight, hard-wearing stitch. Stitch Diagonal Long Armed Cross in rows, completing a cross and then moving down to the next one. When finished with the row, move up to work the next line. Use two plies in your needle, and feel free to use the stitch almost anywhere.

Diagonal Mosaic

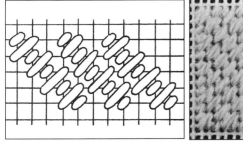

Small, tight, medium-hard wearing, versatile and fun to work—all these describe Diagonal Mosaic. Stitch it in any area, whenever you choose. The only rule to remember is to have fun. You can stitch in one direction, turn your canvas around and continue stitching. Use two-ply Persian wool on 14/1 canvas.

Diagonal Shell

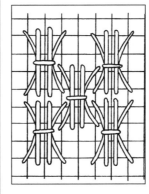

Lumps and bumps on the canvas are the typical result of medium-hard wearing Diagonal Shell. Use two-ply wool on 14/1 canvas for very nice, satisfactory coverage. You may see small, white lines of canvas through your yarn. You can avoid this by first painting the canvas to match the yarn. Try not to pull the stitches too tightly. This could distort the canvas, and you would probably never be able to truly straighten it again. All the tugging you could muster would never square up the canvas. Work the long threads first, and then tie them with the cross hatches.

Diagonal Stem

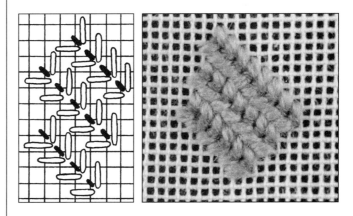

Although the major foundation of hard-wearing Diagonal Stem lies horizontal to the canvas grid, this stitch breaks the rule for upright stitches, as it requires two-ply yarn. The diagonal Continental lines are also in two-ply Persian wool. Use one color for less drama.

Diagonal Wheat

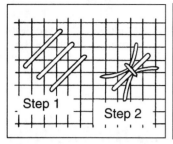

Step 1 Step 2

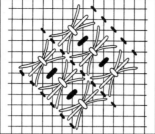

When placing medium-hard wearing Diagonal Wheat, remember that the diagonal lines must run downward, left to right. Keep this in mind when placing it near other dramatic stitches. Notice that the sample shows the stitch in two tones. I recommend this, since one color would not show the beauty of Diagonal Wheat. Two-ply yarn is needed for all except the small diagonal lines that break up the wheat columns. Here, only one ply is used.

Diagonal Wicker

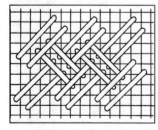 

This light-wearing stitch is exactly like Wicker, only it runs diagonally. The yarn seems to float on the canvas. Two-ply Persian yarn is necessary for good coverage, since the stitch lies diagonally on the intersections of the canvas. For a neat, clean look, take the time to lay the yarn flat on the canvas to ensure that the yarns are not twisted.

Diamond Eye I

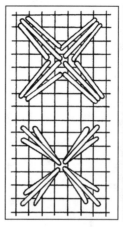 

As an isolated stitch, medium-hard wearing Diamond Eye I can be used as flowers—either representing real flowers or representing a floral pattern on, say, a dress— or as stars in the sky. You can use one of two approaches to create this stitch. Try them both, to see which you prefer. Although the stitch has quite a dainty appearance, feel free to use it on a pillow or other object that may be tossed around. To hide the canvas, use a Tent or other small stitch in the background. For fun, try a French Knot or a seed pearl in the middle. Work the yarns from the outside into the middle for a clean center.

Diamond Eyelet

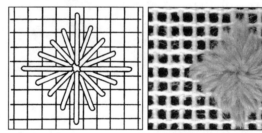

If you look closely, you will see that this medium-hard wearing stitch is actually Algerian Eye I, but with a different count. While Algerian Eye I covers six threads on the canvas, Diamond Eyelet covers four. Stitch it as you do the others, from the outside toward the center.

Diamond Ray

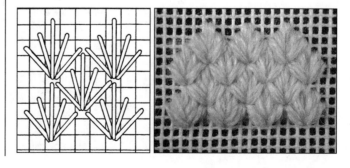

This hard-wearing stitch reminds me of a Washington evergreen forest, or flames in a fireplace. Use a variety of greens to create the effect of a forest or plants around a home. A family of orange shades creates wonderful flames. A single color in your needle will create a fine but dramatic design. Diamond Ray is appropriate for both smaller and larger area on the canvas. Again, two-ply yarn is most appropriate for 14/1 canvas. Work this stitch in rows from left to right. When you reach the end, rotate your canvas and proceed onto the next row.

Diamond Scotch

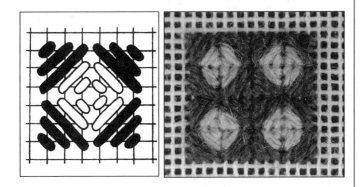

Diagonal Scotch only works as a two-toned stitch. If you were to use only one color, then you would create just plain Scotch. Samplers and other multi-stitched projects are more accommodating for this stitch than a picture of flowers or other definite design. Diamond Scotch crosses three intersections on the canvas, to create a medium-hard wearing stitch.

Diamond Straight

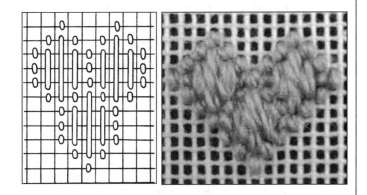

Light-wearing Diamond Straight can be stitched in one or two colors. For a background stitch, use only one color. The graph shows this stitch employed in making a heart. Use your imagination and see what interesting shapes you can make with Diamond Straight. If you use three-ply Persian for 14/1 canvas, the stitch will not show bare foundation.

Diana

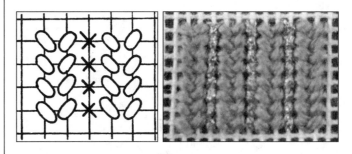

Using two-ply Persian for the Continental stitches, work from the top of your canvas to the bottom. Repeat the process for the second row of Continental. When the foundation has been set, create little Cross stitches between the lines. To create a very delicate look, use very fine metal thread. Although I used a metal yarn, any very fine yarn will work. Do not use one-ply Persian—it is not fine enough to achieve the desired effect. Use this hard-wearing stitch where you would like a vertical line.

Diaper

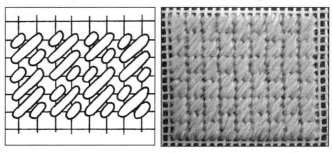

This is a combination stitch, made up of Mosaic and Cashmere stitches. It is simple, and at the same time very versatile. If you do not use stretcher bars, be prepared to do a good deal of pulling when you start the blocking process. Whenever you have a definite square or vertical line, it should be as square as possible. The small Continental stitches add durability to Diaper.

Dillon

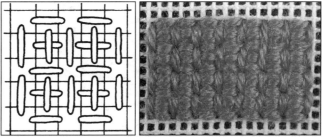

Dillon is another very hard-wearing stitch. Use it anywhere you need durable texture. This stitch produces dominant vertical lines, and softer horizontal lines. It is best in one color. Use two-ply yarn.

Divided Scotch

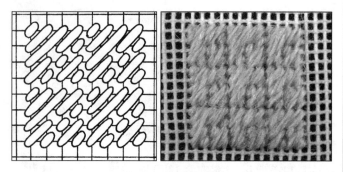

Medium-wearing Divided Scotch is a series of squares divided into smaller stitches. Looking closely, you can detect the tiny squares created by the stitch. Two-ply Persian yarn is the best choice for Divided Scotch. Use this stitch almost anywhere.

Dotted

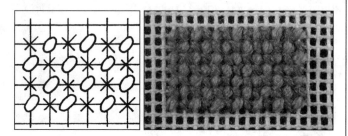

To create hard-wearing Dotted, use two-ply yarn for the Continental stitches, and one-ply for the Cross stitches. Dotted must be stitched in two different colors. If you were to create this stitch in a single color, it would appear almost as Alternating Continental. Work the Continental stitches first, and then the Crosses.

Dotted Scotch

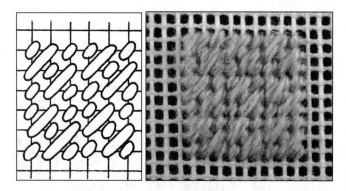

Have a close look at the graph. You can see that Dotted Scotch is stitched as regular Scotch, except for the middle stitch. Dotted Scotch is a stronger stitch. The longest yarn is cut into three Continental stitches, helping to eliminate the possibility of snags from everyday wear. You can use Dotted Scotch in almost any project, since it creates such a small, compact pattern. Use two-ply yarn.

Dotted Swiss

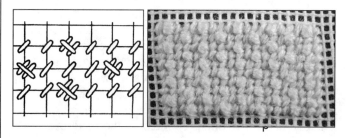

I can just picture little girls wearing Dotted Swiss dresses in a springtime scene! Use two plies in the needle on 14/1 canvas to create this hard-wearing stitch. Work the row from right to left, stitching the three at one intersection at the same time. Turn the canvas and continue stitching. For a fun variation, try the cross hatches in white and the rest in a pastel color. This would give a truer effect for Dotted Swiss.

Double

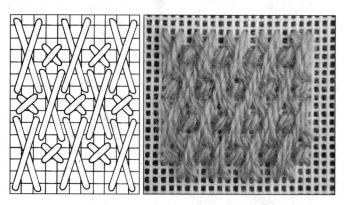

Double creates airy crosses with the appearance of floating on the canvas. Keep in mind from the outset that the canvas will definitely show through the stitch. If you wish to avoid this, paint your canvas to match your yarn before you begin stitching. Because the larger crosses traverse six intersections, this would never be considered a hard-wearing stitch. It is best used in samplers. Work the larger crosses first, and then the smaller ones. For a beautiful piece of work, remember to stitch all the crosses in the same direction, and be sure to keep your tension consistent.

Double Brick

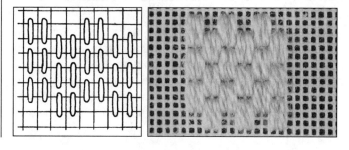

Long, upright stitches are not usually hard-wearing. If you choose Double Brick for a framed picture, you do not need to worry about wear. As for functional items, Double Brick could be over two or four threads. This medium-hard wearing stitch requires three-ply yarn in the needle.

Double Cross I

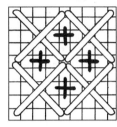 

To create this medium-light wearing stitch, I chose light blue for the larger crosses and dark blue for the smaller ones. When I was finished, to my surprise, I thought that Double Cross I looked like something I might find in a medieval castle—banners on walls or the like. Because of the drama this stitch provides, use it with caution. As always, remember to pay attention to the direction of your cross hatches.

Double Cross Tramé

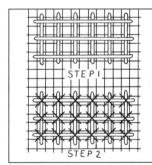 

This stitch requires one-ply yarn in the needle for both the foundation and the crosses. If you use more, the Tramé will not show on the canvas, and the true beauty of the stitch will be lost. The result is amazingly hard-wearing. Any project intended for everyday use will benefit with Double Cross Tramé.

Double Crossed Diamond

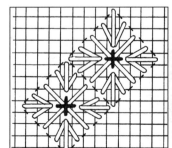 

Hard-wearing Double Crossed Diamond can be used as an isolated stitch or as a grouping. When it is stitched in only one color, the motif is lost, and it looks just like its cousin (note the photo). The small Back stitches that frame the diamonds have been stitched in one-ply Persian wool, and all the other stitches are in two plies.

Double Fishbone

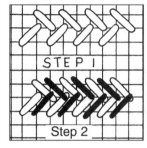 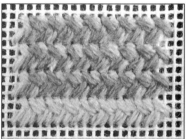

Double Fishbone is a surprisingly hard-wearing stitch. As a rule, use two plies in your needle. You have a choice of one or two colors in each row. Using two colors creates a tweedy effect. One color produces a much softer effect. In one color, you can use this stitch almost anywhere you like. It does not draw the eye too strongly in one direction. Stitch the first row and then, on the same set of threads, work the next row on top of the first. Always work from left to right, stopping at the end of the row, and starting at the left again.

Double Hungarian

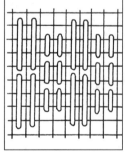 

This stitch requires three-ply Persian yarn. Take the time to strip the yarns, so that the threads lie flat and straight on the canvas. Insert the stitches from an unused hole into a used one for a cleaner result. This also creates a clean underside. The sharper the holes, the better the effect. Large piles of yarn on the back create unsightly lumps on the front of a picture. For lovely, sharp stitches, do not turn the canvas but work back using another count. This medium-hard wearing stitch is best used in samplers and as a background.

Double Knot

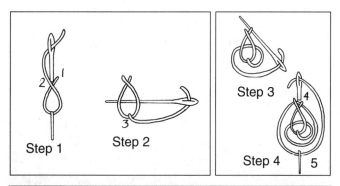

Step 1 Step 2 Step 3 Step 4

Double Leviathan

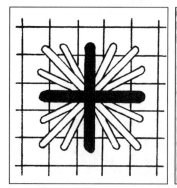

In its own way, Double Leviathan resembles the Pyramid stitch, but with a little difference. The cross in the top gives it the appearance of Hot Cross Buns. It is not a very hard-wearing stitch. For fun, try using Double Leviathan for a background where the motif will support a strong eye appeal. Using two plies in the needle, work the four corners first, and work your way toward the middle. Create the last two stitches in another color. Try Double Leviathan as an isolated stitch or as a grouping.

Double Roumanian

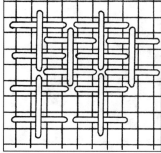

The Double Roumanian is a heavy-looking stitch with a bold texture. The yarn requirement makes this stitch what I like to call a hog. Three-ply yarn is needed for stitching on everyday objects. It is light-wearing and best in one color. On the canvas, stitch Double Roumanian in areas where you prefer the eye to be drawn.

Double Straight Cross

There are many words that can be used to describe Double Knot. A lumpy, interesting stitch, it eats a lot of wool. This is one stitch that cannot be easily compensated. If compensation is required, do not attempt to make a half knot, but create a smaller one. Because of its curves and the fact that it is not tacked down, Double Knot is very fragile. Use it in pictures or other places where hands do not reach. If you must use this on a pillow, remember that this stitch will never hold up to shoe buckles or other rough-and-tumble treatment that comes with children.

Double Knot can be used for borders or anywhere you want extra texture. Of course, the high texture must be used in moderation—too much of a good thing is not always good. This stitch also leaves canvas showing. If you do not want the canvas exposed, fill the voids with Continental. You can use Double Knot as a single stitch, all one size or alternate one large and another small. The choice is up to you.

To start Double Knot, begin with a twisted chain stitch coming out at point 1 and entering at 2. Come out at 3, making a loop under the first one you made. Place your needle under the layer of the twisted chain. Then, make a large chain stitch going in at 4 and back out at 5. You can then choose to make another knot, or finish off with a small anchor stitch. For the photo, two-ply Persian yarn was used.

I would describe Double Straight Cross as striking and quick. This stitch absorbs light, so if you want the individual crosses to show, choose a lighter color. A good deal of yarn is stitched into the motif, making it a hard wearing stitch. The top of the stitches could become fuzzy in time. Keep this in mind when choosing its placement. Try it in a single color, or in a two-color combination.

Doublet
(Courtesy of Mary Lou Helgesen)

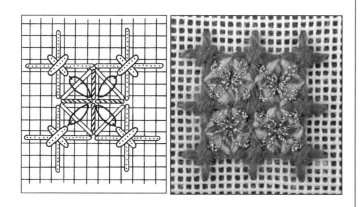

A dark yarn, a dull yarn, a shiny yarn and a metal yarn are all required for creating the medium-wearing Doublet stitch. This is a truly unique stitch. Stitch the large crosses in a dark yarn. Then, insert the diagonal stitches in the middle of the square. For this, use your dull yarn. The inside lines in the center require shiny yarn. Use the metal yarn last to create the isolated chain stitch. This stitch is best used as an all-over pattern, or in a sampler.

Duck's Foot (Courtesy of Chottie Alderson)

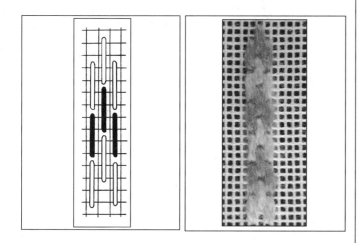

Stitched in three-ply yarn, Duck's Foot can serve as an interesting border. Consider this stitch if you make picture frames or other children's items. It is at its best in two or more colors. Use three plies in the needle for this hard-wearing stitch.

Dutch

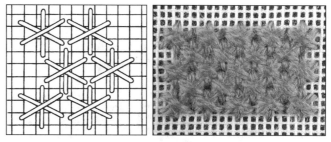

This unique stitch from the Netherlands adds high texture to almost any project, and keeps the eye moving. First, stitch the vertical lines. The horizontal crosses should be stitched last. Two plies provide ample coverage for the medium-wearing Dutch stitch.

Eastern

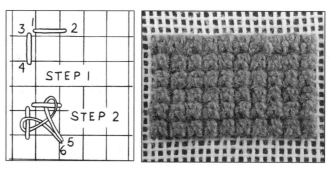

Looking at the graph for Eastern, you would expect this stitch to be airy and lacy. In fact, that is far from the truth. Eastern is a hard-wearing, very tight stitch that may be used in any needlepoint piece you wish. First, make the two lines 1-2 and 3-4. When you finish this, come out at 5, weave in and out as the graph shows and go back down at 6. Use a single ply on 14/1 canvas.

Eddie's Pavane

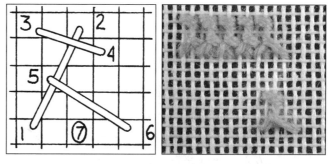

To sum up Eddie's Pavane in a couple of words, I would have to say it is airy and unique. This medium-wearing stitch definitely shows canvas. You can paint it beforehand or using a Tent stitch for the background if you want the canvas covered. Using two plies in the needle, follow the count and have fun. Your next stitch starts at 7.

Edge

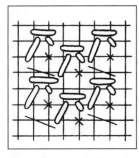 

Hard-wearing Edge requires three types of yarn. You need wool for the "pi (π)" motif. The small Cross stitch is worked in cotton and the slanted stitch is a thin metal. The pi motif uses two plies, and the others require one. The striking result turns everyday projects into works of art. Experiment with different fibers.

Elongated Cashmere

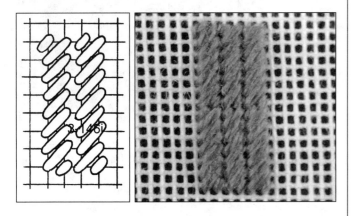

Elongated Cashmere can be any count you choose—use fewer long stitches in a small area. The look is clean and clear-cut, compared with other stitches. The stitch is hard-wearing. Strong horizontal and vertical lines appear when the stitch is finished. The plies do not need to lie as flat and straight as in other stitches. But, for finer work, it is still best to take a little extra time for this step. Use two-ply yarn.

Emily

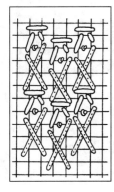 

Stitch the pi (π) signs in two-ply Persian and then the large crosses with a lighter color. Finish the look with shiny rayon French Knots. This hard-wearing stitch could be used for a rose garden. Imagine how it might look on an evening purse. The French Knots give Emily a three-dimensional effect. Three colors are necessary to achieve the effect.

Emily Variation

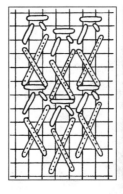 

This stitch differs from Emily in that it lacks the French Knots. The result is a look that is quite distinct from Emily. The sample shows Emily in two-ply Persian wool for the pi (π) and six-ply rayon floss for the large crosses.

Encroached Gobelin

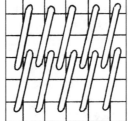 

There are two approved counts for Encroached Gobelin. The diagram shows the stitch crossing three threads on the canvas. Some people stitch Encroached Gobelin over two. The more common method covers three. Two plies in the needle are ample for this hard-wearing stitch. Use it in almost any project.

Encroached Long Cross

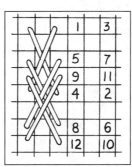 

Encroached Long Cross should be stitched in two-ply yarn, in two columns. Follow the count and you should have no problems. It is medium-hard wearing, but it could be bold on the canvas, so use caution when placing it.

Encroached Oblique

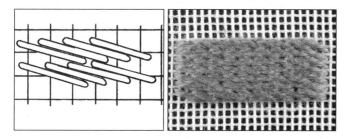

Encroached Gobelin and Encroached Oblique are quite similar to one another. The main difference is that Oblique slants more. Encroached Oblique requires only one ply in the needle, since the stitches are packed together. While it has a soft look, this stitch is quite durable, and it can be used wherever you like.

Encroached Straight Gobelin

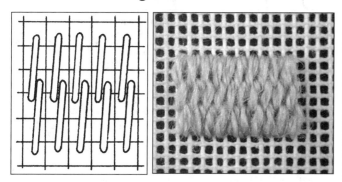

Whenever you want a soft, hard-wearing stitch, think of this stitch. As the stitches intertwine with the preceding rows, Encroached Straight Gobelin offers great durability. Two plies keep the lines firm on the canvas. For items such as pillows, shoes, purses and pictures, Encroached Straight Gobelin will serve you well.

Enlarged Parisian Embroidery

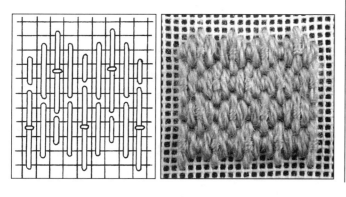

The middle stitch in each group is tied down, which offers some durability to the stitch. Try this one for eye appeal, but use caution, as it adds a lot of texture, and truly draws the eye. It can be too bold if you are not careful. Work the stitches from an unused hole into a used one.

Erin's Ridge (Courtesy of Chottie Alderson)

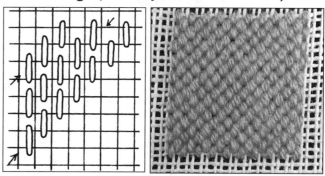

Erin's Ridge is not a stitch, but rather a method. It does not take great practice. In fact, a beginner will often stitch Erin's Ridge better than one who has been stitching for years. To make Erin's Ridge, you need Mono canvas. You will be stitching in vertical rows, making sure no two adjoining rows are stitched in the same direction. Another point to remember is to use the sewing method. Use your needle as though you are hemming a dress. When you pull the yarn through, give it a tug. This distorts the canvas, giving it the effect you want. To see results, you must first finish several rows. The canvas should develop definite ridges moving diagonally right to left. Use three-ply Persian yarn on 14/1 to canvas. The yarn should be heavier than usual. The result is medium-hard wearing.

Eugene

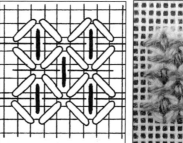

Like so many others, Eugene is made up of several steps. First, lay the foundation by inserting the diagonal lines in one color. Next, add the thin horizontal lines. For interest, use another color or a new shade of the first color. The perpendicular lines are the last to be worked. Here, you can add a metal or another color. In the sample pictured, the third step was stitched in the same color as the second. This medium-wearing stitch creates a great pattern for samplers, or as an all-over motif.

Eye

The hard-wearing Eye stitch can be worked over as many threads as you choose. Eye, or Eyelet, resembles little eyelets on belts, for example. In the picture, you can see it worked over one and two threads on the canvas. Your choice of how many threads to cover depends upon the effect you wish to achieve. When stitching, always make a small hole in the center with a knitting needle. Also, work the stitch from the outside toward the middle. The number of plies required also depends upon the number of threads you choose to cover. For stitches over one canvas thread, one ply is needed. Two or more threads require two-ply Persian yarn. Use your imagination. For an abstract, try making the hole off-center.

Falling Stars

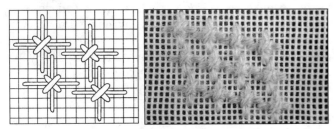

This medium-light wearing stitch shows canvas. If you do not want the canvas to be noticed, try painting it beforehand. You many want to fill the entire area with Continental and then work Falling Stars. The sample picture is made as shown in the graph. Think of other stitches that would complement Falling Stars. This could fill voids very nicely. Two-ply Persian yarn was used in the sample. It is best in contemporary projects.

False Rice

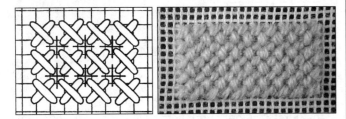

A good amount of yarn is packed into the canvas for False Rice. This makes it quite a hard-wearing stitch. The diagonal crosses seem to disappear when the upright crosses are inserted. You will get definite bumps on the canvas, but the stitch has a fun effect. Feel free to use this in any picture, pillow or other object. Use a single color, or a combination of two colors.

Fancy Cross

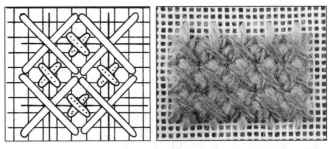

This is another fun-to-work, multi-level stitch. Using two-ply yarn, stitch the long horizontal and vertical lines. Once you have this foundation in place, work the larger diagonal crosses in two plies. The last—and most exciting—step is to stitch the small diagonal crosses. This finishes light-wearing Fancy Cross. For a little more fun, experiment with pearl and metal threads.

Feather Half Cross

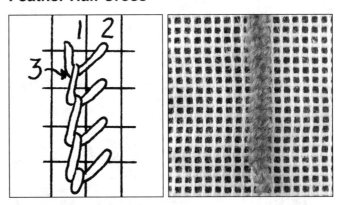

Consider this stitch for a border around a motif or a line that needs to pop up. Feather Half Cross produces a raised line that can neatly top off a curve in need of smoothing. To create the stitch, bring your needle up at point 1 and back down at 2. Before pulling the thread all the way through, pull the needle out again at 3. Repeat this until you finish the row. Stitch subsequent rows all in the same direction. This stitch cannot be worked by turning the canvas. Use one ply for 14/1 canvas.

Fern

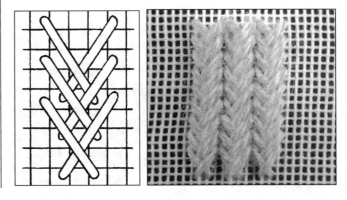

Fern produces light, airy lines. You might think that if you use only two plies in the needle, the canvas is sure to show through. Do not worry—good coverage is achieved with just two plies. Fern cannot be rotated when a row is finished. Stop at the end of the row and begin at the top again. This medium-light wearing stitch is best in samplers.

Fern Variation

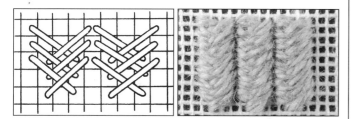

This medium-wearing variation is very close to Fern; the variation is in the count. Original Fern is light and airy, while the variation is tight and soft. When stitching a project, consider using both. Depending upon the area, you may need to choose which would be best. The variation is stitched in the same manner as Fern. Use two-ply yarn.

Fill In

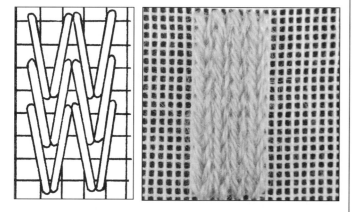

When deciding whether to use Fern, Fern Variation or Fill In, you may wonder really just how different are the effects of the stitches. Examine my samples and compare for yourself. While the other two have been explained already, the effect of Fill In resembles knitting. Consider it for a blanket, sweater or other soft-looking object in a picture project. Use a fuzzy yarn, and brush the stitches for the look of a cashmere sweater. Use two plies for this medium-hard wearing stitch.

Fishbone I

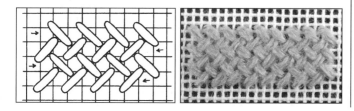

Hard-wearing Fishbone I produces the effect of woven yarns floating over the canvas. The stitches traverse only two intersections on the canvas. This ensures that Fishbone I is a hard-wearing stitch. The canvas is left exposed. To create the stitch, work the diagonal lines, going in one direction. When returning, finish the stitch by working the second set of lines. Two-ply yarn is best.

Fishbone II

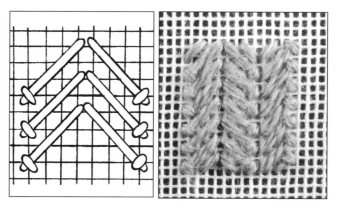

Medium-light wearing Fishbone II is best in contemporary projects. First, stitch a long diagonal line, and then finish it with the small tie stitch. After you have completed both steps, continue to the next long line. Work in a downward row. At the end of the row, tie off your yarn and start again at the top.

Flat I

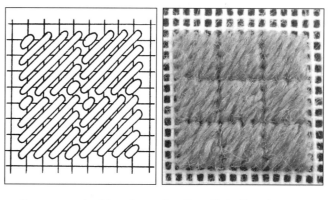

If you are looking for a fragile stitch that is sure to snag, pull and become fuzzy, Flat I is perfect every time. While this may sound discouraging, Flat I's soft texture and pleasing pattern lend it to many uses in various projects—just so long as they are projects that will never be touched, especially by little hands. Exercise caution if you must place Flat I on purses, pillows or other objects that receive everyday handling. To stitch Flat I, start each square in the upper left and work toward the lower right. When the square is completed, go on to the next. Flat I is best in a single color.

Flat II

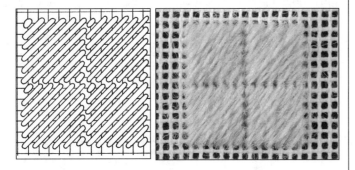

Some people know this stitch as Large Scotch. Both names are correct. You can use any count you wish for Scotch, three, four, or more, and the pattern will appear the same. The only difference is in the boldness of the result. Use caution. If the long stitches are longer than Flat II, the yarns will not lie correctly on the canvas, and a good deal of durability will be lost. Long stitches that traverse anything more than six intersections on the canvas will transform your project into rags.

Flat Woven

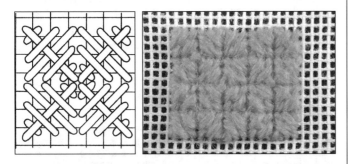

If you simply look at the graph, you would think this is a flat stitch, as the name implies. But, once you work it, you will discover that medium-wearing Flat Woven has many highs and lows. Stitch it as you would Scotch, except, when you have finished, go back to the top and weave every other stitch until the square is finished. Then, proceed to the next stitch. Use one or two colors.

Florentine

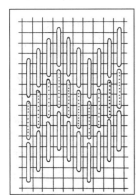

Hard-wearing Florentine is a cousin in the Bargello family with many appropriate uses. Try it for a background, or on purses or tote bags. I imagine it would be wonderful to create an entire chair or settee stitched in Florentine. A pillow in just the right colors could add the perfect finishing touch to a special room. Because it is a vertical stitch, it does require three plies in the needle on 14/1 canvas. You can stitch it in an endless variety of color combinations.

Flower

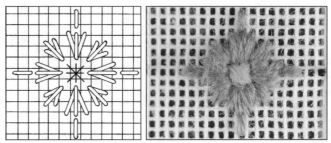

While the name of this medium-wearing stitch implies a single use, certainly you can think of a few other uses for it. For fun, give it a try in a picture project of a night sky. Start by creating a random pattern of flower stitches, and then fill in the canvas with another stitch, such as Continental. The center of the flower does not necessarily have to be the Smyrna stitch. Try seed pearls or rhinestones. A metal yarn could also be added to make the center pop. To create the stitch, begin with the circle of stitches. When you have gone completely around, stitch the four points of the flower, and finish it with the middle.

Four-Way Bargello

The photo and graph are only one example of a use for Four-Way Bargello. This versatile stitch is attractive in any color combination and pattern. To create the stitch, first draw lines from one corner to the opposite in the center of the canvas where you want the motif to start. Then repeat the step, marking the other two corners. Stitching from the center outward, create the pattern you wish to use. All four sides should be identical. Stitch one side, and when you have reached the lines, stop and continue onto the next side. Continue until you reach the last row of stitches. If you wish, find a mirror and lay it perpendicular to the graph. Move the mirror around to decide how you wish to place the pattern on the canvas. Four-Way Bargello can be used as an overall pattern for a pillow, or as a small pattern for a sampler. Try it for a pendant around your neck or a scissors charm for your shears. Use three-ply Persian, and remember to strip the yarn before inserting it into the needle. The size of the stitch determines its durability.

Four-Way Mosaic

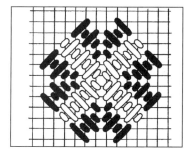 

Like Four-Way Bargello, this medium-hard wearing stitch could be used on a larger design, such as a pillow, or as a small pattern in a sampler. Use two or more colors. Stitching Four-Way Mosaic in a single color is rather a waste of time, as the pattern loses its effect. Use two-ply Person yarn on 14/1 canvas.

Frame

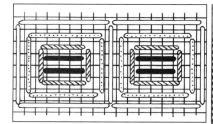 

A versatile but light-wearing stitch, Frame can be used to create two distinct looks. Working the center in a light color, and bleeding into a dark at the outer edges, creates a tunnel effect. The opposite, a dark center and lighter edges, creates a pyramid look. This is one of the great things about needlepoint—the variations do not end with your choice in stitches. They are also affected by your choices of colors, textures, and yarn's fiber content. You can needlepoint your entire life and never stop experimenting with yarn and fiber choices. The Frame stitch requires three-ply yarn.

Frame Variation

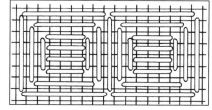 

Stitching Frame Variation in one color creates a square motif of columns with upright marquises. This effect creates a soft stitch that could have a wonderful effect as a background stitch. The sample was worked in two-ply Persian wool. You may find that you have to thicken the yarn for better coverage. If you intend to use the stitch on a pillow or other functional item, use three-ply yarn, as the variation is also light-wearing.

Framed Alternating Flat

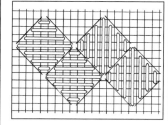 

This medium-wearing stitch requires three-ply Persian wool for the upright and horizontal stitches. You can stitch the long, diagonal stitches in one- or two-ply yarn, depending upon your personal taste. Try using varied yarns for the long, diagonal stitches for a distinctive look.

Framed Cashmere

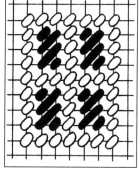 

The sample shows Framed Cashmere stitched in two colors. The stitch can also be done in one color for beautiful results. Because the longest stitch traverses only two intersections on the canvas, this is quite a versatile and hard-wearing stitch. You may prefer to first stitch the Cashmere, and then the Continental stitches.

Framed Diagonal Cashmere

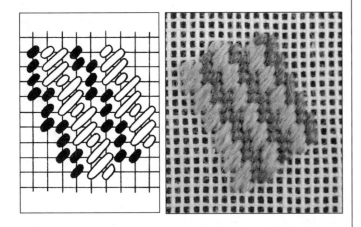

When Framed Diagonal Cashmere is worked in two distinct colors, it produces a bold diagonal line. If that is not the effect you would like, then stitch it in a single color, or two shades that are fairly close to one another. Pink and white might "pop" less than black and white. This medium-wearing stitch is great in multi-stitched projects.

Framed Diagonal Scotch

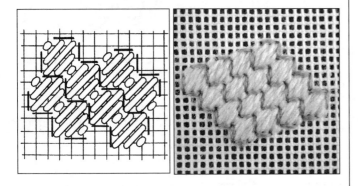

When the Diagonal Scotch part of this stitch is worked in two-ply Persian and the Frame is stitched in one ply, you get a very dramatic, soft result. Stitch the frame in one ply; otherwise, the canvas would "wear" too much fiber, and the extra bulk can distort the grid so that even blocking would be a waste of time. Imagine the effect you might create with Framed Diagonal Scotch, with metal thread highlighting the Diagonal Scotch. This medium-wearing stitch would make a lovely design idea for an evening purse.

Framed Hungarian Brick

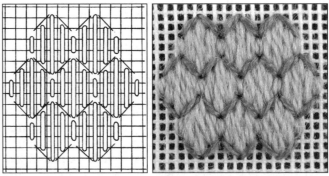

This medium-light wearing stitch is appropriate for creating representations of trees, mountains or flames. Variegated yarn can help you to create a truly unique result. Do not limit your use of Framed Hungarian Brick to backgrounds only. The stitch creates quite a large pattern, but with imagination, this stitch could have many uses. An upright stitch, it requires three plies for the vertical stitches and one ply for the framing stitches.

Framed Mosaic

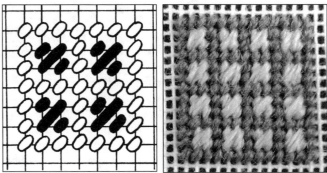

Like Framed Cashmere, Framed Mosaic is a very durable stitch. Everyday items intended for a good deal of handling would make the perfect home for Framed Mosaic. It should be stitched in two-ply Persian wool. Work the Mosaic stitching first, and then finish with the Continental stitches.

Framed Reversed Scotch

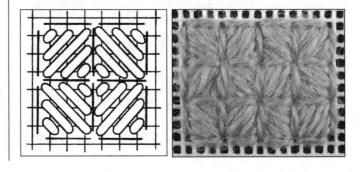

Two-ply wool for the Scotch and one ply for the frame ensure a stitch that holds up to even the roughest wear. Shoes, purses, and children's toys could be stitched in Framed Reversed Scotch. First work the Scotch, and then the framing.

Framed Scotch

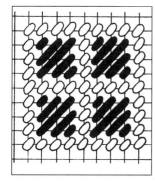

At a glance, you might think that Framed Scotch is just as versatile as original Scotch. Not so. The strong borders make Framed Scotch a very bold stitch. Note the way the Continental stitches form very definite lines around the Scotch. Honestly, you should only choose this stitch where you think the design calls for it, and where you certainly want the viewer's eye to be drawn! To create the stitch, it is the artist's choice whether to stitch the Scotch first, or the Frame.

Framed Scotch Variation
(Courtesy of Chottie Alderson)

This stitch calls for three colors: one for Scotch, another for Continental and a French Knot in the center. The result is a truly unique, hard-wearing, if not completely versatile, look. It may not be appropriate for all projects, but when you do have a project in which to employ the stitch, it creates a great look. Framed Scotch Variation is too dramatic for most classic stitched designs. In a picture project of a room, Framed Scotch Variation might appear as a window—if the count works in the design. You might also try it in a single color.

French I

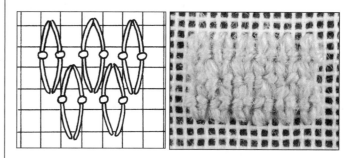

The sheer amount of yarn that is packed into the canvas places this stitch among the most durable. Of course, at the same time, this is reason for caution when stitching it. Too much yarn can also distort the canvas, and throw off your tension and count. The stitch also creates quite a busy motif. The light absorbs enough of the texture, so you can use this stitch in just about any place you choose. In the example, two plies were threaded in the needle. If you want a lighter effect, try one ply and see whether it covers to your satisfaction. Stitch an entire row's worth of long lines, and then go over the line, making the cross hatches. Then go on to the next long line.

French II

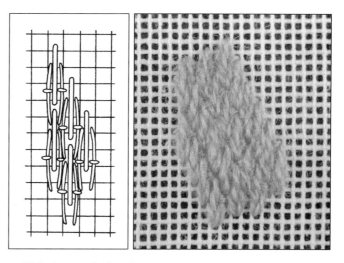

This is a soft, fragile stitch. The sample required one ply on 14/1 canvas. Stitching with two plies stuffs too much fiber into the canvas, causing quite serious distortion. All the blocking you can do will never restore the canvas to its square grid. The single ply also creates a soft-looking stitch that can be placed almost anywhere—anywhere you can place a fragile stitch, that is. This is not the best choice for pillows or other functional objects.

To create French II, first work the curved line and tie it off, and then work the counter-curved line, and again, tie off. Finally, stitch the long line down the middle, and then you may proceed to the next stitch.

French Knot

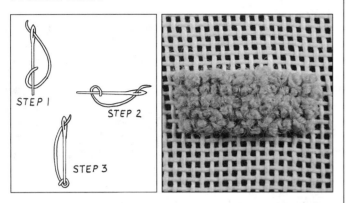

To make a hard-wearing French Knot, bring the needle up at point 1 and while holding the yarn, tuck the needle under. Swing the needle around. Your needle should be straight up, and the yarn should twist once around the needle. Hold the yarn on the needle with your left hand and insert the needle through the canvas into the next available hole. Pull through to complete the knot. This is a great stitch for hair, flowers, leaves, or other areas needing texture.

Frosty *(Courtesy of Chottie Alderson)*

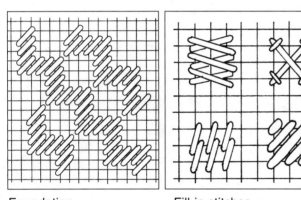

Foundation.   Fill-in stitches.

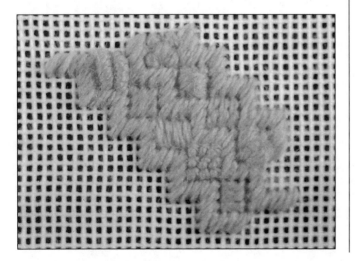

First stitch the zigzag lines, to create the foundation for this quite exciting stitch that uses different colors, fibers and yarns. Fill the blanks with any stitch you choose that fits into the square voids. Create Spider Webs, Knots or Weaves on the available areas. Choose varied stitches, to create highly-piled areas, as well as low, close areas. Keep this stitch in mind for your freer projects, especially when you might have a good amount of scrap yarn in your sewing basket. The graph is only an example, showing just a few ideas you might use. Use your imagination. The foundation requires two-ply Persian, and the rest is up to you. Depending upon your choice of fill-in stitches, this can be a medium-wearing stitch

Ginger Jars

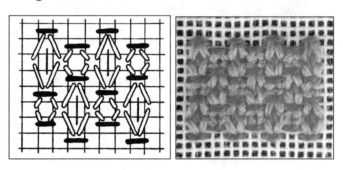

To stitch hard-wearing Ginger Jars, start on the left and make a series of upside-down V's, all the way to the end of the row. Then, when you finish the row, make the next row of upright V's, traveling back to the left side of the canvas. Start another row of upside down V's and continue stitching in this manner until you finish the area. Then, make the perpendicular and parallel straight lines. Like the V's, these are stitches in two-ply yarn, but choose a darker color for the lines. The straight lines finish the stitch.

Gingham

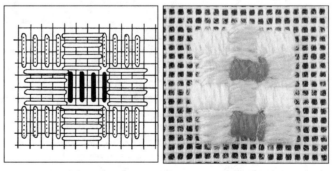

This medium-wearing pattern resembles picnic tablecloths you might remember from childhood. Do not limit this lovely check to tablecloths, but keep it in mind, as well, for a shirt on a man, a dress on a little girl, or even a patch of grass on a mountainside. Gingham requires three-ply yarn for 14/1 canvas.

Gloria

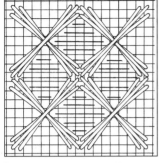

If you compare this light-wearing stitch to its variation, you will see that the two are, indeed, similar. The difference is in the large crosses. In Gloria, they stand out much more. This stitch produces a soft effect, but at the same time, it is quite bold, with a good deal of contrast. Gloria is best in samplers.

Gloria Variation

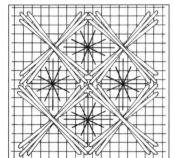

The large Pyramid stitches between the pinwheels lend the variation a good deal more tenacity than the original Gloria. A large texture results. This stitch is a good candidate for samplers that are intended for mounting on a wall. The pinwheels and the pyramid stitches make the stitch quite fragile, which does limit its use.

Gobelin Droit

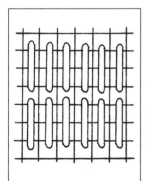

Gobelin is named for its resemblance to famous French tapestry weaving originating in the Middle Ages. The stitch creates well-defined horizontal lines that effect a soft, rolling stitch. While the stitch itself is medium-wearing, it can become fuzzy with abrasion. As with most upright stitches, Gobelin Droit requires three-ply yarn. Even so, the canvas is exposed a bit along the rows. To fix this, you can fill in with Chain, Back or another small line stitch. If that would not be appropriate, consider painting the canvas before stitching. The graph shows Gobelin Droit that traverses three threads on the canvas. You can also stitch this over two threads, if you wish.

Gobelin Tramé

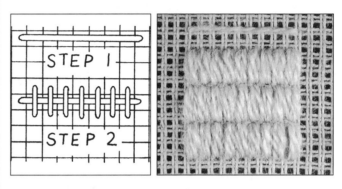

For a definition of Tramé, please look under "Tramé," page 121. The Gobelin Tramé is stitched much like regular Tramé and Cross Stitch Tramé. Lay one-ply Persian horizontally on the canvas. Then stitch Gobelin over the long foundation yarn. The tramé also adds additional padding to the Gobelin. This creates a medium-wearing stitch. Use three plies for the Gobelin on 14/1 canvas.

Half Cross

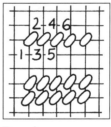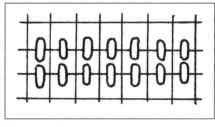

Top of canvas   Bottom of canvas

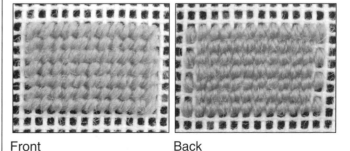

Front   Back

When comparing Continental, Basketweave and Half Cross, it is impossible to tell the difference without also examining the back. All three appear quite the same on the front, but are quite identifiable on the backside of the canvas. If you examine the underside, you can see that Basketweave truly resembles a woven basket. Continental is made up of long stitches, while Half Cross leaves a good deal of the canvas exposed on the underside. Taking this into consideration, you have probably already figured out that Half Cross is the least durable of the three. At the same time, Half Cross uses the least yarn. Depending upon the object you are stitching, the coverage on top of the canvas may not be adequate with Half Cross. Two-ply Persian yarn is required for Half Cross. To create the stitch, follow the count on the graph.

Half Cross Tramé

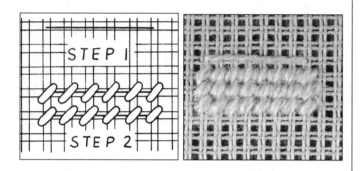

This is just like other Tramé stitches, only here you create the stitch using Half Cross. Lay down one ply of yarn on Penelope canvas to mark your color placements.

Half Eyelet

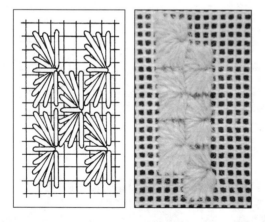

Using two plies in the needle, work each Half Eyelet from the top right, moving around the circle. After completing the first, stitch the next Half Eyelet below the first. Work this row and then start the next in the same manner. For clean, neat holes, poke a knitting needle into the canvas at the center of the eyelet. This is a medium-wearing stitch, best used in samplers.

Half-Framed Scotch

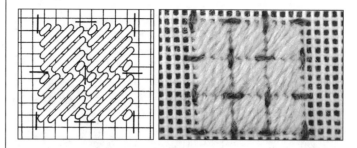

The sample shown required two plies for the Scotch, and one ply for the Half-Framing, to create quite an interesting effect. You might consider stitching the Framing in a metallic yarn, for a distinctive touch. Silk or rayon would also add a bright, dramatic effect to this stitch. An interesting effect has been created. To create the stitch, first work the Scotch, and then stitch the framing. The result is medium-hard wearing.

Half Pyramid with Satin

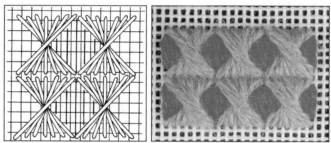

By omitting the right and left sides of the square in the Pyramid stitch, you can create Half Pyramid with Satin, a completely different look. Fill the void area with long Satin stitches. This medium-wearing stitch can be done in a single color or in combinations. The example shows a two-tone combination. For a multi-textured effect that adds interest to a project, choose yarns in combinations of fibers. Try Persian wool for the Pyramids and cotton embroidery floss for the Satin stitches. Use a light tone for the Pyramid stitch and dark yarn for the Satin stitch for a dramatic three-dimensional effect.

Heavy Cross

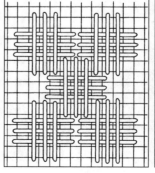 

If you work Heavy Cross as an isolated stitch, and if you have some imagination, you might think it resembles the large buttons you might find on an overcoat. When stitched in a group, the effect of the stitch is soft yet bold. The long lines create a softer appearance, while the crossing adds some drama. Work each part of the light-wearing stitch individually. First, lay the vertical lines, and then the horizontal ones. Remember that all the cross hatches should be stitched in the same direction. Throw caution to the wind, and you are sure to end up with a mess!

Herringbone

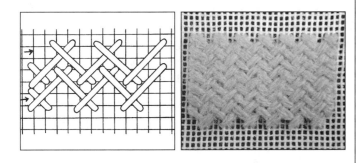

Herringbone is another medium-wearing stitch that looks as though it has been woven onto the canvas. When the yarns lie flat on the foundation, it creates a true Basketweave on the diagonal. The example pictured has been worked in three-ply yarn. Try not to split the yarns during the second, third and fourth rows. One absolute rule to keep in mind is this: Do not rotate the canvas while stitching Herringbone. Instead, tie off the yarn at the end of each row and start again at the beginning of the next. The back of the canvas is not covered by this stitch, which means it is not hard-wearing, but it is economical. Thankfully, Herringbone does not distort the canvas. It is quick, and fun to stitch. You will find that an important part of tying the back is using your imagination.

Herringbone Couching

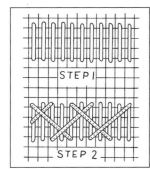 

This medium-wearing stitch closely resembles original Herringbone, except that the first layer of stitching is Gobelin, and then Herringbone Couching is applied over

it. When creating the stitch by following the graph, please note that Gobelin requires three-ply Persian yarn. The Herringbone then requires one ply to finish the stitch. This stitch lends a soft, diagonal plaid look to the canvas. I find that the look is somewhat medieval. The stitch reminds me of the bodice of a woman's dress.

Herringbone Done Diagonally

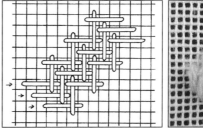 

Follow the diagram to complete this medium-wearing stitch. Even though you work on the straight of the canvas, two-ply yarn is required on 14/1 canvas. Keeping the yarn straight, work the graph moving right to left for every row. This stitch cannot be rotated when you finish a row. Stop at the end, and begin the next row.

Herringbone Gone Wrong

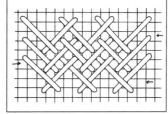 

When stitching Herringbone, you should never reverse the canvas and continue to stitch, as this would not create a true Herringbone pattern. If you ever have been unlucky, or absentminded, enough to make this mistake, then you created Herringbone Gone Wrong. While an accident is an accident, what you do with purpose can make for good art—and this can create a unique, whimsical stitch. Use two plies in the needle and have a little fun. This, too, is a medium-wearing stitch.

Horizontal Brick

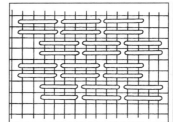 

In the sample pictured, I used two-ply yarn. You may wish to use thicker yarn, depending upon the fiber, texture and color. Darker colors may not cover the canvas as well as lighter shades. Also, consider where you want to use the stitch. Horizontal Brick does not stand up to a great deal of wear. Three plies may be called for if you are stitching a pillow top. For heirloom embroidery, be sure to strip your yarns and take the time to lay them straight on the canvas. Use this medium-hard wearing stitch as a background, or in large areas.

Horizontal Elongated Cashmere

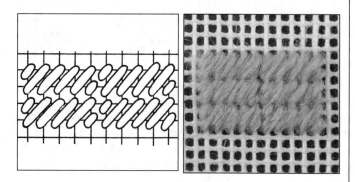

If you were to take the Elongated Cashmere stitch and turn it on its side, you would then have Horizontal Elongated Cashmere. This stitch produces bold lines that run left to right on the canvas. This can be a great stitch for medium to large areas in any project, since the result is quite a hard-wearing stitch.

Horizontal Hungarian

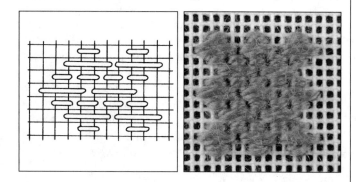

Whether you use two colors or a single shade, Horizontal Hungarian can become one of your favorite stitches in your needlepoint repertoire. The longest stitch traverses four threads on the canvas, while most of the stitch only covers two. If you stitch Horizontal Hungarian in three plies on 14/1 canvas, you can create a very durable stitch. Experiment with your canvas and yarn. Determine for yourself which thickness is best for your individual project.

Horizontal Kalem

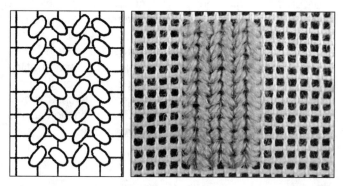

Looking at the example, note the soft lines that run perpendicular to the bottom of the canvas. These lines tend to draw the eye to move vertically, up and down the stitch. You can use this to your advantage—you might use this stitch when you would like to draw the viewer's eye upward on your canvas. Horizontal Kalem is quite durable, as a result of the strong coverage on the underside of the canvas, and the fact that the stitch traverses only one intersection on the canvas.

Horizontal Milanese

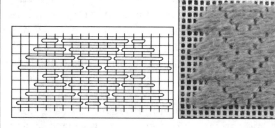

For two graphs that seem so very similar to one another, Milanese and Horizontal Milanese are completely different stitches. While Milanese resembles arrowheads, Horizontal Milanese creates a zigzag pattern. Do not be tempted to use this stitch on any object that will come in contact with little hands. The fine, smooth appearance can be ruined in amazingly short order. Use it in areas that call for drama.

Horizontal Oblong Cross

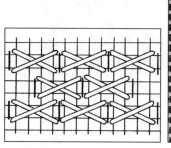

Using two-ply Persian yarn, stitch the crosses and left upright lines as a single unit. You may wish to work in a downward zigzag direction to accomplish the stitch. The long cross hatch on the top could snag on a functional object. Keep this in mind when placing it on your projects. This stitch is best in samplers.

Horizontal Old Florentine

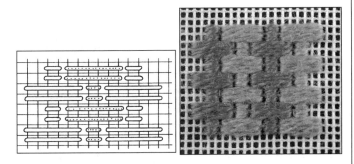

In the photograph, you will notice that the stitch is composed of two-ply yarn. I have used two-ply only for demonstration purposes. For projects in real life, three plies are needed—not only for covering the canvas, but also for the added durability. You can use Horizontal Old Florentine in a single color, or in various combinations. Using a single color, you could use this stitch to create fences or baskets in a picture.

Houser

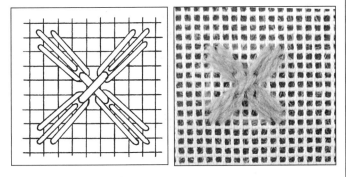

Do not limit this light-wearing stitch to simply samplers. Houser might also be used for flowers, stars, pinwheels, or other whimsical additions to a design. Use two-ply yarn on 14/1 canvas.

Hungarian

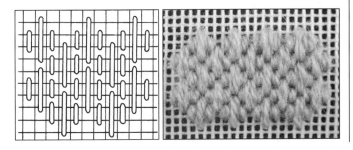

This vertical stitch requires only two plies in the needle. Depending upon the look you hope to achieve, you can stitch Hungarian in a single color, or in combination. For texture alone, use one hue. Hungarian should be stitched as a complete row, without stopping. At the end of a complete row, turn around and continue to the next. This is a medium-wearing stitch.

Hungarian and Stars

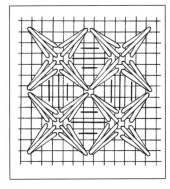

Use yellow for the Stars part of this pattern, and green for the Hungarian, to stitch a meadow of flowers. Add brown French Knots, and your flowers are transformed into Black-Eyed Susans. A blue and white combination might make a wonderful pattern for a girl's dress. Flowered wallpaper in a scene is another possibility for this stitch. Hungarian and Stars requires two-ply Persian yarn. The stitch is medium-hard wearing.

Hungarian Brick

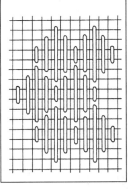

Although the stitch itself is quite large, the visual effect of Hungarian Brick is soft. While it is a nice choice for samplers, it can also be used in picture projects, for backgrounds, brick wall or paths, and fields. The yarn traverses six intersections at the longest point in the stitch. For this reason, it is not the most durable choice of stitches. It could snag or pill quite easily. The standard requirement is three strands of Persian yarn.

Hungarian Diamonds

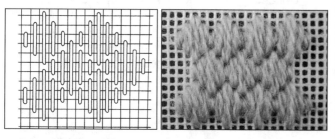

You might think, at a glance, that Hungarian Brick and Hungarian Diamonds are the same stitch. While Hungarian Brick shares its smallest stitch with the next square, creating softer lines, Diamonds does not share this stitch, so it produces well-defined lines. In general, though, wherever one of these stitches could be used, so could the other. The yarn requirement for Hungarian Diamonds, like Brick, is three plies.

Hungarian Ground

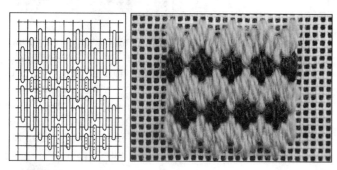

Medium-light wearing Hungarian Ground is another stitch you would normally want to classify in the Bargello family. It creates a lovely, bold effect, as the long stitches border small diamonds. To simplify the look, work the stitch in a single color. Keep this stitch in mind for a larger area, or for a background. Three plies of yarn are required in the needle.

Hungarian Steps

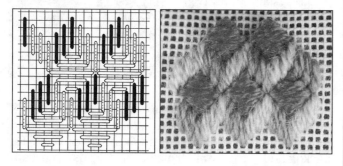

To describe this medium-wearing stitch in two words would not be exceedingly difficult; I would call it large and bold. It is so large, in fact, that I would reserve it for special projects, such as purses. Of, course, like all stitches, Hungarian Steps could be incorporated into samplers. The upright and horizontal stitches are worked in three plies. Send the needle up through holes that do not yet hold yarn, and down into holes that do already hold yarn. At some points in the stitch, fairly large quantities of yarn are inserted into the canvas.

Hungarian Tiles

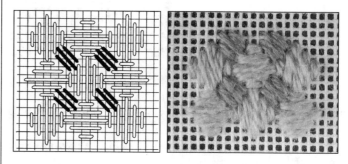

Depending upon your choice of colors and the area on your project, Hungarian Tiles could be used to represent a field of flowers or a grassy meadow. It could also be incorporated into any sampler. The upright stitches are worked first, and they require three plies of yarn. Then, work the diagonal stitches in two plies. Hungarian Tiles is also medium-wearing.

Hungarian Tiles Variation

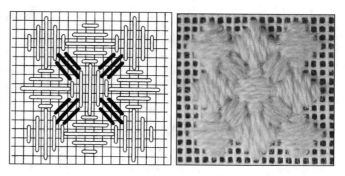

Like Hungarian Tiles, this is a versatile variation that could be incorporated into many various projects, such as pictures, abstracts and samplers. As with its close cousin, work the upright stitches first in three plies, and use two plies for the diagonal stitches. This stitch, too, is medium- wearing.

Hungarian Variation I

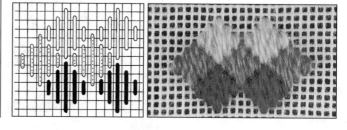

Hungarian Variation I requires multiple colors of yarn. A single color would create Hungarian Diamonds. In the diagram, the white stitches should be worked in your darkest color of yarn. The dotted lines require a medium shade, and the black lines look best in your lightest choice of yarn. This does not mean you must only stitch in one color family—feel free to choose combinations of completely different colors. Three plies of yarn provide ample coverage for Hungarian Variation I.

Indian Stripe

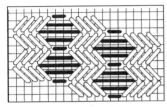 

Indian Stripe creates a very bold look in two tones on the canvas. For this reason, use caution when stitching a project. If you stitch a large area in Indian Stripe, the eye of the viewer will be drawn toward that section. For a softer effect, choose two tones that are very close to one another. Since its longest horizontal line crosses six canvas threads, this stitch is medium-light wearing.

Interlace Band

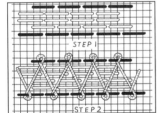 

In brief, this is a three-dimensional stitch. The first step serves as the foundation for the stitch, while the second step brings the stitch to life. While a border is the obvious choice for Interlace Band, it could also be used to create unique lines in a whimsical picture, if you were to use this stitch for a snake or other animal. First, stitch the dark lines in one color, and the light lines in another color (see diagram). Then, with a pearl yarn, weave the curved stitch in step two. Experiment with different fibers and yarns to learn what sorts of effects you can achieve with this stitch.

Interlocking Leaf

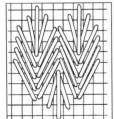 

Among the possibilities for Interlocking Leaf are unique borders and background foliage. You can interlock the rows of the motif to create a pattern. The standard yarn requirement for Interlocking Leaf is two plies in the needle.

Interwoven Herringbone

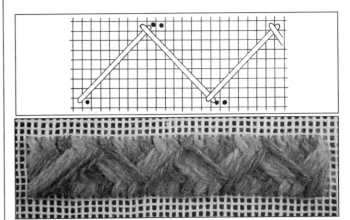

This is perhaps one of the boldest of all needlepoint stitches. Interwoven Herringbone is not necessarily the stitch for just any project—but it is great for projects that can carry a large, dominant line. There are a few things to keep in mind with this stitch. First, do not rotate the canvas. Also keep in mind that the last color you use will be the most dominant hue. You will notice with this stitch that its component stitches are quite long, and that the back of the canvas is not covered. For this reason, you might correctly deduce that the stitch is not so durable. The first line needs to be counted. The second set of stitches goes quickly and easily. To create the stitch, follow the diagram and then, using any combination of four to eight colors, continue to stitch until the row is finished. The set of dots on the graph shows the next set of stitches.

Irregular Gobelin

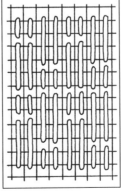 

Irregular Gobelin creates well-defined lines that run parallel to the bottom edge of the canvas. Keep this in mind when placing it in your picture. Perhaps the best use for Irregular Gobelin would be in pillows or picture frames, where you essentially pile borders upon borders. Consider using this to edge a picture project. You might stitch a mock picture frame around the entire piece, and then omit a wooden or metal frame. Hang the project as is for a contemporary look. This is a medium-wearing stitch. Use three-ply yarn.

Italian Cross

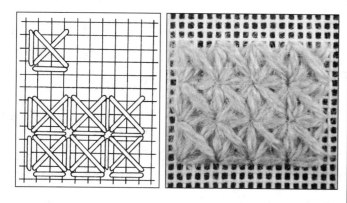

A light, airy stitch, Italian Cross is much more durable than it appears. Two-ply yarn is used, and each stitch is worked as two straight lines accompanied by a cross. Stitch Italian Cross from left to right on all rows. Be sure that the cross hatches are all sewn in the same direction.

Jacquard

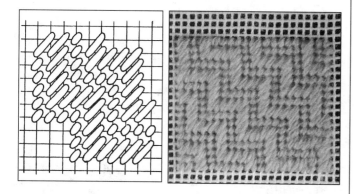

With this medium-wearing stitch, once you have placed the pattern on the canvas, the stitching is actually quite fun to work. You accomplish all the necessary counting in the first row of the stitch. You can lay either all the long stitches first, or all the short stitches. Use two-ply yarn.

Janina

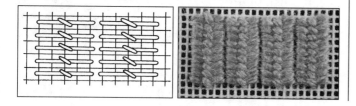

Using two plies in the needle, begin at the top of the canvas, making a long stitch. Then, make a smaller anchor stitch in the middle of the long stitch. Continue on, working the next stitch underneath the first, and repeat to create a row. When the row is completed, tie it off and begin a row again at the top. For the best results in creating even tension throughout the project, complete stitching a row before stopping and putting down the project. Stopping in the middle of a row disrupts the tension. While it might not always be obvious, sometimes it can be.

John

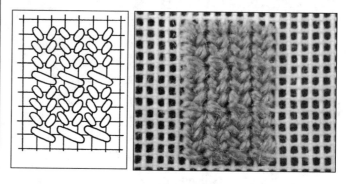

Hard-wearing John can be quite easily compensated. Whether you are stitching in a curved or square area, you can fit John in anywhere. Two-ply yarn covers the canvas quite nicely.

Jus

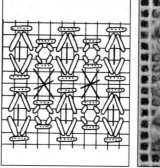

To stitch Jus, begin on the left-hand side of the canvas, making a series of upside-down V's, all the way to the end of the row. Then, make the next row of upright V's from the right to the left. Start another row of upside-down V's, and continue stitching rows in this way until you have filled the area. Once the area has been filled, you are ready to stitch the straight, perpendicular lines. These lines are also stitched in two plies, but in a darker color. Then use a metal thread to make the upright, straight lines. For a finish on the example, large crosses with a hatch were stitched in rayon thread. Apply hard-wearing Jus on such items as belts, purses and evening shoes.

Jus Variation

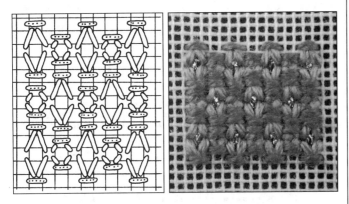

Jus Variation is stitched much like original Jus, with the exception that the design does not include Cross stitch. While the effect of the stitch is less dramatic than Jus, the variation is just as versatile and just as hard-wearing.

Kathy

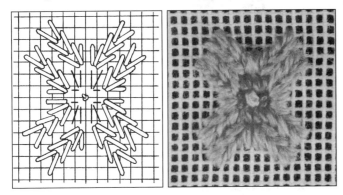

Kathy is a hard-wearing center stitch that is not equal on all sides. Exercise caution when using it. Either you must surround the stitch with Continental, or it will be surrounded by void canvas. You can see an example of this stitch on the "Scissors Charm." To create the stitch, make the straight, center lines in pearl cotton. The slanted V's should be stitched in two-ply Persian, and the French Knot in the center is made of rayon floss. Take care when counting—it can be a bit tricky.

Ken A

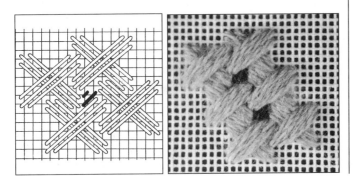

With two-ply yarn, stitch a large, bold cross. Two colors are required to make the motif. The large crosses are stitched in one color, and a darker hue is used for the small fill-in stitches to make a bold motif. Ken A is quite delicate, in terms of durability. Use this stitch in samplers and other multi-stitched projects that might require a larger pattern.

Kennan

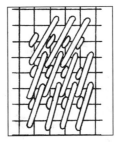

If you were to look at the diagram without seeing a sample of the stitch, you might not assume that this stitch has a softer effect. In Kennan, the short stitches seem to disappear. In the sample pictured, I used one ply—but, if you find that one ply does not offer enough coverage, then increase your yarn to two plies. Kennan is well-adapted for cases where you want to turn the canvas in order to continue the rows.

Kip

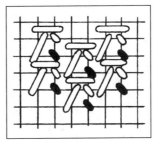

This hard-wearing stitch is a close cousin to Edge. If you want to add a little glitter to your project, but not too much, consider Kip. The small motif can be incorporated into many projects. Two-ply Persian wool is used in the pi (π) and the small slanted line is in metal.

Knit One Purl One

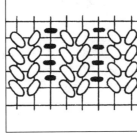

I was inspired by a knitted sweater to create this hard-wearing stitch. The front of the sweater had a motif of V's. If you closely examine the stitch, you will see little lines between the V's. Those who knit will understand why the stitch has its name. To create the stitch, use two-ply Persian yarn to make a column of V's down the area to be filled. Then, skip a thread on the canvas and repeat the row of V's. To fill the void, make small horizontal stitches down the canvas in a thin yarn or in one-ply Persian.

Knitting I

Knitting I resembles a knitted pullover sweater. The tight stitches lend the stitch a good deal of durability. Do not limit your use of Knitting I to places and projects that require you to copy the look of a knitted fabric, but use it anywhere you want texture and a good amount of eye appeal. To create the stitch, think of the motif as rows of V's running down the canvas. Stitch the V's together. When you reach the bottom of the area, stop and begin the next row at the top.

Knitting II

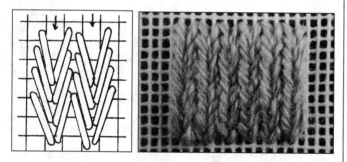

This stitch closely resembles Knitting I, but it calls for a different count. Instead of crossing two threads on the canvas, Knitting II travels down three. Use Knitting II anywhere you would use Knitting I. Use two-ply yarn.

Knitting III

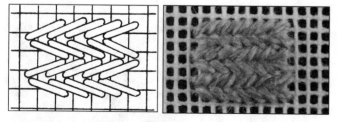

Depending upon the area, you may wish to create the effect of knitting that stands upright or on a diagonal, or that lies horizontally. Whatever direction you need to observe, this stitch can be adapted to suit your needs. Load your needle with two shades of green at one time, and you can create a stitch that resembles grass in a field. Because Knitting III is quite durable, you can use it in almost any project.

Knotted I

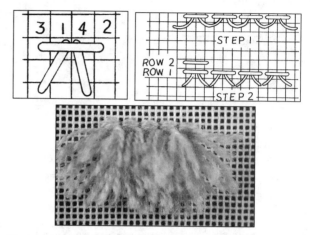

Knotted I is completely different from Knotted II and III. This first is considered a pile stitch. For this reason, it "eats" a good deal of wool. To create the stitch, start with three plies in the needle.

Bring the needle down at point 1 and, without pulling through, come out at 2.

Pull the yarn through the canvas, leaving about one inch of yarn from point 1.

Go down again at 3 and pull the yarn tight—but not to the point of distorting the canvas.

Come back out at 4.

For one individual stitch, cut the yarn off at this point (see the first diagram).

To make a continuous line, do not cut the yarn, but go to the next stitch.

When the row is finished, cut the yarn. Work from the bottom to the top of your canvas. After stitching an entire row, you are ready to give the area a "haircut." With a sharp pair of scissors, cut the loops, and then trim the entire area to make an even pile on the canvas (see the second diagram). For areas such as a head of hair or a peach, where you would want the edges of the motif rounded, trim as close as needed. Do not be afraid to cut. The piles will not fall off your project.

Knotted II

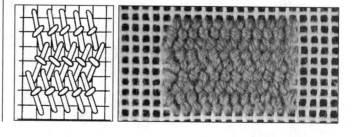

This stitch is nothing like Knotted I. This stitch shares the name of Knotted because the long stitches are knotted, or tied down, with a small Continental stitch. These Continental ties lend durability to Knotted II. The texture is an eye-catcher, but it is versatile enough for just about any area. As with all stitches, you should experiment to determine what you want in any special area. To create Knotted II, make the long stitch first, and then tie it off with a small Continental. Then, move on to the next stitch. Rotate the canvas to make the next row.

Knotted III

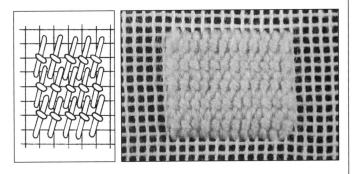

Knotted III closely resembles Knotted II, except in the direction the long stitches lie on the canvas. Work this stitch just as you would Knotted II. Use two plies in the needle for even coverage.

Lace Wheels

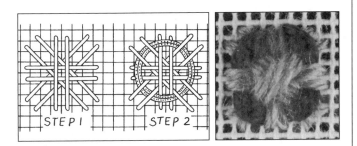

In its own way, Lace Wheels resembles marine life preservers. It is considered an isolated stitch, but you can also work several of them close together, to fill an entire area with Lace Wheels. Do not limit this stitch to Persian yarn. Wonderful wheels can be made on a foundation of pearl cotton or embroidery floss. The round circle in the stitch can be stitched in any fiber, from traditional yarns to metals.

First lay the foundation on the canvas. Then, coming out to the top of the canvas, begin weaving the yarn over and under the long stitches. For a neater appearance, come out and go back down under a long stitch that you will be weaving. This makes the circle appear to be one continuous movement, and not a start and stop (see the photo).

Laced Chain

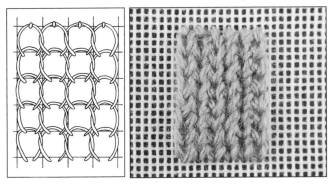

Take a close look at the diagram for Laced Chain, and you might think this is a hard result to achieve. It looks to be definite loops that resemble rows of Chain stitches—but, when the stitch is worked, the result is actually quite different. Compare the diagram to the photograph and you will see that Laced Chain appears as more of a series of curves. Consider this stitch for any area where you want extra impact. This is medium-hard wearing, so you can feel relatively free to use it in any project. To create the stitch, make a row of Chain stitches. Then, stop the yarn and start again at the beginning of the next row. Come out to the top, and, before going back down, slide your needle under the stitch next to it—and then go back under the canvas. Return to the top of the canvas, anchoring the previous loop. Continue until the row is complete, and then move on to the next row. Just keep in mind that you should start and finish your rows in one direction.

Large Brick

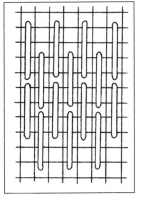

Using three-ply yarn, you can stitch Large Brick over four or six threads on the canvas. Exercise some caution in employing this stitch—it is not well suited for such projects as foot cushions or other functional items that receive everyday wear. Be sure to keep the plies lying straight on the canvas while stitching.

Large Checker

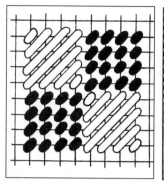 

Large Checker truly resembles a checkerboard. In a single color, the pattern is much less busy than in two colors. To stitch Large Checker, make the large square first and then the Continental stitch. Then go on to the next large square. Stitch in one long line, and then reverse the canvas and stitch the next line. The square traverses four intersections on the canvas, making this a medium-light wearing stitch.

Large Diagonal Mosaic

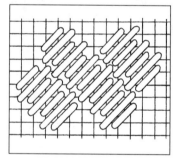 

Large Diagonal Mosaic produces very bold diagonal lines that really draw the eye, so place the stitch with caution. Although it covers three intersections on the canvas at its longest point, Large Diagonal Mosaic holds up to a considerable amount of wear. The yarns may pill, however. Use two-ply yarn in your needle.

Large Diagonal Scotch

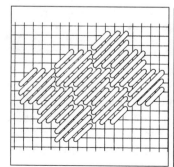 

For a large area or background, try Large Diagonal Scotch—but think twice when applying this motif. At its largest section, it traverses four intersections. These longer threads can catch or grab, possibly resulting in ripped yarns. For this reason, do not use the stitch on items intended for regular use or wear. Stitch down the row, and then turn the canvas around and continue on to the next row.

Large Horizontal Parisian

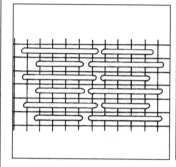 

Skies, oceans and pastures can all be created using Large Horizontal Parisian. With three plies in the needle, stitch down a row, and when you reach the bottom, return, stitching upward. Continue until you complete the area. Insert the needle downward into the canvas, into a hole that already holds yarn, and return to the top of the canvas through an empty hole to ensure sharp, clean stitches. Use three plies to create this light-wearing stitch.

Large Interlocking Gobelin

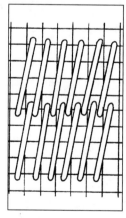 

This stitch produces very soft, delicate, horizontal lines on the canvas. The stitch is remarkably strong, when you consider that the yarn traverses four threads on the canvas. Because the stitches interlock, this is an easy pattern to place on the canvas. Regular Gobelin produces the same hard, horizontal lines. Use two-ply yarn for this stitch.

Large Knitting

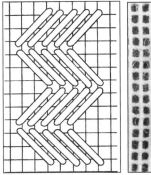

Like many other large stitches, Large Knitting is not a very durable stitch, and it is best used in a sampler. It crosses three canvas intersections. The diagonal lines limit the stitch's usefulness for backgrounds in picture projects. For this reason, give thought to its placement in projects. Use two-ply yarn.

Large Moorish

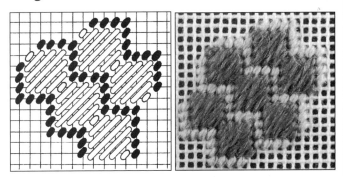

The long, diagonal stitches traverse four intersections on the canvas, which can cause Large Moorish to snag or pill through with use. Use this stitch on projects such as pictures or other items that will be subjected to handling. First create the Diagonal Scotch, and then lay Continental stitches in the void areas. Two plies make an appropriate thickness for both sets of stitches on 14/1 canvas.

Large Oblong Cross I

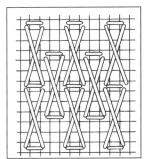

Using two-ply Persian yarn, stitch the large crosses and the top lines as a single unit. Then you can make half cross hatches along an entire row and return to finish the upper hatch, or you can complete each unit fully before moving on to the next. I recommend the second choice. It allows you to create a much neater appearance on the underside of the canvas. Because of the large crosses, Large Oblong Cross I is not a hard-wearing stitch. Try this stitch for a linen look. A simple Tent in the foreground lends greater texture to this stitch—and the combination is fun to work.

Large Rice

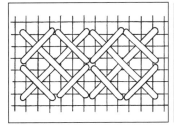

Large Rice is a lacy, fragile stitch. Use it sparingly in most projects. Think of this stitch when you want an airy texture. Consider using Large Rice for samplers and other multi-stitch projects. Both counts of the pattern require two plies for stitching, and you absolutely must strip the yarn.

Leaf

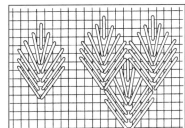

The color you choose to stitch this medium-wearing pattern determines the feeling that the stitch evokes. Autumn is created using combinations of red and gold, while bright greens give life to a summer scene. Do not limit the use to topping trunks of trees. Anywhere you need a true leaf pattern, keep this stitch in mind. Two-ply yarn ensures correct coverage.

Leaf with Smyrna

Diminutive shrubs or the flames of a campfire can be the effect of Leaf with Smyrna. As with the Leaf stitch, this medium-hard wearing pattern does not have to be limited to isolated use. Consider it for background cover. Either make the stitches at random or space them evenly, and then fill in with Continental, or another small pattern. Use two-ply yarn on 14/1 canvas.

Ley's Trail *(Courtesy of Chottie Alderson)*

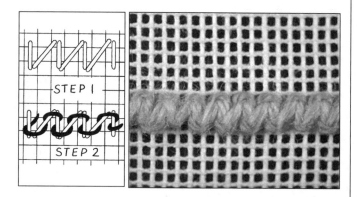

Light-wearing Ley's Trail is great for creating a frame around a picture project. Stitched borders are fun to create, and can add a lot to a project. It resembles the effect of rickrack that might be used to trim a dress. If you were to stitch a series of rows in several colors, the needlepointing would take on the look of fabric, and you could create an interesting pattern for an accent pillow. In the sample, two shades of one color were used. To create this stitch, first lay the foundation as indicated in the diagram, step one. Then, with the second yarn, come out of the underside and weave the yarn in and out of the foundation yarns. Never return under the canvas until you finish the row.

Lipperts

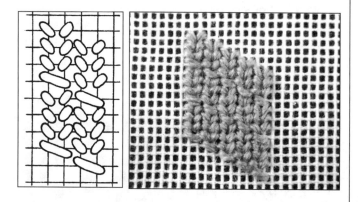

When stitching Lipperts, think of the two sets of Continental and the long line as a single unit. Work your way down the canvas in rows. This is a hard-wearing stitch.

Long Armed Cross

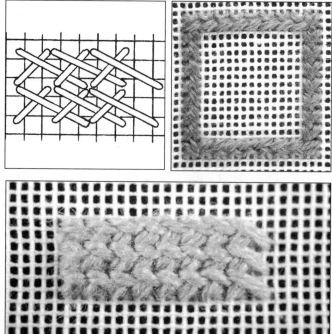

Long Armed Cross is a versatile choice for adding texture in smaller areas. The smaller stitches that tie down the longer ones add durability to the stitch, so it is an excellent candidate for purses, pillows, and functional projects. Just remember, always stitch left to right. If you allow your stitching to travel in both directions, the crosses will not be sewn correctly. Use two-ply Persian yarn.

Medallion

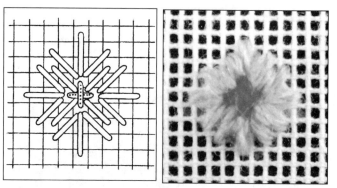

Medallion could be used to create sweet little flowers in a green, grassy field, or the whimsical eyes of an animal, or a dramatic, stylized sun. While it is a large, bold stitch, Medallion is also hard-wearing. Work the outer lines first and then fill the middle with a cross. Use two-ply Persian for both colors.

Medium Checker

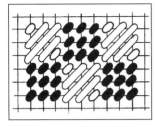 

You have two options for stitching hard-wearing Medium Checker. Either you can work the Continental first and then go back to fill in the Flat stitches, or you can work both components as you go. If you follow the first method, your Continental stitches are more likely to end up with a finer, smoother appearance, and the Flat stitch is more likely to have an even tension throughout the project. Of course, as both methods are correct, the technique that you follow is entirely your choice. Try both approaches, and see which works better for you. Because the stitches lie diagonally, two-ply Persian yarn is a good choice for 14/1 canvas.

Medium Rice

Medium Rice is not a very durable stitch. This is for two reasons—first, the underside is not covered very well; second, although the stitch requires two-ply yarn, it tends to show canvas once in a while. Small cross hatches over the large X bolsters the durability some. Considering all these factors, you might use Medium Rice in pillows, pictures and other items that might be handled some, but certainly not as a rule. Use two-ply Persian yarn.

Medium Rice Checker

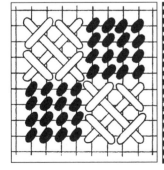 

As does Checker, Medium Rice Checker produces a bold pattern. The squares, which are the Rice stitch, add a richer design to this stitch. Because of the bold motif, though, give some thought to its placement in a project. Keep in mind, too, that you can mute the effect of the stitch some by using a single color, rather than a color combination. This stitch calls for two-ply yarn.

Melrose

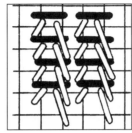 

Hard-wearing Melrose might be used for shoes, purses and pillows. Make the long and short slanted stitches in rows, moving downward on the canvas. Then insert the horizontal stitches. Each horizontal stitch is tucked under the check above it. Use a thin metallic thread for Melrose to create drama with the stitch.

Mettler

This medium-wearing stitch can become quite busy if you do not use some caution when using it. It creates a lumpy texture, which tends to draw the eye. To create the stitch, work each cross completely and then continue to the next. Two-ply Persian wool provides sufficient coverage.

Mettler Variation

When it is worked following the methods of original Mettler, the variation tends to allow canvas to show. To remedy this, you have two options. First, you can paint the canvas, preferably with an oil-based paint. Second, you might fill the voids with Continental or another simple, small stitch. Mettler Variation has a modern look, and might work best in contemporary projects. It is also medium-wearing.

Milanese

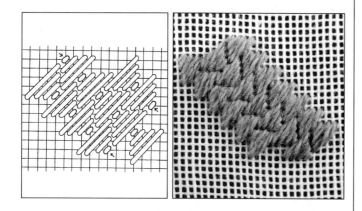

Milanese produces the effect of arrowheads traveling diagonally. Because the yarn traverses four intersections on the canvas, Milanese is not a durable stitch. Save it for projects that will not be handled much. Work diagonally, moving left to right. When you finish a row, move to the next and stitch right to left. For clean lines, always have your needle go up through a hole that has not been used, and back under through a hole that already holds yarn. Use two-ply yarn, and try the stitch in a single color or in combinations.

Milanese Color Variation

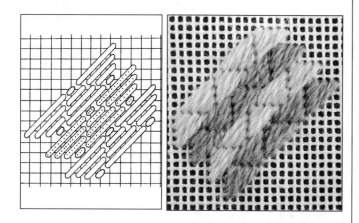

Unless the two colors that you use are closely related, Milanese Color Variation produces bold diagonal lines. Use it on samplers or similar projects. The motif is too bold for many designs, so use it sparingly. Use two-ply Persian yarn.

Mixed Milanese

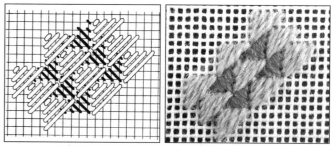

Oriental IV and Mixed Milanese are close cousins, as you can tell by comparing the two graphs. Mixed Milanese traverses four intersections at its longest point, however, where Oriental IV covers six. You can create either a very bold design or a more tranquil one. Your color choice determines the effect of the stitch. Two-ply yarn is required for good coverage of the canvas. Consider using it in samplers. Stitch the large arrowheads first and then insert the smaller stitches. The second set lies under the longest stitch in the arrowhead.

Mixed Up Cross

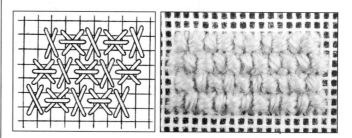

Mixed Up Cross is a tight, hard-wearing stitch with terrific eye appeal. I think this stitch would be an appropriate choice for a blanket on a bed, or curls on the head of a small child. Really, though, the possibilities for placing this stitch are endless. Try stitching several different colors in one area. Incorporating black for one cross and red for another, you can create the look of a lumberjack's flannel shirt. Stitch a row in one direction and rotate the canvas to continue with the next row.

Montenegrin

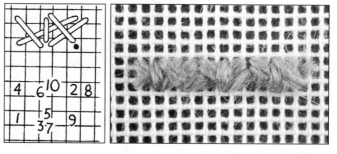

Follow the number pattern in the graph to produce an interesting, hard-wearing border stitch. The actual size of this stitch is very small. If a larger line is desired, try doubling the count of threads on the canvas that the stitches need to traverse. In the sample, two-ply yarn was threaded in the needle.

Montenegrin Cross Adaptation

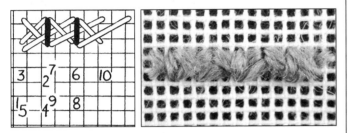

When comparing this diagram with that of original Montenegrin, I find that the looks of the stitches are quite similar. The same holds true for the actual stitch texture. As with Montenegrin, the size is small but changes can be made. Two plies are required in the needle. To create the stitch, follow the count in the diagram. Then apply the vertical stitches. The sample shows two colors. Of course, you can always stitch in a single color for a different effect.

Montenegrin Variation

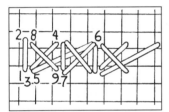 

Montenegrin Variation is tighter and more tightly packed than the other two Montenegrin stitches. This forms a more rounded line. Consider this variation if you would like to add a higher texture to your work. Use two-ply Persian yarn.

Moon

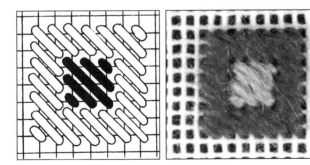

This stitch evokes the feeling of a moon on a cloudy night—but do not let that prevent you from using it in other capacities. You might use it for a square pillow, or for a picture hanging on a wall—and, of course, there are always plenty of backgrounds to think about! Your only limit is your imagination. Even though the threads are quite long in this stitch, it is considered medium-hard wearing, which broadens the range of projects for which you might choose it. Use two-ply yarn.

Moorish I

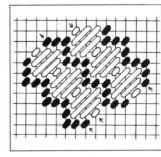 

Just because a stitch has components that traverse more than three intersections on the canvas does not necessarily mean that the stitch must be fragile. Moorish I is considered medium-hard wearing. In two colors, this motif can become busy, but one tone can help to keep it quiet. In one color it creates a soft pattern with some texture. To create the stitch, use two-ply yarn and follow the arrows on the diagram.

Moorish II

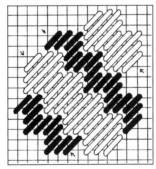 

Not much can be said about Moorish II that has not been already said about the first. Moorish I features a small zigzag between the larger diagonals. Moorish II is wider in its main line as well as its smaller one. Moorish II does not wear as well as the first. It is worked in the same way.

Mosaic

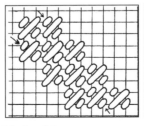 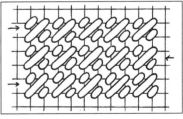

Method 1   Method 2

There are two correct methods for stitching hard-wearing Mosiac. You should choose your methods according to the area you intend to fill with the stitch. Your options include working Mosaic horizontally or diagonally. In the picture, you can see both approaches. The darker shade is in horizontal, while the lighter is diagonal. As you can see, the top side does not have a difference, but the underside changes. Either method of stitching Mosaic will cause your canvas to distort. For this reason, you should always use stretcher bars or a scroll frame. See page 26, for more information on these tools.

Mosaic Stripe

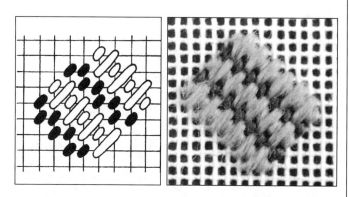

Mosaic Stripe produces strong diagonal lines. It is quite a durable stitch, but keep its bold lines in mind when choosing a home for it on canvas. To tone down the heavy lines, use two closely related colors. Use two plies for both yarns.

Narrow Oblong Cross

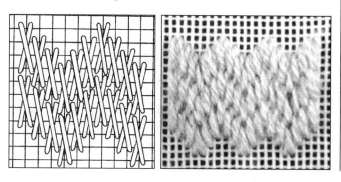

Narrow Oblong Cross is a close cousin to Bargello. Except for the crosses, the vertical effect of the stitch resembles flames. Compare the textures of Bargello and Narrow Oblong Cross. Notice how Narrow Oblong has a unique, soft look that recedes into the canvas, while Bargello is bold and flat. Besides this difference, Narrow Oblong Cross does not have as prominent vertical "flame" movements. Consider this stitch for adding a good deal of texture without the bold, defined lines of some other highly textured stitches. Like all other Cross stitches, remember to stitch all the top hatches in the same direction. This is a medium-wearing stitch.

New-Cah's Walk
(Courtesy of Chottie Alderson)

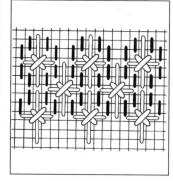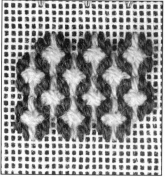

New-Cah's Walk resembles flowered wallpaper. Stitching it in two colors, as is done in the photo, you can create a much bolder, even three-dimensional, look than you would create stitching it in monochrome. In the sample, two-ply yarn was sufficient for good coverage. Even the upright stitches cover the canvas satisfactorily with this yarn thickness.

Nine Cross

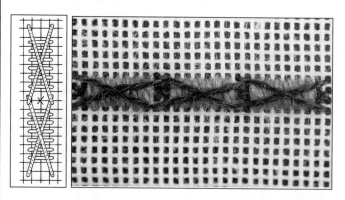

Light-wearing Nine Cross might resemble a Native American motif if you stitch it in colors that evoke a Southwestern feel. Change the color combination to create a completely different look. Nine Cross can be used to create beautiful borders around picture projects, or you might use it in multiple layers for an overall motif. The stitch's long crosses make it very delicate to handle. Of all the Cross stitches, it is most imperative in Nine Cross that the larger crosses lie in the same direction. Just one glance will reveal any yarn lying in the wrong direction. Use two-ply yarn.

Nobuko

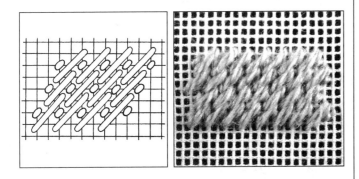

Nobuko is a soft-looking, and yet medium-wearing, stitch. The small stitches in the pattern lend it a good deal of versatility. Use two-ply yarn.

Norwich

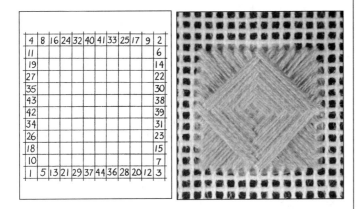

In the Norwich diagram, you will see a number pattern, as opposed to lines where the stitches would go. Use two-ply yarn and follow the numbers. Go up at point 1 and down at 2, up at 3 and back down at 4, and continue until you reach number 44. The final set of stitches finds you in the middle of the square. When all of this has been accomplished, you have a diagonal square on top of another. This creates a dramatic motif when used in isolation as a single stitch, or in a grouping for a larger area, such as a background. You can fiddle with the size of the square by adding to or subtracting from the number of stitches. For true Norwich,

the square must be equal on all sides. Of course, you may want to be inventive, and experiment with rectangles of varied sizes. There are no true rules for this light-wearing stitch.

Oatmeal

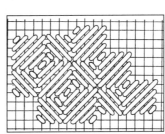

How this stitch got its name is a good question. When I worked this sample, I chose a light brown color, just to see whether the stitch actually resembles oatmeal. I have to say, I cannot see oatmeal here. As a matter of fact, the large and small squares create quite an interesting texture. The larger stitches traverse over four intersections on the canvas, making this a medium-light wearing stitch. Consider using Oatmeal any time you need some movement, but a flat lying stitch, on the canvas. Like all other diagonal stitches, Oatmeal requires two plies in the needle. When working Oatmeal, begin by stitching the larger squares diagonally. After you have laid this foundation, go on to stitch the smaller squares, working in the opposite direction.

Oblique Slav

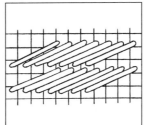

Oblique Slav features definite lines that lead the eye horizontally. Because is it medium-hard wearing, pillows or other items intended for use would be fine for Oblique Slav. As a matter of fact, just about any project you choose would be fine for this stitch. To stitch Oblique Slav, begin stitching a row from left to right and when the row is finished, rotate the canvas and continue on to the next one. Use two-ply yarn.

Oblong Cross

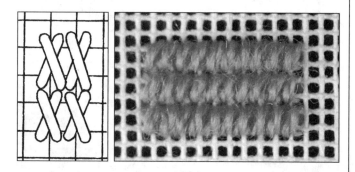

Using one-ply Persian wool, make the crosses just as you would in any other Cross stitch. Run the first set of hatch marks all in one direction, and then finish the stitch by doing the same in the opposite direction. Continue on to the next set of stitches. This is a medium hard-wearing stitch.

Oblong Cross Tramé

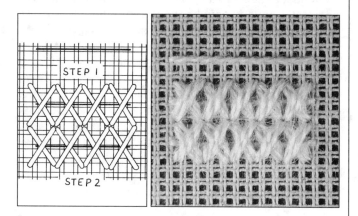

The first step in stitching medium-wearing Oblong Cross Tramé is to count the motif on the canvas. Take care of the count, as usual, with one ply in the needle. Count the number of crosses that must be worked in a particular color, and lay the yarn over the required number of canvas intersections. You should lay the yarn in the center of the two threads that make up each intersection. Continue counting the motif using the graph for the project. Like all other Tramé stitches, never lay a count for a large number of stitches with one continuous thread. Use the count from one to five. If a color requires a longer row, break it up, and use a couple of separate threads. For example, you need nine Cross stitches. Lay the Tramé across four intersections, and then across five, and then continue on to the next color. When the entire motif has been counted out, begin making your Crosses as you would for any other Cross stitch. For 14/1 canvas, use two-ply yarn for the Crosses and one ply for the Tramé. Penelope canvas requires three-ply yarn for the Crosses.

Oblong Rice

The graph shows little cross hatches covering large crosses. When the stitch has been applied to the canvas, the larger crosses tend to disappear, creating a very tight texture. Feel free to use Oblong Rice for items such as purses, shoes or throw pillows. It holds up to little hands and the wear and tear that comes with them. Use two-ply yarn.

Oblong with Back

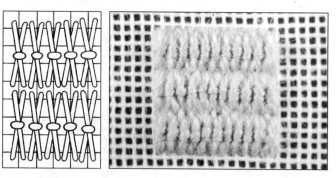

Oblong with Back creates a definite horizontal line, although the major part of this stitch is large crosses. It is not as important to stitch all the cross hatches in the same direction, since they are covered by back stitches. Of course, I argue that there is more to stitching than looks—the personal satisfaction of creating an heirloom cannot be underestimated. This is a durable stitch, so you can apply it to any project, including those that are handled often. Use two-ply yarn.

Old Florentine

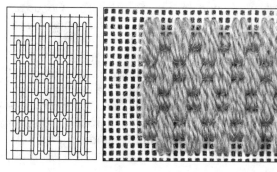

This old upright stitch requires three-ply yarn. As the yarns traverse six threads, it is hardly a hard-wearing stitch. While it is certainly a lovely choice for samplers, it could also make an elegant detail for an evening purse, if stitched in, say, white silks and silver metallic threads. Pillows that will not come in contact with too many young hands are all right, too. Consider using a color family to shade an area, such as a field or sky in a picture project. One solid color of Old Florentine is a wonderful fill for a background.

Oriental I

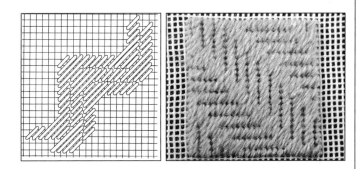

When this sample was stitched, the canvas was distorted quite severely. At the corners of this motif, the yarn passes over more than five intersections of canvas. The only truly effective way to achieve correct tension is to keep the canvas lying flat. For this, stretcher bars are indispensable. Oriental I produces a large motif that truly requires a larger area to accommodate it. Do not be daunted; Oriental I would also look great in patchwork areas. It is light-wearing, and at its best in an area that has enough space to really showcase its design.

Oriental II

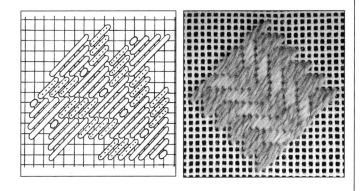

While this stitch shares a name with the previous stitch, the two are actually very different from one another. At the same time, wherever you might use Oriental I, you could also incorporate Oriental II. For a little dazzle, make the smaller slanted lines a deeper color than the rest of the motif, to add depth to this light-wearing stitch.

Oriental III

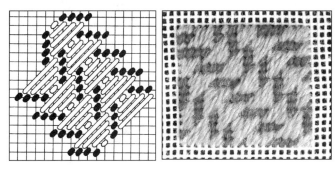

The only difference between this stitch and Oriental II is the presence of the small stitches between the arrowheads. Oriental II features small stitches traversing two intersections, while Oriental III has only one intersection between arrowheads. Use two-ply Persian yarn.

Oriental IV

When stitching light-wearing Oriental IV, work the larger arrowheads first (the white lines in the diagram) and then the smaller ones (the dark lines). The dark lines must be worked under the longest of the white lines (for further instruction, see the picture). This creates the illusion of a straight, uncompensated line. Use two-ply yarn.

Oriental V

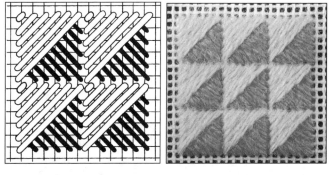

Stitch Oriental V just as you would stitch Oriental IV, first the white lines, and then the black. Tuck the black lines under, for the appearance of a straight line.

Outline I

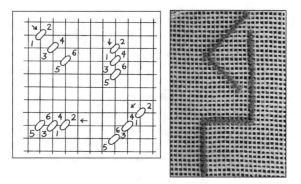

Outline I is not used as a unit, but as a border for other areas where there needs to be a strong cut-off between two stitches. The diagram shows four directions in which Outline I can travel. You can take the stitch in any one, or any combination, of directions. The example shows how Outline I can be applied to the canvas. There is really only one great rule to remember, and that is this: Never allow the stitch to resemble Continental Gone Wrong! If you are working in a right hand direction, do not worry that the stitches do not touch one another. When everything is completed, the eye fills in the void. Keep in mind that needlepoint, as a medium, has its limits—and one of those limits is its inability to truly curve. Think of yourself as an Impressionist painter, and you will sleep better.

Outline II

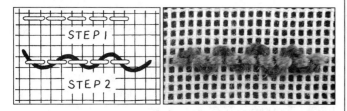

Outline II is created of Back stitches with yarn woven in and out of the foundation. The Back stitches are very hard-wearing but, because the weaving is not tied down except at the beginning and end, this stitch can snag. For a variation of Outline II, lay it over Continental. Use silks and metals for the weaving. This would never stand the wear required of everyday items, but for an evening purse or special occasion dress Outline II would create a wonderful special effect. Outline II would also make an elegant border for a picture project or a pillow.

Overcast

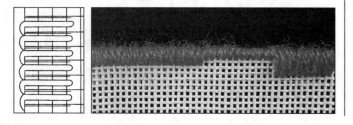

Medium-wearing Overcast is the simplest choice for binding the edges of raw canvas. It does not create much texture. At times, when you truly want the focus to be on the center of the piece, it can be a wise choice to use a low texture edging to accent the project. To work the stitch, come out to the top of the canvas four threads in from the edge. Wrap the yarn around the edge of the canvas, to the back, and come out directly below where you previously came up. The yarn becomes something like a spiral binding on a notebook. For a variation, you can stitch over one, two or three threads on the canvas. This stitch works well for plastic canvas. For any canvas other than plastic, never stitch over an edge that has not been turned under. Plastic canvas does not need to be turned under.

Padded Cushions

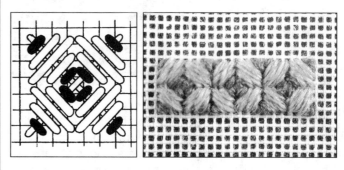

Padded Cushions produces a three-dimensional effect on the canvas. Your options for placing this stitch are truly endless. You could use it for a border. In two colors, for a field, it has a completely different effect. Use two plies in your needle for Padded Cushions.

Padded Double Cross

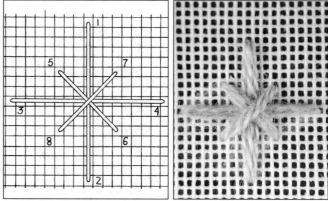

Light-wearing Padded Double Cross is a great candidate for such jobs as large centers in a motif. A project such as the "Scissors Charm" featured in this book, or center on a pillow, could accommodate this stitch quite nicely. You can use any number of plies in the needle; determine the number you need by considering how bold an effect you wish to create. Use your imagination when placing this stitch. If you do not wish the canvas to show, place Padded Double Cross over Continental stitches.

Padded Gobelin Droit

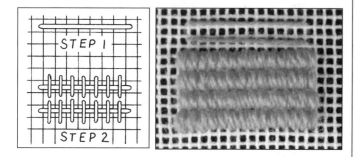

You may want some areas of stitching to be raised above others, to add interest to the project. To achieve this end, you might simply pile yarn on the canvas—or, you might choose such a padded stitch as this. Padded Gobelin Droit is just like the original Gobelin Droit, only it is raised on the canvas. To create the stitch, make long, horizontal stitches, and then go over the area again with Gobelin Droit stitches.

Papermoon
(Courtesy of Anne Dyer)

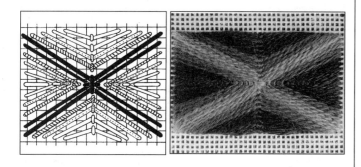

Papermoon is one of the most fragile stitches I have known. The middle yarns traverse so many intersections on the canvas that it becomes very easy to snag. The foundation of Papermoon is one large Cross stitch anchored in the middle with a small Upright Cross. After this has been laid, the next series of stitches are Rococo, becoming smaller and smaller until the middle has been filled. You can stitch Papermoon in any size you wish. The only rule is that you need to move over and down an even number of threads on the canvas. In the picture, the count is over 36 threads and down 20. For the shading, the large cross is a light blue, then two medium blue, two dark blue, three black, and five gray Rococo stitches on the short side. The longer side was stitched the same, but two dark gray stitches were added. Use two-ply Persian yarn.

Parisian

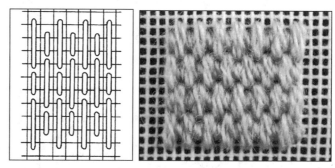

A versatile stitch, Parisian can be placed in both large and small areas. The texture is soft. I would say that this stitch is medium-light wearing. It does tend to snag, so use discretion when choosing its placement in projects. It requires three-ply yarn on 14/1 canvas. Remember to take stitches from clean holes into holes that hold yarn for a sharp, clean look.

Parisian Cross

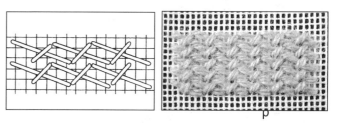

With its long stitches traversing six threads on the canvas, this could never be considered a hard-wearing stitch. In the sample photo, you may notice canvas showing through the stitch. This is another reason for the stitch's delicacy. If you do not want the canvas to show, then you must paint it to match your yarn before stitching the project. The sample shows the stitch in two-ply yarn. Experiment on a scrap canvas before placing the stitch in a project, to see whether you prefer it in three-ply yarn. On a pillow or other functional object, I recommend three plies. Always stitch left to right. At the end of the row, stop your yarn and start again on the left.

Parisian Stripe

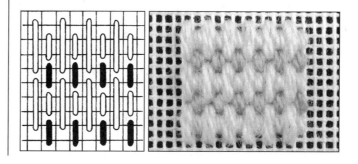

The sample was worked in two plies. You may need to thicken the yarn, depending upon the project you are stitching. Pillows may require thicker yarn. This stitch is medium-wearing, since it traverses four threads at its longest point.

Paul and Lin

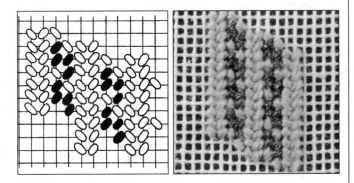

Hard-wearing Paul and Lin is at its best when you choose two contrasting colors. Work the foundation first, and then fill in the voids. The graph is easier to read this way. Put some thought into the placement of this stitch, as it does have a definite design. Do not place it in projects where the design would complicate or conflict with a motif.

Paul and Lin Variation

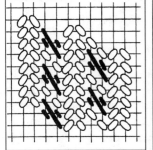

Everything that I mentioned for the original Paul and Lin goes for the variation, as well. In the sample, the center of the motif was worked in pearl cotton. Try both the original and the variation, to determine which you prefer.

Pavilion Boxes

In the photo, note the three-dimensional effect that this stitch has. The bold pattern places this stitch at its best on such projects as samplers or very large designs. Purses and pockets would be fun in Pavilion Boxes. Since the yarn is packed into the canvas, the stitch is medium-wearing. Work the squares first in three-ply yarn, and then stitch the diagonal lines in two plies.

Perspective

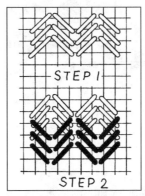
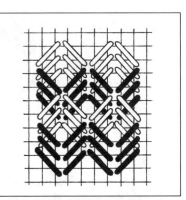

Working this stitch in two tones of a single color allows you to create a three-dimensional motif. Use two-ply yarn to produce a medium-wearing stitch that is appropriate for placement in almost any project you might imagine. When working Perspective, first stitch the light lines, left to right, and follow with the darker lines, and then the lighter lines again, followed by the darker lines. You can also stitch Perspective in a single shade, or in a pair of contrasting colors.

Peter's

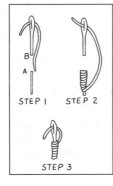

Light-wearing Peter's is a very close cousin to Bullion Knot, but with a few variations. Because the stitch requires you to roll many loops around the needle, a longer needle is required. Also, use a needle that is larger than the thickness of your yarn requirement, to help the yarn pass through the loops. To make Peter's, bring the needle out at point A and down again at B. Do not place points A and B too far apart. Come out at A again, but do not pull the needle out of the canvas. Wrap the yarn around the needle several times—two to three times the required amount for Bullion Knot. Insert the needle in B again and begin to pull the yarn tight. The number of times you wrap your yarn around the needle determines the size of the stitch. The completed stitch should resemble strange looking animals or plants. Peter's is not so much a pattern for a stitch, as it is a whimsical technique for accenting special areas.

Petit Point

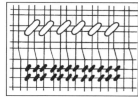 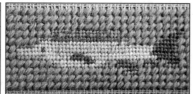

Often, the details we want to include in picture projects cannot be accomplished using the larger stitches. For example, let us say you are stitching, in Continental, a picture of a woman sitting in a chair, reading. The woman's face, bust and arms might require finer stitches than the rest of the projects. Petit Point is the perfect solution for this type of job, but it can only be stitched on Penelope canvas. On the diagram, you will see large Continental stitches. This is Demi Point. The smaller stitches are made by splitting the vertical and horizontal threads on the canvas to make petite intersections. Each Demi Point equals four Petit Point stitches. This allows you to add delicate details to a picture. When placing Petit Point, use it in combination with Basketweave or Continental stitches. Half Cross does not create a pleasing combination.

Pinched Cross

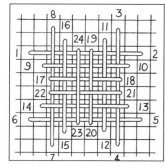 

If you compare the diagram to the photographed sample, a great difference should be immediately apparent. When the count has been completed, it creates a diagonal "X." To make Pinched Cross, come out at point 1 and down at 2. Stitch up 3 and down at 4. Continue doing this until you reach number 24. The yarn that piles up in the middle of the stitch adds to its durability, making Pinched Cross a medium-hard wearing stitch. Use Pinched Cross as an isolated stitch.

Pisces

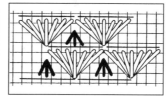 

For a medium-hard wearing border that can take you just about anywhere, try Pisces. The sample shows this stitch in a family of blues. Pisces can miter nicely to travel around a picture. To create the stitch, first make the white lines that compose the large triangles. Then, work the smaller triangles, and finally, the long lines that combine the entire look. Pisces requires two-ply yarn, and one-ply for the long horizontal stitches.

Plaited

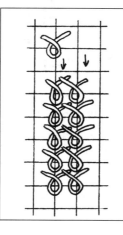 

Plaited is a very hard-wearing stitch with many potential uses. Think of Plaited for areas such as fence posts, tree trunks or lines that run parallel with the lines of the canvas. Use this stitch in a family of colors such as light blue to black, changing colors as you move from one row to the next. An entire pillow stitched in Plaited can have a very interesting visual effect. It would also be a fun stitch to try for a sunset. The diagram shows the first stitch isolated on the top. Do not skip threads on the canvas. Stitch from top to bottom. When you reach the bottom, start again at the top, at the next thread on the canvas, and again, work downward. Plaited requires two plies in the needle.

Plaited Algerian

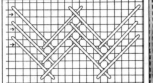 

Because its stitches traverse six intersections on the canvas, Plaited Algerian is a light-wearing stitch. From a distance, it appears as a lovely, soft zigzag. Take care to lay the two-ply yarn smoothly on the canvas, to create a soothing texture on the canvas. Consider Plaited Algerian when your project calls for a bit of added texture, but you do not wish to pile yarn on the canvas. Stitch the rows from left to right. When you reach the right, stop the yarn, and begin anew on the left, making large zigzags across the canvas.

Plaited Gobelin

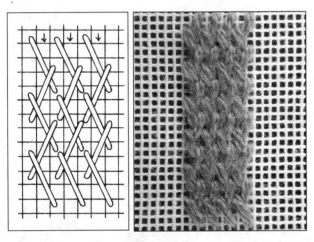

Plaited Gobelin is similar to Plaited Algerian, only it is stitched perpendicular to the bottom of the canvas. Use this medium-light wearing stitch anytime you want to use Plaited Algerian but prefer an upward movement. Stitch this just as you would Plaited Algerian. Two plies in the needle ensure a very satisfactory result on 14/1 canvas.

Point de Tresse

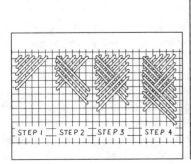 

In the diagram, this appears to be a complicated stitch. Quite the opposite is true. In step 1 you can see there are five stitches that start over one intersection and progress onto five intersections. The lines in step 2 represent the next set of stitches that move over five intersections on top of the previous ones. Step 3 shows another set of three stitches that run in the opposite direction again over five intersections on the canvas. The last step repeats the previous set, but in a perpendicular direction to the last step. Continue stitching this pattern until you reach the end of the row. If you are stitching a border, you can stop there and change directions. You can always stop and start at the top of the canvas again to double or triple a row. This is a hard-wearing stitch.

Point Russe I

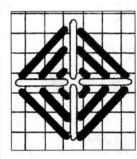 

You can use this stitch to create a squared-off little life preserver. If you change the colors and add French Knots, Point Russe I resembles flowers. Regardless of what you use it to make, the Point Russe I produces a versatile, medium-hard wearing stitch. Have fun with this stitch, trying it in a variety of colors. Use it as an isolated stitch, or stitch it in a group. First lay the diagonal stitches, and then the straight.

Point Russe II

Your choice of colors determines whether medium-wearing Point Russe II produces a two-dimensional or three-dimensional effect. By choosing dark centers and moving outward in lighter tones, you can create the illusion of deeper centers. Three colors are not required for the stitch, but a variety of tones creates a striking result. All of the component stitches require two-ply yarn, except the framing, which requires one.

Princess

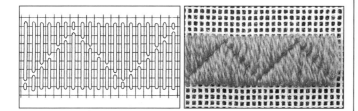

Princess is a large, soft, light-wearing border stitch that makes a wonderful accent for picture projects. You can stitch it in a single color, or create a two-color design. One color on the top, and a second color on the bottom, very nicely pull a motif together. On 14/1 canvas, Princess requires three-ply yarn.

Princess Variation

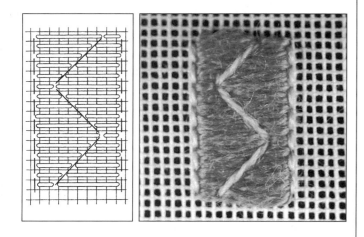

The great difference between Princess and this variation is in the application of the zigzag to the stitch. Use single-ply Back stitches along the sides to add the look of banded trim. You might like to miter the corners around a picture to make the stitch stand out.

Pyramid

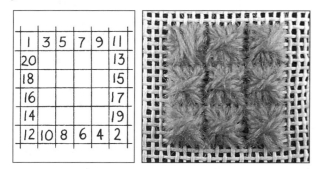

Pyramid closely resembles Double Leviathan. Because the yarn that is piled in the center of the stitch

tends to fuzz, Pyramid is not a very hard-wearing stitch. You can make a larger or smaller stitch, as you prefer. With two-ply yarn in the needle, begin the stitch by coming up at point 1. Following the number sequence, travel around the square. The yarns should resemble a spiral.

Queued Diamonds

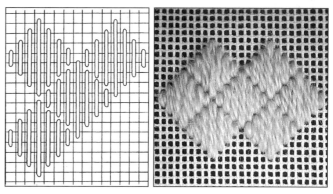

Keep light-wearing Queued Diamonds in mind when you need to create a large motif on the canvas. As with other large stitches, think twice before placing this one on the canvas. I recommend it for projects such as samplers and pillows, or for an interesting background. Use three-ply Persian yarn on 14/1 canvas.

Raised Cross

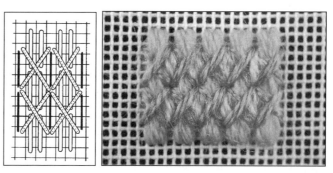

Medium-light wearing Raised Cross requires three colors to complete the look. Use three-ply yarn for the upright stitches, and two-ply for the crosses. Lay the upright stitches first, in pairs. Then incorporate the single upright lines in two-ply. This combination serves as the foundation for the Cross stitches, which you should work as you normally work Cross stitches.

Raised Work

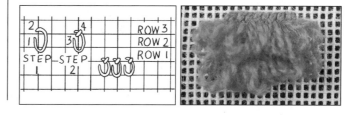

Along with most pile stitches, Raised Work is quite a hard-wearing stitch. When you complete this stitch, you will have produced a series of loops on the canvas. You can use the stitch to fill an entire area rug, or you can incorporate it into a motif, to an area where you would like to lead the eye. Note the numbers in the diagram. First make the loop (stitches 1 and 2), and then tie it off with a Continental stitch. Take care to make even loops. You can use a knitting needle or other rod-shaped instrument to create straight, equal loops. Make the first row of Raised Work at the bottom of the canvas and work toward the top to keep your existing loops from interfering with your work.

Random Bargello

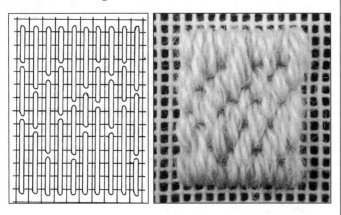

Not a true count, Random Bargello is more a technique of placing the yarn on the canvas. Random Bargello is a series of long and short upright stitches that traverse three or more threads on the canvas. For pillows, I recommend that you do not make the stitches longer than four intersections; for pictures, you can make them up to eight. To begin, stitch any pattern of Bargello you wish. Stitch the second row in the pattern like the first. Continue doing this until you have finished the area. As with all upright stitches, make sure your yarn lies straight on the canvas, to keep the project neat, and to create heritage embroidery.

Random Byzantine

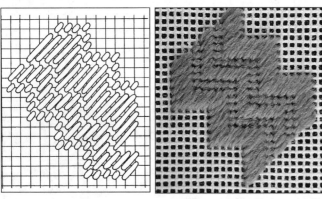

Working any stitch length, follow the true diagonal over one, two, three or four intersections on the canvas. Then follow with another row, stitching the same. Your combination might be 2, 4, 3, 1, etc. There is no required count for Random Byzantine. You can use a different count each time you stitch it. Just remember to be consistent with your steps. Use two-ply yarn to create this light-wearing stitch.

Random Continental

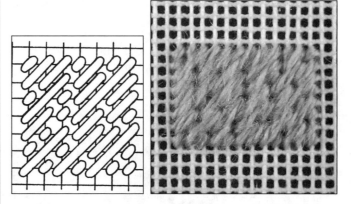

This is another stitch that does not have a true count. While the stitches are all Continental, the sizes vary. Stitch on a true diagonal, traversing one, two, three or four intersections at a time. Each time you use this medium-hard wearing stitch, it will be a little different. Random Continental creates a very unusual effect. Place this stitch anywhere. Because the Continental stitches are all different, you do not need to compensate.

Ray

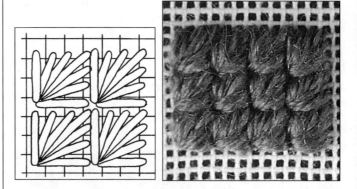

Two strands of Persian yarn in the needle create an extremely versatile, hard-wearing stitch. Definite squares appear on the canvas. The fact that this stitch does not pop out and "shout" adds to its versatility. You can place it almost anywhere. It is best to poke a small hole with a knitting needle for the seven stitches in the corner. All stitches should come up from the sides and down into the lower left-hand corner.

Raymond

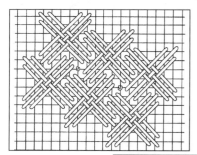

Using two-ply yarn, begin by making a large triple cross. Note: The diagonal stitches are woven in and out of each other. After you finish the crosses, make French Knots where you see dots on the diagram. You can make the French Knots in the same color as the crosses, or you can make them in an accent color, for a different effect. This is a medium-light wearing stitch.

Raymond Variation I

The variation is stitched in the same way as original Raymond. The difference, however, is that this variation is not woven. The stitch requires two-ply yarn on 14/1 canvas—and remember to make sure the yarns lie flat on the canvas.

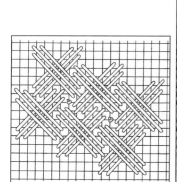

Raymond Variation II

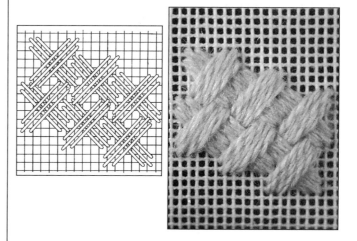

This second variation is very similar to the first, only here the crosses have been moved on the canvas. Stitch with two-ply Persian in the needle. For Raymond Variation II, the tips of the crosses are tucked under the previous rows. The completed stitch produces the effect of a large diagonal weave.

Reinforced Cross

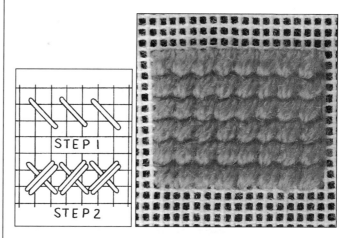

At first glance, it is difficult to detect whether true crosses are the result of this stitch. The motif has the appearance of large, padded Continental stitches. The first step in the diagram shows the usual way to make Cross stitch. Then, when you return to the row, make the cross hatch twice for each cross. Any place that would call for a Cross stitch would also be well suited to medium-hard wearing Reinforced Cross. One ply was used in the example. You may wish to thicken the yarn.

Renaissance I

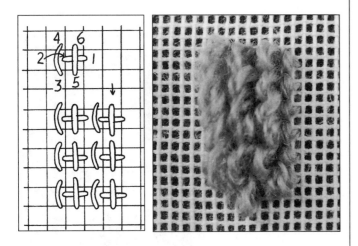

If you are looking for a stitch that is durable enough to use on a rug, consider Renaissance I. Stitch it from the top of the canvas downward, and keep an extra needle handle to pull the loops, to keep them even. Two-ply yarn was sufficient for the sample. To make the stitch, follow the steps, 1 through 6, on the diagram.

Rep

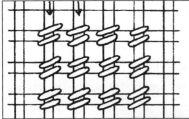

Rep is a slow stitch to make, but the results are worth your patience. The result is a hard-wearing stitch and a delicate-looking pattern. Keep two rules in mind when working this stitch. First, you must always use Penelope or Double mesh canvas. Using Mono or Interlock canvas creates quite a different stitch. Second, work Rep in a downward motion on the canvas. Because the stitch only covers one thread as it moves down, and two threads as it moves over, the stitch only requires one ply in the needle. Split the Penelope canvas intersection into two parts.

Reverse Cross

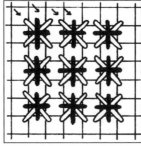

Two steps are required to achieve this hard-wearing stitch. First make the white crosses, working left to right, from one corner to the other. Then insert the darker lines. The sample required two-ply yarn in the needle. Reverse Cross can be used in almost any project.

Reverse Eyelet

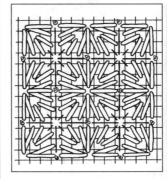

Medium-hard wearing Reverse Eyelet reminds me of squared-off daisy flowers on a trellis rod in a garden. In yellows and browns, this stitch could represent little Black-Eyed Susans. To create the motif, first make Ray stitches. Then, insert the lighter lines. The dots on the diagram indicate French Knots. Use two plies for the Ray stitches, and one ply for the frames. The French Knots are up to you.

Reverse Tent I

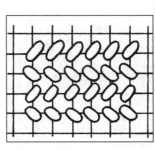

If you are interested in finding just a slight change in design, try Reverse Tent I. It is like Basketweave in that all its stitches are clean. Of course, this is because you create the stitches by working from a clear hole into one that already holds yarn, creating heirloom quality work. Stitch from right to left and then left to right, using two-ply yarn in the needle. Place this very hard-wearing stitch anywhere multi-stitches can be used.

Reversed Cashmere

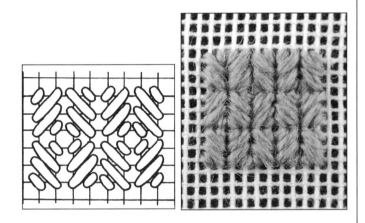

Work hard-wearing Reversed Cashmere in groups of alternating squares. When you finish the area, the stitch creates a distinctive pattern. Consider Reversed Cashmere when you wish to incorporate a small stitch with a little extra texture. Use two plies in your needle.

Reversed Mosaic

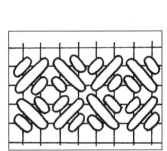

Hard-wearing Reversed Mosaic is a small stitch with a great deal of eye appeal. At first glance, you may think that it does not offer much texture. However, when it has been worked on the canvas, it creates a much bolder pattern than original Mosaic. Use two-ply yarn.

Reversed Norwich

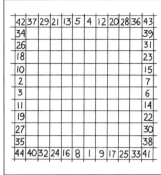
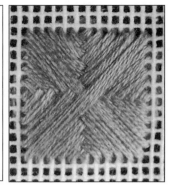

42	37	29	21	13	5	4	12	20	28	36	43
34											39
26											31
18											23
10											15
2											7
3											6
11											14
19											22
27											30
35											38
44	40	32	24	16	8	1	9	17	25	33	41

Follow the count on the diagram using six-ply embroidery floss or two-ply Persian yarn. Light-wearing Reversed Norwich creates a flat stitch with a little texture. You can employ it as either an isolated stitch, or a grouping.

Reversible Alternating Tent

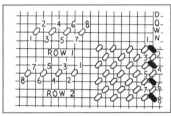

When I was working Alternating Tent, it reminded me of Chottie's Plaid, and I asked myself whether this stitch might also be reversible. In short order, Reversible Alternating Tent was created. The great aspect of this stitch, like Chottie's Plaid, is that it can be used for such items as clothing and coasters. Objects that are intended for viewing from both sides—the front and the underside of the canvas—are good candidates for Reversible Alternating Tent.

Ribbon Cross

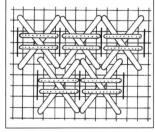

Medium-wearing Ribbon Cross creates the appearance of rows of ribbons couched onto a canvas. Of course, this stitch can always be used as a border, but with a bit of imagination you might think to fill an entire pillow of different colors or varied shades to accent a room. The sample is stitched in a family of blues. You might use this stitch to create the basic pattern of a motif, and then add silks and metal threads, to create a pillow that is not only elegant but also a one-of-a-kind piece. To create the stitch, begin with the large crosses. Follow with the parallel lines, and finally, the perpendicular lines. Use two-ply yarn.

Ribbon Cross Upright Cross

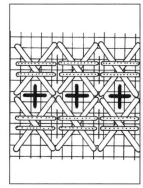 

Everything assumed about Ribbon Cross can also be assumed for Ribbon Cross Upright Cross, but there is one great difference between the two. This stitch creates the effect of weaving across the canvas. Like Ribbon Cross, though, its two horizontal stitches and its perpendicular stitches truly resemble couched ribbon. Work the stitch just as you would Ribbon Cross, and then add the small upright stitches. You can choose from an endless variety of color combinations for this pattern.

Rice Variation

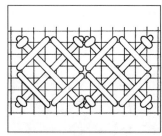 

Because this variation of Rice leaves some canvas exposed, it creates a lacy effect. As you would with any open stitch that leaves some canvas exposed, first paint the canvas with an oil based paint to hide the foundation, allow it to dry completely, and apply the stitches to the canvas. To create the pattern, first stitch the larger crosses, and then tie it down with half hitches. Use two-ply Persian yarn.

Ridges

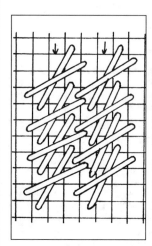 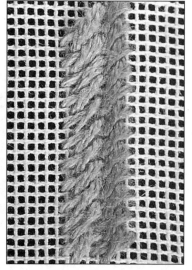

As this stitch traverses several intersections on the canvas, it would be silly to ever expect it to be very durable. Have a look at the example—this texture is appealing whether stitched in a single color or a whole rainbow. Imagine creating this stitch lying on its side, in the colors of a sunset. While it is highly textured, in the right motif, this stitch could be a tool toward creating a masterpiece. To create the stitch, use two-ply yarn, and make downward rows, stopping at the end (bottom), and beginning again at the top. Follow this rule whether you stitch in a single color, or many colors.

Rococo

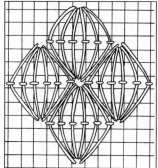 

Rococo, as it is called in England, was a very popular stitch in the seventeenth and eighteenth centuries. It was commonly employed to create geometric patterns, fruits and flowers. The Victoria and Albert Museum in

London features many samplers that employ Rococo stitches. These samplers are stitched on fine linen, and worked in silk—and sometimes even silver threads. In America, Rococo is referred to as the Queen stitch. On this side of the ocean, it was used a great deal in the eighteenth and nineteenth centuries. Because of the relatively high cost of silk, only smaller items were worked in the fine fiber. Examples of these small objects would be pin cushions and pocketbooks.

Using two-ply yarn for Rococo, you would have to insert a good deal of yarn into the canvas. One ply, however, creates lovely, clean, soft stitches. Although Rococo creates quite a busy pattern, its overall look is really quite versatile. Save it for areas that will require very little compensation. Begin the stitch by coming out at the top and back down at the bottom, keeping the yarn loose. Tie off the stitch with a small Back stitch on the side. After completing the first, make the next one the same but anchor it to the next thread on the canvas. Each Rococo stitch is made up of six stitches. Work in rows from left to right, and then move right to left. Always use a lighter amount of yarn than usual.

Rosemary

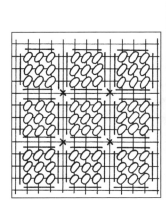 

Rather than a stitch all its own, medium-wearing Rosemary is actually a combination of stitches. Each square uses three long stitches and nine Continentals in the middle. The corners require small Cross stitches. This medley creates a pleasing, soft motif. Think of Rosemary for areas such as blankets, flooring or clothes in a picture project. In more abstract stitching projects, the uses are endless. Use two-ply Persian yarn for the Continental stitches, and stitch the small crosses and long lines in one ply. Experiment with different colors and fibers, and you might find that Rosemary becomes one of your favorite stitches.

Rotating Flat

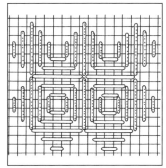 

The example shows Rotating Flat in two colors. Depending upon your project, you can stitch it in a single color, or in two. Use three-ply yarn for 14/1 canvas. This light-wearing stitch is best used in samplers.

Roumanian Couching

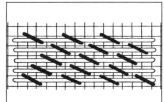 

For a free-form couching stitch that does not require a true count, try Roumanian Couching. Use a count of any combination you like. If you want to add durability to your couching, make several ties on the long yarn. For an airy effect, make the ties far apart from each other. To stitch each row, first make a long stitch and then couch it down with your second yarn. The next row repeats the same procedure, except that you work in the opposite direction. Use two sets of needles and yarns. Try couching with different fibers and numbers of plies in your needle. Your choices of patterns are virtually never-ending with Roumanian Couching.

Round Braid

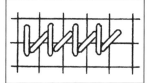 

For a clean, hard-wearing stitch, try Round Braid, in two-ply yarn. This is a great choice for any space in need of a finished edge. It adds an interesting texture to smaller areas on samplers. Try Round Braid in several colors, piling one row on top of another for a pillow top.

Rubato *(Courtesy of Chottie Alderson)*

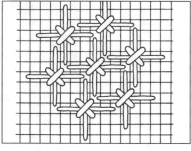

Foundation.

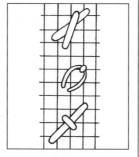

Fill-in stitches.

Lay the foundation in two-ply Persian wool. Then stitch, using all one stitch, or a combination of stitches, to fill in the voids on the canvas. The fill-in stitch can be worked in cotton or any other fiber you choose. Use this medium-wearing stitch as an over-all pattern in samplers.

Running Cross

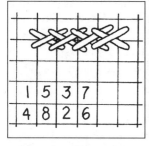

Running Cross creates a tight, durable, smooth stitch. If you follow the count in the diagram, a braid will appear on the canvas. Pile a few rows on top of one another to create definite horizontal lines. This is a great stitch for borders or frames. You can make several rows around a picture project, in colors taken from the motif, to beautifully tie the project together. Use one or two plies in the needle.

Saint George and Saint Andrew

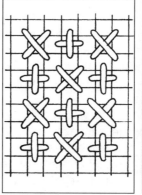

At first glance, this looks like the common Cross stitch. A closer look, though, reveals the unique feature of this stitch: every other cross is stitched in the opposing direction. Like the Cross stitch, it requires two plies. Work the first row from left to right, and the second row from right to left. The small pattern ensures that compensation for this stitch is a simple matter. Try this medium-hard wearing stitch in two colors.

Sand Shells

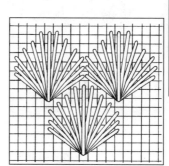

No name could be more appropriate for this stitch. The count creates bold, large shells—so, of course, you should use consideration when placing the stitch on a project. The long stitch prevents Sand Shells from being a very durable stitch. All stitches should be made from outside the shell toward the middle, to ensure sharp lines in the center. When I stitched the sample, I found it simplest to start the count on the top, and work the two sides simultaneously. Use two-ply Persian yarn.

Sandy's Slide
(Courtesy of Chottie Alderson)

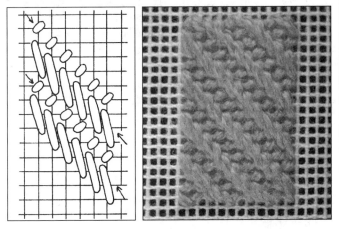

If you examine the underside of the canvas after stitching Erin's Ridge, you will see a definite pattern. This is Sandy's Slide. It is created by working Erin's Ridge on the underside of Mono canvas. Remember to pull tightly, and do not make stabbing motions, but sew the stitch. Using stretcher bars will not achieve the desired effect for Sandy's Slide. The yarn requirement is three plies on 14/1 canvas. Because of the high texture this stitch creates, save it for smaller areas—and certainly, I would not use it for a background stitch.

Satin

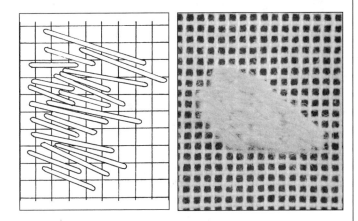

Here, the diagram really only depicts a suggestion for the creation of the Satin stitch. It does not have an exact count or direction. You can use long and short, or equal-length, stitches. Remember, the shorter the stitch, the more durable. To cover a large area, I recommend a combination of large and short stitches. Satin is used in "Unicorn in Captivity." Take a look at the unicorn's head and neck. The stitches travel up his nose to the tip of the ear. The beard begins downward, working its way into curves. For a smooth effect, split the tip of the previous stitch to blend the fibers.

Scotch

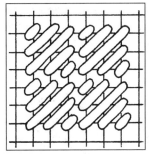

Scotch is one of the most commonly used stitches. Its simplicity makes it quite versatile. The squares lead the eye both horizontally and diagonally, making Scotch appropriate for most projects, and both large and small areas. Its versatility makes Scotch a favorite. Two-ply Persian is required for 14/1 canvas.

Scotch Worked Diagonally I

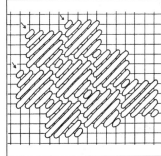

With two plies in the needle, stitch medium-light wearing Scotch Worked Diagonally I in rows from the upper left toward the lower right. When you finish a row, stop the yarn and begin again at the top. Follow this procedure until the area is filled. The design will be bold, so use it in medium to large areas. Smaller areas do not showcase the pattern well. Think twice before using this stitch for a background, as it can create a busy effect. Use two-ply Persian yarn.

Scotch Worked Diagonally II

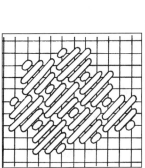

Using two-ply yarn, lay Scotch Worked Diagonally II on the canvas. When you finish a row, continue by stitching the next row in the opposite direction. The rows share the small Continental stitch at all times. This medium-light wearing stitch can be used on large or small projects.

Sean

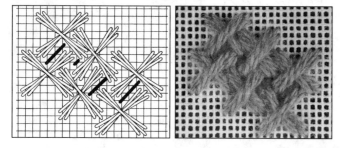

Sean is a light-wearing stitch that creates a pattern of large pinwheels. As with all Cross stitches, you should work the cross hatches in the same direction. Sean is more appropriate for larger areas than it is for smaller ones. Notice the different sizes of Continental stitches filling the voids. You can do this in the same color, or use a different one, as I did in the example. Use a darker color to accentuate the pinwheels.

Shaded Stripe

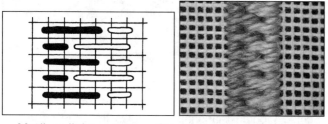

Medium-light wearing Shaded Stripe creates the best effect in two shades. Using colors that are closely related creates a softer effect, while two starkly contrasting colors add drama. Three-ply Persia n ensures good coverage. Apply Shaded Stripe as a border, in one or more rows. One row might also make interesting fence posts. Two or more could fill an entire side of a building. Use two-ply Persian yarn.

Shadow Mesh

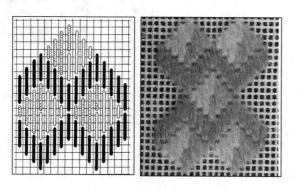

Unlike universal stitches such as Continental, Mosaic, and Cross, Shadow Mesh is not for very many projects. It is best used as a pattern, without other stitches or samplers. This is not to say it does not have practical uses. Pillows, purses, shoes and other items are fun to stitch in Shadow Mesh. The yarns traverse four threads on the canvas, so it is not a very durable stitch. The color combinations, however, are endless. Have fun using a variety of yarns. Again, for 14/1 canvas, three-ply Persian yarn is needed.

Sheaf II

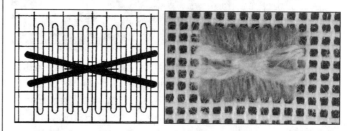

I used two-ply yarn to stitch the sample. Feel free to experiment. For objects that are not intended for a great deal of handling, this is a nice, light-wearing stitch. A pillow may require three-ply yarn. Stitch the long, upright lines first, and follow with the large cross. The last step is the small tie on top of the cross. Two colors make a prettier stitch compared with a single color. You can use Sheaf II as an isolated or cluster stitch. Staggering the rows creates an interesting pattern design. A pillow stitched entirely in Sheaf II would resemble a brick wall.

Shell I

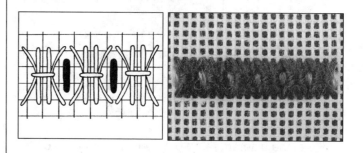

Use one or more rows of this stitch for a border. For an interesting effect, try piling a row on top of another. Depending upon the shape of the area you are working, this stitch can be a challenge to compensate. Square areas are usually better. With two-ply yarn, this stitch packs a good deal of yarn into the canvas, so it is quite durable. I like to stitch the small upright stitches between the clusters in a lighter color, to create a three-dimensional effect. Make the clusters first, and then the upright stitches.

Shell III

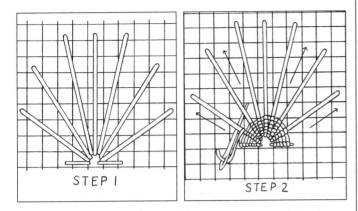

STEP 1   STEP 2

For a unique accent stitch, try Shell III. This is both stitched and laid on top of the canvas. Once the foundation has been stitched, the needle rarely goes back under the canvas. First, lay the long lines on the canvas. For a clean foundation, stitch into the middle of the "star." Then, bring the needle out to the top of the canvas as close to the center of the "star" as you can. Loop the needle under, then over, the first thread, and pull it through. Then put the needle under the first and second thread and pull it through. Loop over the second one and then go under the second and third threads. Follow this procedure until you finish all nine threads, keeping the loops as close to the center as possible. Then bring the yarn under the canvas and back up to make the next set of loops.

This next row will again be as close to the center as you can make it. The quality of the shell depends upon how close the loops are on the foundation threads.

When making the rows of loops, you will notice that the canvas threads will be filled. You want this. When no more loops can be loaded on a thread, move up to the next thread and start the next row. Your last set of loops might only cover the top three threads in the shell. With a little practice, this will be fun to add to your projects. Use two-ply yarn for the foundation, and one ply for the loops.

Shell IV

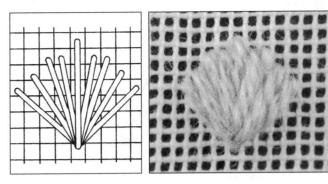

Work medium-light wearing Shell IV as you would Ray, Algerian Eye or other stitches that have yarn piled up in the center. Use a knitting needle to open the hole. This allows you to insert the needle and pull it through without much effort. First stitch the middle and outside lines, and then the northwest and northeast lines. Fill the voids so that the center hole lies smoothly on the canvas. Use two-ply yarn.

Shell Variation I

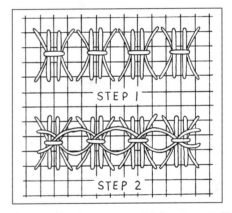

STEP 1

STEP 2

The foundation of Shell Variation I is the same for Shell I. Lay the clusters of stitches on the canvas. Weave in and out of the short tie stitches. Weave from left to right. The second woven row is the same, but it is woven in the opposite direction. This creates little loops over your clusters. The stitch is durable, but remember that the loops may tend to pull. The pulling is easy to correct. Use two plies for the foundation, and one ply for the loops.

Shi Sha, Acorn Method

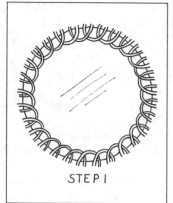

STEP 1

STEP 2

Acorn Method (pearl)　　　Acorn Method (mirror)

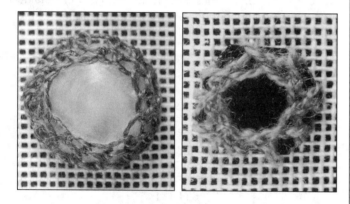

Shi Sha mirrors are glass mirrors quite unlike the regular mirrors we use every day. From India, they are made of thicker glass with a washable backing. This thicker glass is less breakable than vanity or compact mirror glass. Hand wash Shi Sha mirrors.

Jewels, beads, mirrors or other items you wish to attach to the canvas can be applied by using the Acorn method. The first row of stitches follows the exact shape of the item.

With the mirror held in place where you want it, bring your needle up to the top of the canvas. Come up as close to the mirror as possible. Make a series of loops all along the side of the mirror by working Back stitches around the mirror. Do not pull the yarn snugly. Do not return the needle to the canvas after the first row has been laid. For the second set of loops, make a series of chain stitches in the loops of the first row. Continue adding loops until you have the desired depth around the mirror. Weave the yarn through the loops to reach the edge of the mirror. After you tuck the yarn under the canvas, tie off the stitch. This medium-light wearing method can use any number of plies you wish.

Shi Sha, Buttonhole Method

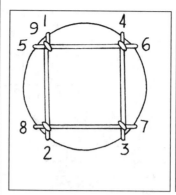

Step 1

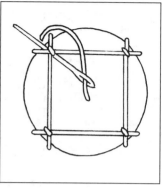

Step 2

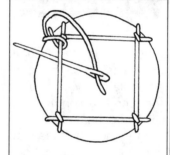

Step 3

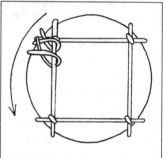

Step 4

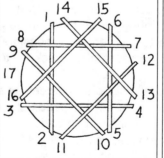

Step 2 (square)

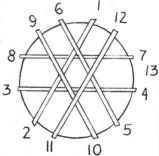

Step 2 (triangle)

The Buttonhole method can be used to apply many items to the canvas, such as flat gemstones, coins or Shi Sha mirrors. If you attach them properly, they will be quite secure, and add a great deal of drama to your project. With the right method of securing the object, and good quality stitches, a mirror can last for years. Use any type of thread.

There are three anchoring options for attaching the Shi Sha. These include tic tac toe, two triangle, and two square. Usually, I use the tic tac toe frame. Follow the number sequence to lay the foundation, to ensure that the mirror will not fall out.

Secure your yarn under the canvas. Lay your mirror in its place on the canvas. Bring your needle up at point 1 as close to the side of the mirror as possible, and go back down at 2. Follow the same steps, coming out at 3 and down at 4. Now, you have two parallel threads over the mirror. Bring the needle out at 5 and before going in at 6, make a loop under and over the first and second thread. Repeat this process with the next set of stitches, 7 and 8. To create a tight foundation, bring the needle up at 9. This locks the foundation.

Now the fun begins. Each loop is made in two steps, moving left to right. Slide the needle under the intersection of threads on the mirror, and move from the center out. Pull the yarn snugly. Insert the needle on the right side of the loop and come up on the left. Make a small chain from right to left along the side of the mirror, until you make a complete circle. You may need to adjust the tension as you go to make a neat donut around the mirror. Slip the needle under the first stitch to create the appearance of a continuous circle.

To make the two triangle and two square methods, work the same stitch around the foundation. Be sure to follow the number sequence for each.

Slanted Gobelin I

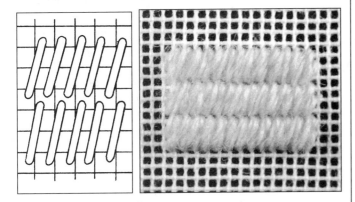

Medium-wearing Slanted Gobelin I is a close cousin of Gobelin Droit. The two are very similar, except that Slanted Gobelin I covers intersections and Gobelin Droit does not. For this reason, Slanted Gobelin I should be stitched in two-ply Persian yarn. Anywhere Gobelin Droit can be used, so can Slanted Gobelin I. Work one row completely, and then move down to the next and continue. For the best results, return the needle down into used holes on the canvas. Use two-ply yarn.

Slanted Gobelin II

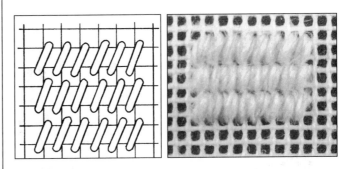

Slanted Gobelin II can be stitched in many different ways. You can make the up stitches cross two or three threads on the canvas. This determines the size and boldness of the pattern. The stitch is very durable, and you can use it on just about any project. Use two-ply Persian yarn.

Slanted Gobelin III

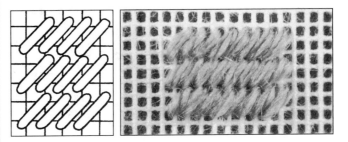

Because the stitches are on a true diagonal, hard-wearing Slanted Gobelin III is more dramatic than the other Slanted Gobelins. It requires two plies in the needle.

Slanted Gobelin IV

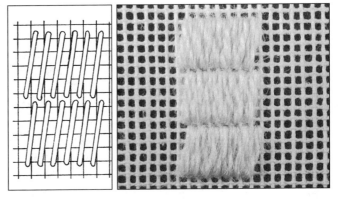

Two-ply yarn makes Slanted Gobelin IV's stitches soft and lovely. It creates defined horizontal lines on the canvas, and it leaves the canvas threads exposed. If you do not want the canvas threads to show, then you must paint the canvas before stitching. This light-wearing stitch crosses five threads on the canvas.

Slashed Cross

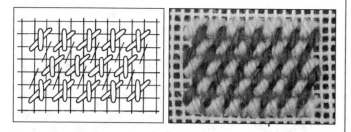

The sample shows the well-defined diagonal lines of Slashed Cross. Using a single color eliminates this effect. Slashed Cross produces a small, versatile pattern, and a hard-wearing stitch. Use two-ply Persian for the crosses and slashes. Use two plies for both colors.

Slashed Oblong

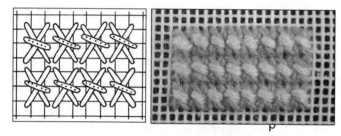

Slashed Oblong begs to be stitched in two colors of yarn. Metal threads, if used to tie off the Oblong crosses, would add wonderful sparkle and drama to the stitch. Imagine a fun evening purse in Slashed Oblong. Work the row of crosses as you normally would, and then finish the row by making the slashes.

Slipped Multiple

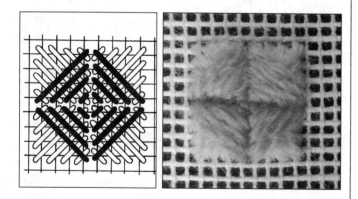

Slipped Multiple is a medium-wearing, highly piled stitch. For this reason, the long stitches could snag or fuzz with age. Use it as an isolated stitch or as a group. Both sets of yarn require two plies.

Small Checker

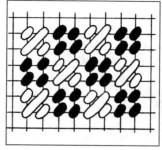 

When I first learned this stitch, I made a sample in green and orange. The Continental stitches were orange. When it was finished, it reminded me of an orange tree. For the sample, I used two tones of the same shade, and the effect is a checkerboard. Small Checker is versatile, hard-wearing, easy to compensate and fun to work. Two-ply yarn covers 14/1 canvas very nicely.

Small Rice

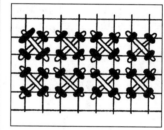 

Stitch the crosses first, then go back and insert the small cross hatches in one-ply yarn. Two colors produce very fine diamonds on the canvas. When I worked the sample, it reminded me of a medieval dress bodice. Be creative with hard-wearing Small Rice—there are endless possibilities for you to discover. I used one ply for the example. You may wish to thicken the yarn.

Smyrna

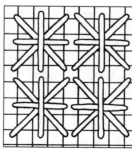 

Since Smyrna covers four threads and intersections on the canvas, it could never be considered a hard-wearing stitch. In addition, as the yarns are piled on top of one another in the middle, they tend to snag and pill. For this reason, use Smyrna in projects that can afford to be fragile. By all means, though, do use Smyrna. It can add interesting dimensions to your project. Two plies cover 14/1 canvas quite satisfactorily.

Spider Webs

Foundation (1)

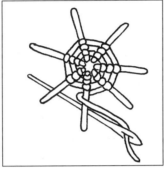

Whipped under (2)

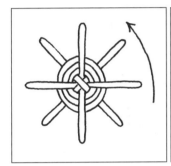

Over and under

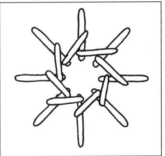

Open middle

Spider Webs

People claim that no two spider webs are alike. This can also be true of this stitch. There are as many ways to make Spider Webs as there are people. The diagrams show just a few, but your imagination will allow you to create many more. Vary the shapes, textures and sizes when you stitch this wonderful family of webs. The variations depend upon the number of foundation threads, and how you lay them on the canvas. Whether the whipping yarn travels over, under or woven through the foundation is another factor. In the wagon wheel-shaped diagram, Spider Webs should be stitched from the middle outward. Bring the yarn out near the middle of the wheel, up over the yarn and then under it along with the next. You should whip over every foundation yarn. Remember, the needle should not go under the canvas while you whip around the wheel rungs. The webbing spirals until you reach the outer ends of the wheel. For the best results, pack the whipping tightly on the rungs of the wheel. To do this, pull the yarn snug toward the center.

The diagram shows a wheel woven over and under its foundation. This web is not hard-wearing, because it has an even number of spokes. For harder-wearing Spider Webs, the number of spokes should be odd. You can also see a web with a hole in its middle. Make the hole by whipping over or under, or weaving the yarn.

Split Florentine

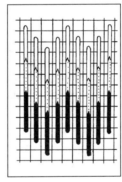
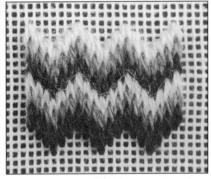

One look you can create using Split Florentine is that of old Indian blankets. The interlocked stitches create a versatile, soft-looking, medium-wearing stitch. As a background, the stitch has a plush appearance. For shading, the possibilities are endless. Imagine this stitch as a sunset over mountains or a sea. The sample shows the yarn crossing three threads on the canvas, while the diagram shows four. The choice is yours. Follow the diagram from top to bottom, starting with compensating stitches. Never start on the main line, and never split the compensating lines. When working the stitches, always insert the needle into the previous row. Use three-ply Persian yarn.

Split Gobelin

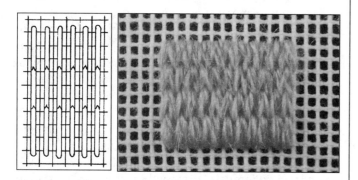

Split Gobelin is very similar to Split Florentine, except that the rows cross the canvas threads in a straight direction. The stitch's soft effect makes it very versatile. You can use it in almost any project you might imagine. Work from the top to the bottom, and insert the stitches in the previous row. Use three-ply yarn on 14/1 canvas.

Split Slanted Gobelin

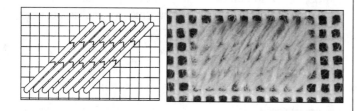

Split Slanted Gobelin creates soft, small, hard-wearing stitches that are easy to compensate, and can be used on any area of the canvas. The stitch is most effective in round, squared, and oblong areas. The yarn covers only three intersections on the canvas, making Split Slanted Gobelin very hard-wearing.

Sprat

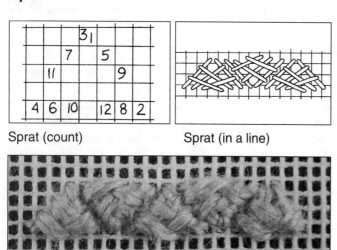

Sprat (count)   Sprat (in a line)

Hard-wearing Sprat seems to scream "Borders!" Imagine stitching it in a square, layer on top of layer. Sprat is a low pile stitch so when it is combined with other stitches, it not only creates an interesting visual effect, but it is also interesting to touch. Follow the count in the diagram when working the stitch. Sprat does leave canvas exposed. If you do not want the canvas to show, stitch over only one thread on the canvas. Use two-ply Persian yarn.

Sprat's Head

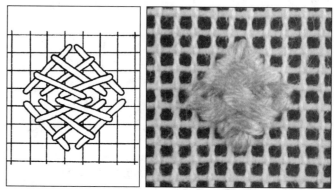

Follow the number pattern in the diagram for Sprat, and repeat the procedure on the row below the first, to create a very interesting stitch. Sprat's Head can be used as an isolated stitch or as a group, although, when clustered, it does have a heavier effect, so think twice. Think of Sprat's Head for a row or for an accent at each corner of a project. Two-ply yarn will cover 14/1 canvas quite satisfactorily.

Square Cross

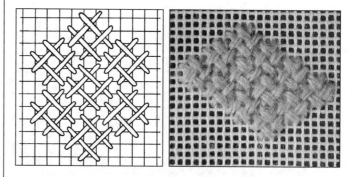

Square Cross produces a soft, woven effect. It is medium-wearing, and can be placed almost anywhere. The cross is actually doubled on the canvas—and a closer look reveals that the cross hatching is woven. This adds more durability than you would think possible for this stitch. The pattern works in a downward motion that seems to fit better in curved areas.

Square Herringbone

Use two plies in your needle and follow the number pattern to discover what you can create with this pattern. The numbers on the diagram do not tell as much as the sample photo does. This stitch is not really intended for objects that receive much wear, such as pillows or shoes. The yarn traverses many intersections on the canvas before being inserted again underneath. It could add great drama to a sampler, though. This should be used sparingly since the motif is heavy looking.

Staggered Cross

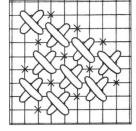

Staggered Cross adds a three-dimensional effect to an area. First, work the large crosses, and then the smaller ones. Two plies work best for the larger crosses, and one ply for the smaller. Take care to stitch the cross hatches in the same direction. This medium-wearing stitch's simplicity keeps it versatile. Use it in any area that does not require much texture or eye appeal.

Staggering Crosses

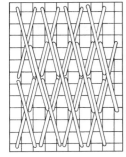

A pattern of large stitches, all running in different directions and crossing six intersections of canvas, can never be expected to be durable. At the same time, do not let that stop you from using wonderful motifs like Staggering Crosses. This stitch could be used to add interest to many projects, adding a little pop to special areas. Two plies nicely fill the surface.

Staggering Flat

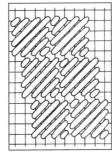

Staggering Flat is a beautiful, medium-light wearing stitch. The durability factor is a result of the four intersections that the yarn crosses on the canvas. Still, do not fret about the fragility of the stitch. Just use it on appropriate objects, and enjoy its beauty. Because the squares shift over one thread for each row, the pattern is easier on the eye than Flat stitch. Begin on the left, and work toward the right. Finish each square and continue to the end of the row. When you finish the row, stitch as you did the first row, only in the opposite direction.

Staircase

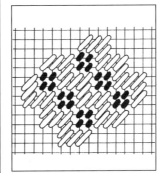

Use green for the zigzags and pink for the Continental stitches to make flowers. Switch the pink with orange to create the look of oranges on a tree. Of course, there are many other uses for Staircase, which you will discover, with a little imagination. The large zigzag and the Continental stitches are both worked in two-ply Persian wool. Staircase is a medium-hard wearing stitch.

Starry Crosses

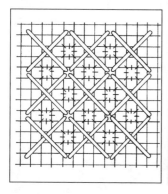

At first glance, Starry Crosses has a three-dimensional appearance. The large crosses rather appear as long, continuous lines filled with small eyelets. The large crosses tend to snag, but do not be afraid to use Starry Crosses. I think this stitch would be appropriate for the bodice of the dress of a medieval princess in a picture project. Stitch the crosses in two plies, and the eyelets in one. Have fun experimenting with silks, metals and specialty yarns.

Stem

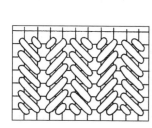

Stem creates a hard-wearing stitch, with a definite pattern of parallel lines. Begin at the top of a row, and work downward until you reach the bottom, and stitch the next row from the bottom to the top. For pleasing, even rows, make sure you have enough yarn to complete the line. Heirloom quality embroidery requires that you complete an entire row before putting the project down.

Step

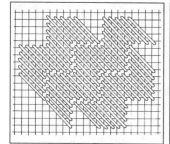

Step Is a very large, light-wearing stitch that cannot be placed just anywhere. The yarn covers four intersections on the canvas in one stitch, so the motif is best used as a background or overall pattern for a project. Two-ply yarn covers the canvas sufficiently. Try to keep the plies straight when stitching to ensure neat work.

Straight Cross

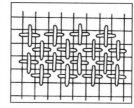

Follow this diagram to create a very small diamond motif. In brief, Straight Cross is hard-wearing, simple and textured, which makes it a good choice for any area where you want an interesting effect without too much design. There are no very definite lines that need to be considered. Use Straight Cross in any project you wish.

Straight Rice

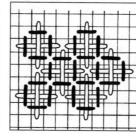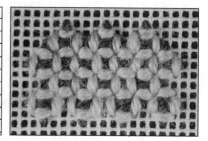

In medium-wearing Straight Rice, stitch the upright crosses first, then incorporate the perpendicular cross hatches. Stitch both sets in two-ply yarn. Experiment to determine whether you prefer one ply for the cross hatches. This, of course, does depend upon the project. Purses and pillows are best stitched in two-ply yarn.

Strap

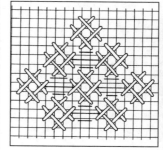

Strap can be described as a fun, busy stitch. It could never be used in all projects, with its definite pattern. The crosses leave canvas exposed—so, as always, if you do not want the canvas to show, paint it before stitching, to match your yarn. Make sure the paint is completely dry before stitching. Stitch the woven crosses first in two plies, and then the three horizontal lines, also in two plies (for 14/1 canvas).

Sturgeon Trail

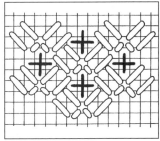

Sturgeon Trail tends to show canvas. A quick application of oil-based paint quickly solves this annoyance. Use greens to achieve a leafy effect. Use other colors for wall flowers or blankets. The sample shows the small cross in metallic yarn, pearl cotton for the small Continental, and Persian wool for the foundation. The mix creates an interesting pattern. Experiment with different fibers and yarns. The motif is medium large, but if used with good judgment, it can add a creative touch to many projects. Work the long diagonal stitches first, and follow with the small Continental stitches. Add the upright crosses last. Sturgeon Trail is a medium-hard wearing stitch.

Sugar Buttonhole

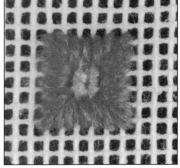

At first glance, this diagram looks like it will produce a large stitch—something that resembles a throw pillow. Actually, Sugar Buttonhole produces a small, tight fitting pattern. I imagine it would be a fun stitch to do in a variety of colors and fibers. As a background, or as an entire project, Sugar Buttonhole is fun to stitch. Stitch the center eyelet in one-ply wool and the rest of the motif in two-ply yarn, for a stitch that can stand some real abuse.

Surrey

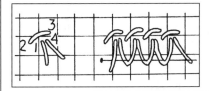

Entire rugs are made with this stitch. In the first half of the twentieth century, Berlin work used Surrey. Many table rugs had yards of wool yarn in sheared piles. Some were sculptured and others had straight edges. Because it is a pile stitch, Surrey is very durable. Unless the project is made entirely with Surrey, use caution in placing it. The diagram shows the correct count for the stitch. On the right, the diagram shows a continuous line when making a row. Use a knitting needle or other rod to ensure even loops—but do not fret if they are not even. Start your rows on the lower part of the canvas, and work toward the top. This enables you to work without being bothered by the previous row's loops. When you complete the area, you will give it a "hair cut" to trim the pile to the height you like. You can cut them quite short without their becoming loose.

Suzann's Bicentennial Star

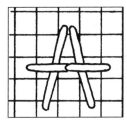

Suzann's Bicentennial Star is just that—a star. It was designed for flags and other similar items. To create the hard-wearing stitch, first stitch the long, diagonal lines. Then stitch the left cross hatch and come out at the far right. Finally, insert the needle into the middle of the first hatch. You can have great fun playing with plies and fibers with this stitch.

Suzie's Garden

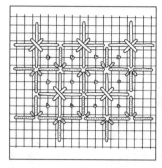 

When stitching the samples for this book, at one point, my eyes looked at a motif and my mind thought of another. I had stitched the foundation before discovering the mistake. Rather than rip out the error, I laid it aside and gave it some thought. Later that afternoon, I picked up the sample and started playing with the void areas. Within an hour, I had created a new look for the foundation. I think of a garden trellis with little flowers climbing on it. This was the birth of Suzie's Garden. The pattern is very large, so use caution when placing it. Suzie's Garden would make a fun, medium-hard wearing, over-all pattern on a purse or small pillow. Use various fibers and textures of yarns. Stitch the large crosses first and then the long and short ones. The dots indicate the placement of French Knots.

Tent

This is the correct name for Petit Point, Demi Point and Gros Point. The three names indicate the size of the Tent stitch. This stitch can also be used in the same projects, at the same time, as with Continental, Basketweave and Half Cross. Think of it as a basic stitch. See also Continental, Basketweave and Half Cross.

Texas Mosquito

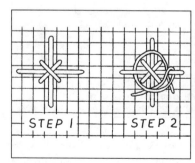 

For an isolated stitch that adds a little pizzazz, try Texas Mosquito. Follow the diagram on the left of the graph to stitch the foundation. On the right, you have the beginning, whipping and ending of the final part of the stitch. The yarn comes up out of the canvas and weaves

under the long horizontal bar. Then weave in and out until you reach the same bar where you started. Weave under the entire area and pull the yarn under as shown. The size and thickness of the yarn are determined by how big or small a Mosquito you need.

Three Layer Web

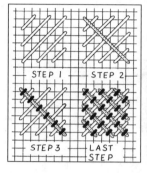 

Use two different colors in one ply, for both step 1 and step 2, to create this unique stitch. Use a third color for the Continental stitches in the third step. If you use only one color, you will notice no difference between Three Layer Web and Tent. Three Layer Web is a durable stitch. Feel free to use it in any project you wish.

Tied Cashmere

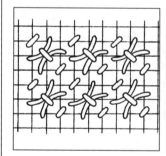 

When you look at Tied Cashmere, you may wonder whether the tying makes a great difference. The result of the tying is a textured, durable stitch that can be used in almost any project. To create the stitch, stitch Cashmere as usual, and then tie the two longer stitches with a Tent stitch. Use two-ply Persian wool on 14/1 canvas.

Tied Down Cross

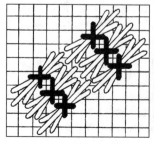 

In the stitched example, you can tell that the top cross has been stitched in a different color. This creates an interesting, hard-wearing variation. Use Tied Down Cross in areas where you want the eye of the viewer to be drawn. To tone it down, use a single color. In two colors, the stitch tends to make a diagonal line. Two plies on 14/1 canvas make a very durable stitch. First, stitch the diagonal lines, and then add the small, upright crosses.

Tight Pinched Cross

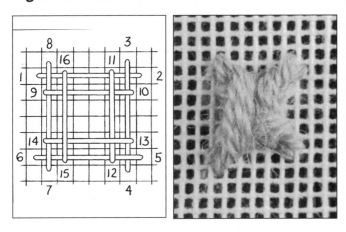

The finished product here is quite different from what you might expect, looking at the number pattern. First, you might expect the stitch to produce a large square—but the result is actually an upright, thick, large cross. I worked the sample in two-ply Persian wool, but you may work this stitch in virtually any fiber and thickness. Think of Tight Pinched Cross as an isolated stitch, for use as a bold accent to a project.

Tip of Leaf

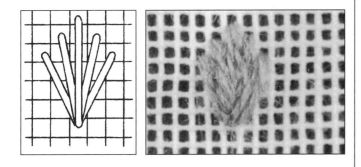

Tip of Leaf could be used for small bushes, leaves, or flames. Use a larger version of Tip of Leaf for larger plants and smaller stitches for "new growth." Add texture and variety by adding varied shades of green. Begin at the top of the stitch and work downward. Work the center line first, and then the middle of each side, followed by the two stitches on the sides. This is a medium-wearing stitch.

Tom

Because the large pinwheels in the diagram traverse eight intersections on the canvas, Tom is a very light-wearing stitch. It is best used in samplers. Make the large crosses in two-ply Persian wool. Work the Smyrna crosses in one-ply wool. For a bold effect, try a metal or shiny yarn in the center of the pinwheels.

Tramé

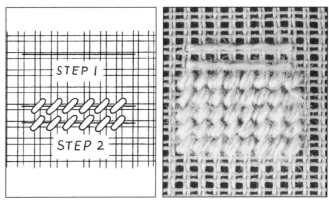

Rather than a stitch, Tramé is a technique used to apply a motif to canvas. Think of Tramé as a method of under stitching. Many people like to first apply a design on the canvas, then stitch the entire piece. You could paint the picture to lay it out, but painting may not always give you the details or accuracy you need. Tramé allows you to mark exactly where every stitch should be on the canvas, eliminating the guesswork. You can choose from two techniques for laying out the design. Your first choice is to make a full-size drawing of your design and outline it on the canvas. Second, you could use a graph and count the design out on the canvas (for transferring designs onto canvas, see Chapter Two).

Tramé can only be applied on Penelope canvas, using Tent stitch, because the one-ply yarn is inserted between the two sets of threads that make up the intersection. Once the design is on the canvas, take one strand of Persian wool and lay it horizontally along the weave of the canvas. Then use Continental stitches to cover the thin horizontal yarns. Use two plies for the Tent stitching. The stitches will have a slightly padded appearance, but this is not the only reason for keeping the yarn thin. Although the Tramé is not seen, the one ply adds extra strength to the stitches, making it a good choice for projects such as seat cushions or prayer kneelers. The Tramé also adds dimension to the work.

A few rules to remember: If a line calls for a large number of stitches in one color, break up the number into two or more counts for the same color (for example, 14 stitches in green should be covered as five, then four, and another five). This ensures that the Tramé foundation is less likely to snag before you stitch it. It is also to your benefit to stagger the Tramé foundation as much as possible, to keep your project smoother, with no unsightly lumps. Do not be tempted to pull the Tramé too tightly, or let it hang too loosely. If you need added tension, use stretcher bars when counting. The durability of this stitching technique makes it versatile enough to employ in any project.

If you are trying to decide on a stitch for a project, you might also want to see Cross Tramé, Half Cross Tramé Oblong Cross Tramé and Gobelin Tramé.

Triangle

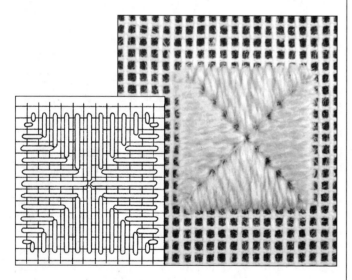

To stitch Triangle, start at one corner and stitch around the square until your ends meet. The sample was worked in two plies. You may wish to thicken the yarn. As it crosses six canvas threads at its longest point, Triangle is a light-wearing stitch. Use it as an isolated stitch, or in groupings.

Triple Cross I

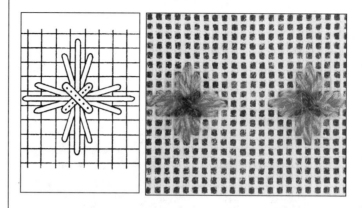

While this hard-wearing stitch is called Triple Cross I, it should not be thought of as simply a large cross. It has, in fact, many purposes, such as stars in the sky or flowers in a field. To add interest to a motif, stitch random Triple Crosses in various colors all over your canvas, and fill in the background with a Tent stitch. The overall effect would be fun as a pillow. Try using different colors or yarns to make the last cross.

To create Triple Cross I, first make the large cross, and then stitch the small cross to interlock all the larger ones.

Triple Cross II

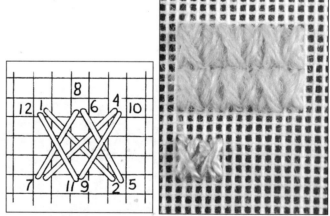

As an isolated stitch, a continuous border or a pattern, Triple Cross II can be added to almost any project. The result is a medium-light wearing stitch, only because the last stitch traverses four threads on the canvas and tends to snag. Keep the plies straight, and be sure they lie flat, for the best effect. Triple Cross II is not easy to compensate. It can be done, but an area with an exact count would be better. To make Triple Cross II, follow the number count on the diagram.

Triple Diamond Cross

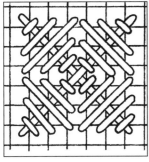 

This stitch is a very close cousin to Alternating Flat. Looking closely at the two diagrams, you will notice that Triple Diamond Cross has a large cross as a foundation before the flat stitches are inserted. This stitch also has a padded feel to it that makes it more luxurious. Begin by stitching the large cross in two-ply yarn. Then work all four flat stitches and continue onto the next motif. Use it in almost any project in need of texture.

Triple Leviathan

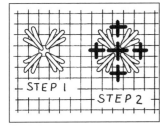 

Triple Leviathan is a very tight, hard-wearing stitch. Try placing the stitch in random order on the canvas and then filling the background with Tent, for a lovely pattern to be used on purses, belts or shoes. For a fun, glittery evening look, stitch shoes and a purse in silks and metals. Begin by stitching the foundation, following the first step in the diagram. Then fill the voids with the upright crosses. Use two-ply Persian yarn.

Tuft

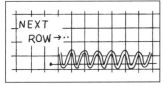 

Unlike other pile stitches, Tuft is not hard-wearing. This is because its loops are not tied. The method is to stitch in and out of the same hole, working down the row. Use thicker yarn than what you usually would for your chosen canvas size, to help keep the loops from coming undone. Make the first row at the bottom of the canvas, and work your way up. For even loops, use a rod or knitting needle to measure the circumference.

Two Color Herringbone

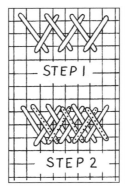 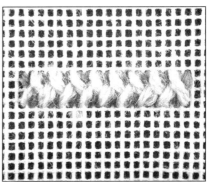

Hard-wearing Two Color Herringbone is a wonderful border stitch. Follow the first step in the diagram, then stitch over the same with a zigzag in another color of yarn. This second color really brings the stitch to life. Try using a metal yarn over wool. This stitch begs for experimentation with varied yarns and fibers.

Two-Sided Cross

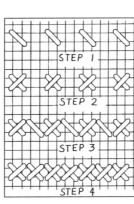 

Needlepoint that is stitched on the flap of a purse or pocket needs to be either stitched very neatly on the underside, or have a lining to cover the mess. If you want to show off your talent by not hiding the underside, try using Two-Sided Cross. When this stitch is worked, the underside has the same appearance as the front. Follow the diagram, moving toward the right until you reach the end of the row. Then, work the row toward the left. Repeat until you reach the left of the row. You should have voids and crosses along the entire row. Follow the diagram to fill the voids. This takes you back to the right, when you can begin the final step. At the left end of the row, you have finished the stitch and are ready to being a new row. While the steps may seem redundant, the result is heirloom quality embroidery.

Two Tied Gobelin

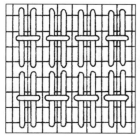 

Two Tied Gobelin creates defined rows of stitches. Tying the stitches off in the center adds durability, which makes Two Tied Gobelin versatile enough for any project you wish. Work the long stitches in sets of two and tie them off, then follow with Gobelin stitches. Use two-ply Persian yarn on 14/1 canvas.

Two Tone Starburst

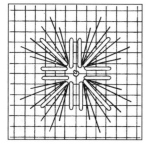 

Two Tone Starburst makes a fun isolated stitch. Use one-ply Persian yarn, a shiny yarn and silk floss. First, stitch the diagram's white lines in shiny yarn. Note, too, that the center of the square has a void intersection on the canvas. Then, with Persian yarn, stitch around the star, and use silk to make a French knot in the center. This is a medium-hard wearing stitch.

Upright Oriental

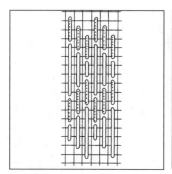 

Whether one or two tones are used for Upright Oriental, it creates a light-wearing, bold pattern on the canvas. As with other large design stitches, a background or other similar area is appropriate for Upright Oriental. Three-ply Persian yarn is required for 14/1 canvas.

Van Dyke

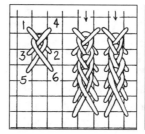 

Follow the steps in the diagram to create the pleasing, tightly fitting, parallel rows of Van Dyke. The first stitch is a cross, requiring the needle to travel under the canvas in two parts. After this, the needle does not return to the underside of the canvas until the stitch is complete. Work from the top of the canvas toward the bottom. Tie off at the end of each row and begin again at the top. For even stitching, be sure you have enough yarn to start and finish the row without needing to restart your yarn. Use two-ply Persian yarn, and place Van Dyke where a definite vertical line is called for.

Velvet I

The hard-wearing, piled texture of Velvet I requires more than one step in its creation. The first step shows two-ply Persian worked in a zigzag. Lay a strip of paper over this row and continue. Step 2 is applied the same way, but this time the zigzags cover the first set of stitches. You will stitch one thread on top and beneath the first set on the canvas. Step 3 is the same again, adding a wider row on top of the previous row. When you finish the stitching, cut all the layers except the first. This is why you place a layer of paper over the first set of stitches. The pile should not pull out of the canvas, but white glue on the back of the canvas adds extra security.

Vertical Milanese

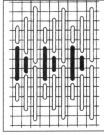 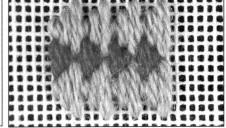

Depending upon the color combination in the motif, Vertical Milanese can be bold or subtle. Highly contrasting color combinations should be reserved for samplers, while single colors create a striking background for a project. This light-wearing upright stitch requires three plies in the needle.

Victorian Step

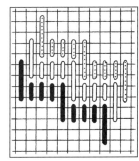 

For a simple project, use medium-wearing Victorian Step as an overall pattern on a pillow. Choose colors to accent a room, and begin at the top of the canvas, stitching downward. Any color combination works nicely. For consistency, use one family of colors, picking four or five shades ranging from light to dark. Because the size of the stitch is small, your pillow can be any size you wish.

Wall Flowers

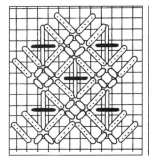 

To create Wall Flowers, first insert the long, diagonal stitches in wool. Then work the small Continental and parallel stitches in pearl cotton. Finish with the horizontal stitches in a metallic yarn. This medium-hard wearing stitch is best in samplers.

Weaving

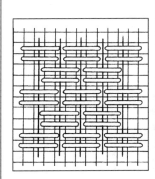 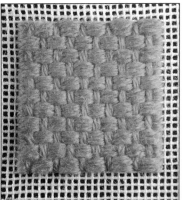

This medium-light wearing stitch is perfect for representations of baskets. Imagine a basket of flowers on a table as a great beginning for a picture. Begin with a basket and then think of all the hard-to-place stitches. Then think of isolated ones, creating the picture as you go. If the flower looks a bit strange, you can always rip it out and start another. This would be a great way to use up bits of leftover yarn. To stitch Weaving, use two-ply Persian yarn. Be sure to strip the yarn and lay the plies flat on the canvas. First lay the foundation of horizontal stitches. Then, with a long yarn, weave the parallel stitches into place. The parallel lines only travel under the canvas at the start and finish of each row.

Web

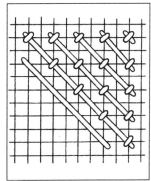 

This medium-wearing stitch creates the look of a weave on the true diagonal. Do not limit your use of this stitch to weaving. Its possibilities are endless. To create Web, first make the long stitches, then couch them with the small Tent stitches. Note the difference when you use two colors. The effect of the stitch as a whole is quite different. Use two-ply yarn.

Wicker

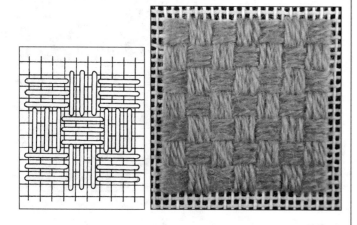

This light-wearing stitch is very close to Weaving, especially in appearance. The difference is in the method of creation. For Wicker, stitches are worked in sets of three. This is a simple stitch to compensate.

Wicker Variation

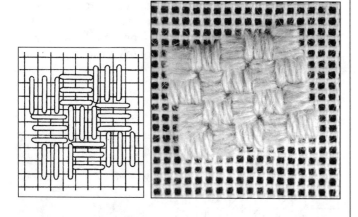

Let us say you want the effect of a weave, but you do not want a squared appearance. In this case, try Wicker Variation. It is a medium-light wearing stitch, which you can use in almost any project to create a good amount of texture. Of course, if all your other stitches are square, you may wish to choose a square weave stitch for continuity—Wicker placed in the middle of such a project may look more like a mistake. Use two-ply Persian wool.

Willow

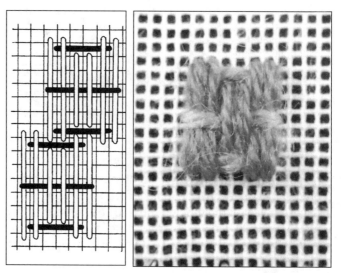

Notice in the diagram how the stitches are set off from one another, creating perpendicular lines that lie close to one another at some points and far away in others. Consider using medium-wearing Willow as an isolated stitch, or in a group. The vertical stitches require three plies, while the rest of the stitch is done in two-ply yarn.

Woven Checker

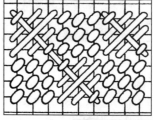

I rate the Woven Checker as medium-wearing, only because the long yarn traverses three intersections on the canvas. It may tend to snag. Woven Checker can be adapted to fit many areas. Begin by making the long stitches on the diagonal. Follow by filling the spaces with Flat and Tent stitches. Use two-ply Persian wool.

Woven Cross I

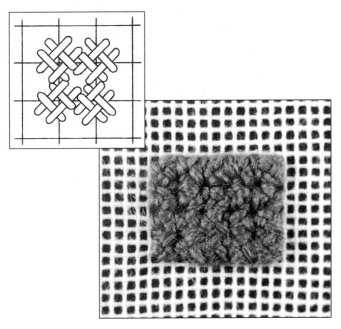

Woven Cross I creates a tight, busy effect. In the picture, the crosses are difficult to identify. This is why the motif is very busy. Do not let this keep you from using it in your projects. The weaving makes Woven Cross I quite durable, making it a good candidate for shoes, purses and other projects intended for use. Two plies in the needle offer ample coverage on 14/1 canvas. Depending upon your project, you may opt to use one ply.

Woven Cross II

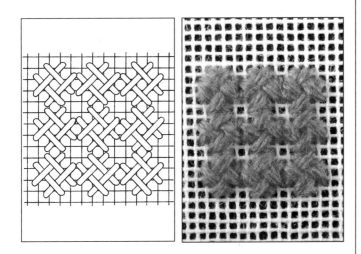

For a lacy look that leaves canvas exposed, try Woven Cross II. If you do not want the voids to show, cover the canvas with oil-based paint before stitching. Use two-ply yarn. In Woven Cross II Variation (the next entry), you can see small crosses. This may be a better answer for the person who is bothered by bare canvas threads.

Woven Cross II Variation

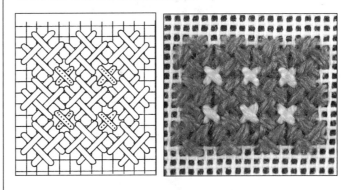

This stitch is just like Woven Cross II, with small crosses added to fill the void. The large woven crosses are worked in two plies and the smaller crosses are in one-ply pearl yarn.

Woven Scotch

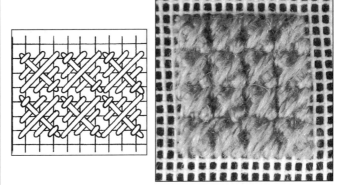

For a little more texture than Flat, and a notch less than Oatmeal, try Woven Scotch. This stitch adapts to any area in most projects. Although the long left-to-right stitch traverses three intersections on the canvas, I still consider the stitch to be medium-wearing. Use Woven Scotch in any project you wish.

Zed

With two-ply Persian yarn, begin by making the large diamond foundation. Follow by filling the voids as indicated on the diagram. The French Knots make up the final step to the stitch. Zed is best in multiple colors. Its bold, light-wearing pattern is best in samplers.

Zed Variation

Begin Zed Variation with the same foundation as Zed, in two-ply Persian yarn. Then fill the center. The smaller diamonds have Oblong Cross, Detached Chain and a French Knot, all in one-ply Persian yarn.

Zigzag

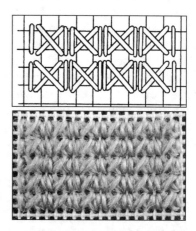

Zigzag requires one-ply Persian on 14/1 canvas to create a light, delicate stitch. The horizontal lines show—but do not let this aspect keep you from using the stitch in your pictures and pillows. The crosses do not dominate the stitch, but they do keep the stitch from having a solely vertical movement. If you want a harder wearing stitch, try using two plies in the needle. One ply was used in the sample.

Note the variety of effects you can achieve in needlepoint projects by varying stitches, canvas and yarns.

Consider the stitches and projects pictured as a springboard. In the world of needlepoint, anything is possible

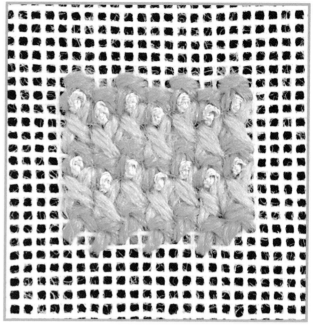

EMILY

French knots in shiny rayon add sparkle. See page 66 for details and instructions.

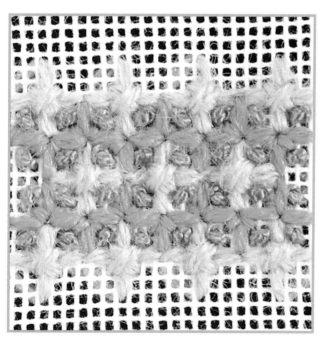

SUZIE'S GARDEN

The trellis-and-flower motif would be charming on a small pillow. Refer to page 120 for details and instructions.

JUS

Metallic detail in this stitch makes it great for belts or purses. Refer to page 82 for details and instructions.

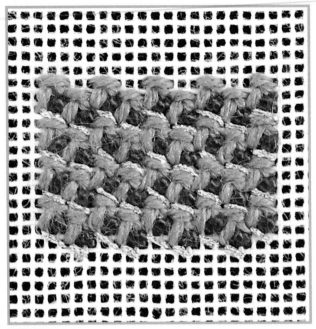

EDGE

Edge is a hard-wearing stitch that ensures a striking result. For details and instructions, see page 66.

TWO TONE STARBURST

This stitch is great fun when used in isolation. For details and instructions, see page 124.

STURGEON TRAIL

This medium-large, medium-hard wearing stitch adds a creative touch to projects. See page 119 for details and instructions.

ZED

In multiple colors, Zed makes a fine detail stitch. Refer to page 128 for instructions.

Details accentuate the nautical theme of this project. Courtesy of Janlynn Corporation.

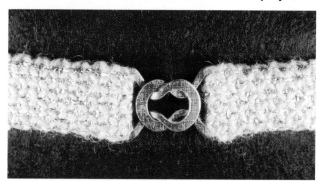

Stitched belts are relatively simple, and make a lovely gift. Stitch shoes to match!

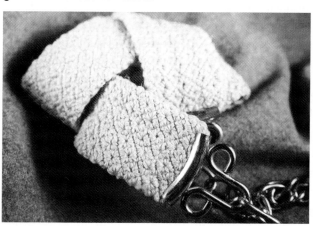

A close-up of the boat detail.

"Unicorn" pillow, courtesy of Dot Clark.

"Unicorn in Captivity" and close-ups. Courtesy of Alice Peterson.

In the close-ups, note the variety of stitches used to complete the project. The variety ensures texture and a play of light.

"The Theater" also employs a variety of stitches and techniques for texture and interest.

Varied stitches reflect a
diversity of hair types,
colors and styles.

"The Butterfly"

Shiny yarns and smooth stitches complement one another for a finely detailed effect.

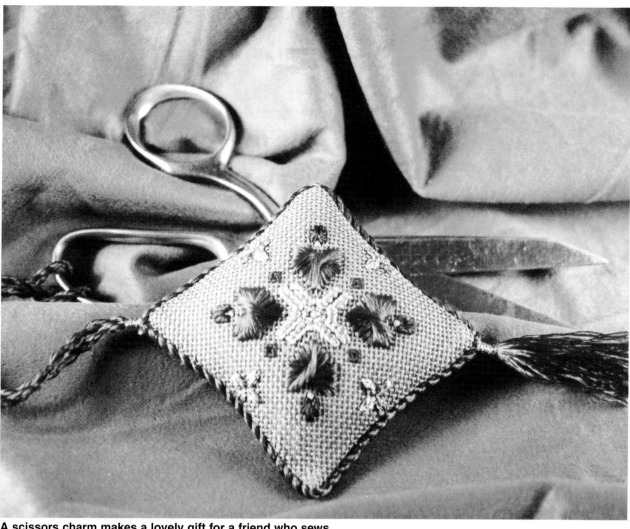

A scissors charm makes a lovely gift for a friend who sews.

Relatively simple stitches in carefully chosen yarns, placed on a colored canvas, ensure an elegant result.

This butterfly yarn organizer lends convenience to stitching projects.

Coasters make great projects for beginners! These examples are stitched on plastic canvas.

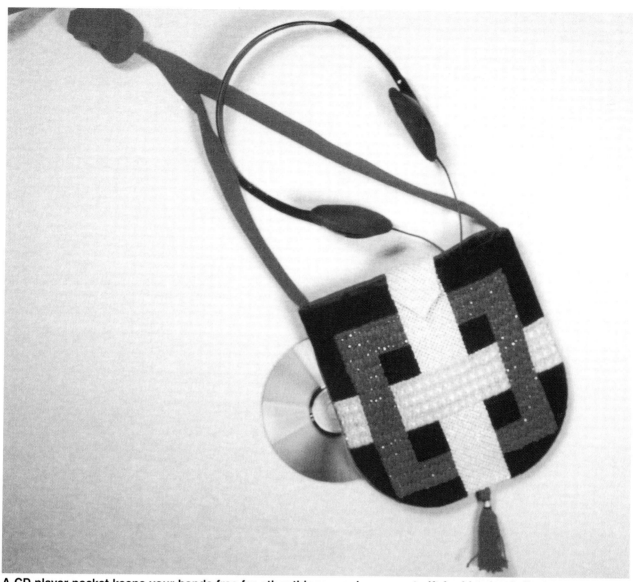

A CD player pocket keeps your hands free for other things—makes a great gift for friends of all ages.

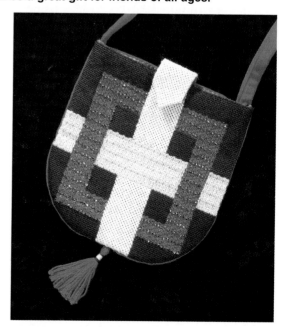

Beads add sparkle.

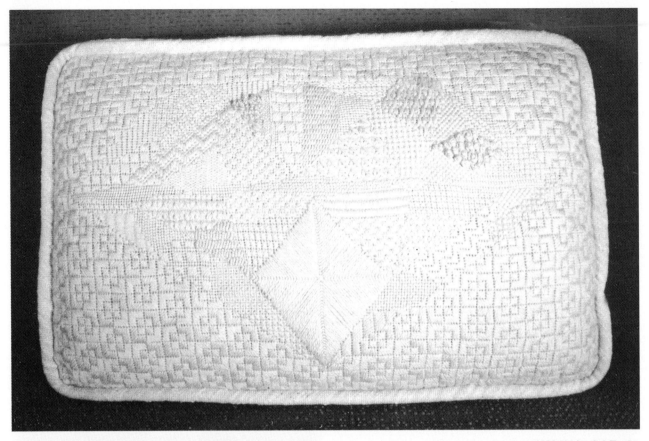

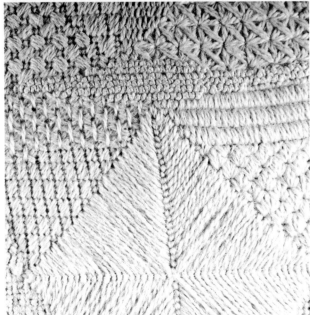

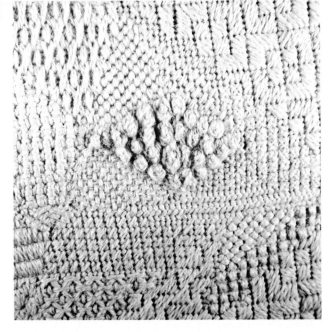

This diamond pillow showcases a variety of stitches.

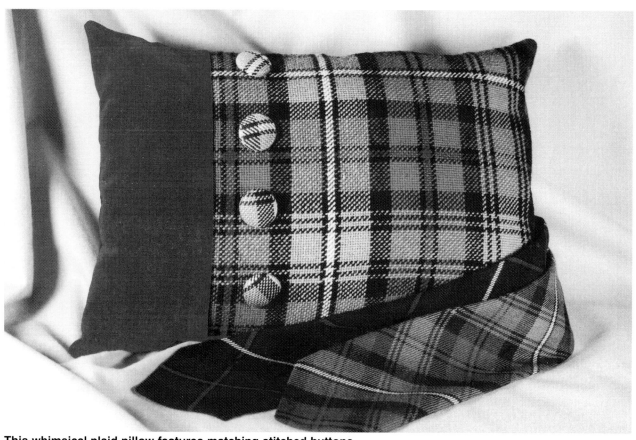

This whimsical plaid pillow features matching stitched buttons.

Tassels finish this gold and white pillow.

Stitched tote (large side). Plastic canvas makes this project easier.

Narrow side view.

Embroidered upholstery adds a touch of elegance to any room.

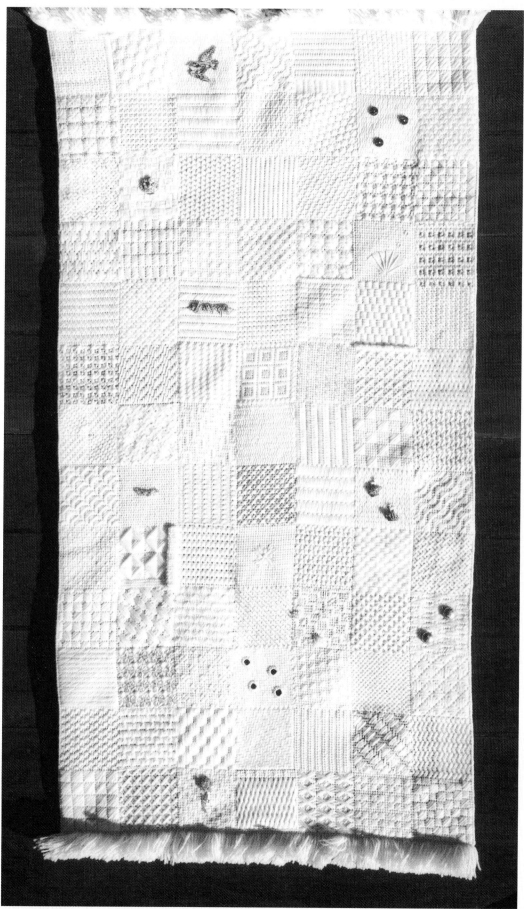

Showcase a variety of stitches and "found" objects in a tapestry like this one.

As an alternative to painted pictures for home décor, consider a stitched portrait. Here, "Blue Boy," courtesy of Éts Steiner Frères, S.A.S.

"Pinky"

Add a cozy feeling to any office with a hand-stitched mouse pad.

This stitching adds an individual touch to a Western style shirt.

Light switch plates add homey detail.

Stitch Durability

Stitch	Light	Med. Light	Med.	Med. Hard	Hard
Algerian Eye I					X
Algerian Eye II					X
Algerian Eye Variation					X
Alternating Flat			X		
Alternating Scotch				X	
Alternating Scotch Variation				X	
Alternating Tent					X
Alternating Tied Gobelin		X			
Ant Weft Edging					X
Arrowheads			X		
Arty's				X	
Ashley		X			
Astrakhan Velvet				X	
Aubusson		X			
Back					X
Banded Cross Weave					X
Bargello		X	X	X	X
Basketweave					X
Bath		X			
Battlement	X				
Beau Ridge	X				
Belly Feathers	X				
Ben	X				
Bokhara Couching	X				
Bow					X
Boxed Stepped		X			
Brazilian			X		
Breton	X				
Brick					X
Brick Cashmere				X	
Brick Variation I		X			
Brick Variation II		X			
Brighton		X			
Bucky's Weaving	X				
Bullion Knot					X
Butterfly					X
Butterfly Variation					X
Button					X
Buttonhole			X		
Buttonhole Flowers			X		
Buttonhole Half Moons					X
Byzantine I					X
Byzantine II	X				
Byzantine III					X
Byzantine IV	X				
Byzantine V	X				
Byzantine Scotch		X			
Carl			X		
Carla B.	X				
Cashmere					X
Cashmere Checker					X

Stitch	Light	Med. Light	Med.	Med. Hard	Hard
Chain					X
Chain Couching			X		
Check		X			
Chevron				X	
Chinese Loop Knot	X				
Chop Sticks					X
Chottie's Plaid					X
Closed Cat					X
Continental					X
Continental Gone Wrong					X
Continuously Woven Scotch		X			
Coral				X	
Corn Field		X			
Couching	X				
Cretan		X			
Criss Cross Hungarian					X
Cross I					X
Cross II					X
Cross Corners III					X
Cross Cushions		X			
Cross Mosaic				X	
Cross Stitch Gone Wrong				X	
Cross Stitch Tramé					X
Cross Tied Gobelin					X
Cross with French Knot					X
Crossed Scotch			X		
Cushion I			X		
Cut Turkey					X
Dana			X		
Darning	X				
Darning Variation	X				
David	X				
Detached Chain	X	X	X	X	X
Diagonal Butterfly					X
Diagonal Cashmere					X
Diagonal Cross					X
Diagonal Fishbone					X
Diagonal French					X
Diagonal Hungarian Ground				X	
Diagonal Knit					X
Diagonal Leaf					X
Diagonal Long Armed Cross					X
Diagonal Mosaic				X	
Diagonal Shell				X	
Diagonal Stem					X
Diagonal Wheat				X	
Diagonal Wicker	X				
Diamond Eye I				X	
Diamond Eyelet				X	
Diamond Ray					X
Diamond Scotch				X	

Stitch	Light	Med. Light	Med.	Med. Hard	Hard
Diamond Straight	X				
Diana					X
Diaper					X
Dillon					X
Divided Scotch				X	
Dotted					X
Dotted Scotch					X
Dotted Swiss					X
Double	X				
Double Brick				X	
Double Cross I		X			
Double Cross Tramé					X
Double Crossed Diamond					X
Double Fishbone					X
Double Hungarian		X			
Double Knot	X				
Double Leviathan		X			
Double Roumanian		X			
Double Straight Cross					X
Doublet			X		
Duck's Foot					X
Dutch			X		
Eastern					X
Eddie's Pavane			X		
Edge					X
Elongated Cashmere					X
Emiley				X	
Emiley Variation				X	
Encroached Gobelin					X
Encroached Long Cross					X
Encroached Oblique					X
Encroached Straight Gobelin					X
Encroached Parisian Embroidery			X		
Erin's Ridge				X	
Eugene			X		
Eye					X
Falling Stars		X			
False Rice					X
Fancy Cross	X				
Feather Half Cross					X
Fern		X			
Fern Variation			X		
Fill In				X	
Fishbone I					X
Fishbone II		X			
Flat I		X			
Flat II	X				
Flat Woven			X		
Florentine					X
Flower			X		
Four-Way Bargello				X	
Four-Way Mosaic				X	
Frame	X				
Frame Variation	X				
Framed Alternating Flat			X		
Framed Cashmere					X
Framed Diagonal Cashmere				X	
Framed Diagonal Scotch			X		

Stitch	Light	Med. Light	Med.	Med. Hard	Hard
Framed Hungarian Brick		X			
Framed Mosaic					X
Framed Reverse Scotch					X
Framed Scotch					X
Framed Scotch Variation		X			
French I					X
French II		X			
French Knot					X
Frosty			X		
Ginger Jars					X
Gingham			X		
Gloria	X				
Gloria Variation	X				
Gobelin Droit			X		
Gobelin Tramé			X		
Half Cross			X		
Half Cross Tramé			X		
Half Eyelet			X		
Half-Framed Scotch				X	
Half Pyramid with Satin			X		
Heavy Cross	X				
Herringbone			X		
Herringbone Couching			X		
Herringbone Done Diagonally			X		
Herringbone Gone Wrong			X		
Horizontal Brick				X	
Horizontal Elongated Cashmere					X
Horizontal Hungarian					X
Horizontal Kalem					X
Horizontal Milanese		X			
Horizontal Oblong Cross	X				
Horizontal Old Florentine	X				
Houser	X				
Hungarian			X		
Hungarian and Stars				X	
Hungarian Brick		X			
Hungarian Diamonds		X			
Hungarian Ground		X			
Hungarian Steps			X		
Hungarian Tiles			X		
Hungarian Tiles Variation			X		
Hungarian Variation I			X		
Indian Stripe		X			
Interlace Band	X				
Interlocking Leaf			X		
Interwoven Herringbone	X				
Irregular Gobelin			X		
Italian Cross	X				
Jacquard			X		
Janina				X	
John					X
Jus					X
Jus Variation					X
Kathy					X
Ken A.	X				
Kennan				X	
Kip					X
Knit One Pearl One					X

Stitch	Light	Med. Light	Med.	Med. Hard	Hard
Knitting I					X
Knitting II				X	
Knitting III					X
Knotted I					X
Knotted II					X
Knotted III					X
Lace Wheels				X	
Laced Chain				X	
Large Brick	X				
Large Checker		X			
Large Diagonal Mosaic		X			
Large Diagonal Scotch			X		
Large Horizontal Parisian	X				
Large Interlocking Gobelin			X		
Large Knitting	X				
Large Moorish		X			
Large Oblong Cross I		X			
Large Rice	X				
Leaf			X		
Leaf with Smyrna				X	
Ley's Trail	X				
Lipperts					X
Long Armed Cross					X
Medallion					X
Medium Checker					X
Medium Rice		X			
Medium Rice Checker				X	
Melrose					X
Mettler			X		
Mettler Variation			X		
Milanese		X			
Milanese Color Variation		X			
Mixed Milanese		X			
Mixed Up Cross					X
Montenegrin					X
Montenegrin Cross Adaptation					X
Montenegrin Variation					X
Moon				X	
Moorish I				X	
Moorish II	X				
Mosaic					X
Mosaic Stripe					X
Narrow Oblong Cross				X	
New-Cah's Walk		X			
Nine Cross	X				
Nobuko			X		
Norwich	X				
Oatmeal		X			
Oblique Slav				X	
Oblong Cross				X	
Oblong Cross Tramé			X		
Oblong Rice					X
Oblong with Back					X
Old Florentine	X				
Oriental I	X				
Oriental II	X				
Oriental III		X			
Oriental IV	X				

Stitch	Light	Med. Light	Med.	Med. Hard	Hard
Oriental V	X				
Outline I					X
Outline II	X				
Overcast			X		
Padded Cushions			X		
Padded Double Cross	X				
Padded Gobelin Droit			X		
Papermoon	X				
Parisian		X			
Parisian Cross			X		
Parisian Stripe			X		
Paul and Lin					X
Paul and Lin Variation					X
Pavilion Boxes			X		
Perspective			X		
Peter's	X				
Petit Point					X
Pinched Cross				X	
Pisces				X	
Plaited					X
Plaited Algerian	X				
Plaited Gobelin		X			
Point de Tresse					X
Point Russe I			X		
Point Russe II			X		
Princess	X				
Princess Variation	X				
Pyramid			X		
Queued Diamonds	X				
Raised Cross		X			
Raised Work					X
Random Bargello			X		
Random Byzantine	X				
Random Continental			X		
Ray					X
Raymond		X			
Raymond Variation I	X				
Raymond Variation II	X				
Reinforced Cross				X	
Renaissance I					X
Rep					X
Reverse Cross					X
Reverse Eyelet			X		
Reverse Tent I					X
Reversed Cashmere					X
Reversed Mosaic					X
Reversed Norwich	X				
Reversible Alternating Tent					X
Ribbon Cross		X			
Ribbon Cross Upright Cross				X	
Rice Variation		X			
Ridges		X			
Rococo			X		
Rosemary			X		
Rotating Flat	X				
Roumanian Couching			X		
Round Braid					X
Rubato			X		

Stitch	Light	Med. Light	Med.	Med. Hard	Hard
Running Cross					X
Saint George and Saint Andrew				X	
Sand Shells	X				
Sandy's Slide			X		
Satin		X			
Scotch			X		
Scotch Worked Diagonally I		X			
Scotch Worked Diagonally II		X			
Sean	X				
Shaded Stripe		X			
Shadow Mesh	X				
Sheaf II		X			
Shell I					X
Shell III		X			
Shell IV		X			
Shell Variation I			X		
Shi Sha (Acorn)		X			
Shi Sha (Buttonhole)				X	
Slanted Gobelin I			X		
Slanted Gobelin II					X
Slanted Gobelin III					X
Slanted Gobelin IV	X				
Slashed Cross					X
Slashed Oblong				X	
Slipped Multiple			X		
Small Checker					X
Small Rice					X
Smyrna			X		
Spider Webs	X	X	X		
Split Florentine			X		
Split Gobelin				X	
Split Slanted Gobelin					X
Sprat					X
Sprat's Head					X
Square Cross			X		
Square Herringbone		X			
Staggered Cross				X	
Staggering Crosses			X		
Staggering Flat		X			
Staircase				X	
Starry Crosses		X			
Stem					X
Step	X				
Straight Cross					X

Stitch	Light	Med. Light	Med.	Med. Hard	Hard
Straight Rice				X	
Strap		X			
Sturgeon Trail				X	
Sugar Buttonhole					X
Surrey					X
Suzann's Bicentennial Star					X
Suzie's Garden				X	
Texas Mosquito	X				
Three Layer Web					X
Tied Cashmere					X
Tied Down Cross					X
Tight Pinched Cross			X		
Tip of Leaf			X		
Tom	X				
Tramé					X
Triangle	X				
Triple Cross I				X	
Triple Cross II		X			
Triple Diamond Cross			X		
Triple Leviathan					X
Tuft	X				
Two Color Herringbone					X
Two Sided Cross					X
Two Tied Gobelin					X
Two Tone Sunburst			X		
Upright Oriental	X				
Van Dyke					X
Velvet					X
Vertical Milanese	X				
Victorian Step			X		
Wall Flowers				X	
Weaving		X			
Web			X		
Wicker	X				
Wicker Variation			X		
Willow			X		
Woven Checker			X		
Woven Cross I					X
Woven Cross II			X		
Woven Cross II Variation			X		
Woven Scotch			X		
Zed	X				
Zed Variation	X				
Zigzag					X

Canvas, Needles and Yarn

This chart is for slanted stitches. Upright stitches, such as Bargello, require thicker yarn in the needle. For the best results, always experiment first with a scrap of canvas. Test for the perfect thickness if you intend to stitch heirloom quality work.

Canvas (Stitches per inch)	Yarn and Thickness (Plies)	Needle Sizes
3 -5	3-ply Rug 9-ply Tapestry	13
7	4- to 5-ply Tapestry 12-ply Persian	13
10	3-ply Persian 1-ply Tapestry 6-ply Medici 14-ply Cotton floss #32 Kreinik briad 1/8-inch Kreinik Ribbon 3-ply Caron Watercolours	16
12	2-ply Persian 5-ply Medici 12-ply Cotton floss 1-ply #3 Pearl 2-ply Caron Watercolours	18-20
13	2-ply Persian 5-ply Medici 9-ply Cotton floss 2-ply Caron Watercolours 3-ply Caron Wildflowers 6-ply Caron Waterlilies 2-ply Caron Impressions	20-22
14	2-ply Persian 9-ply Cotton floss 6-ply Kreinik Mori 6-ply Splendor silk #16 Kreinik braid Kreinik Tapestry 1-ply #5 Pearl 2-ply Caron Watercolours 3-ply Caron Wildflowers 6-ply Caron Waterlilies	20-22
16	1-ply Persian 7-ply Cotton floss 1-ply #5 Pearl 3-ply Caron Wildflowers	22
18-20	1-ply Persian 2-ply Medici 2-ply Appleton 3-ply Kreinik Mori 6-ply Cotton floss 4-ply Splendor silk 1-ply #12 Pearl 1-ply Kreinik Serica #8 Kreinik braid 1/16-inch Kreinick ribbon 1-ply Caron Watercolours 2-ply Caron Wildflowers 4-ply Caron Waterlilies 1-ply Caron Impressions	22-24
22	2-ply Kreinik Mori #4 Kreinik braid 1-ply Caron Impressions	22-24
24	(Persian is too heavy) 4-ply Medici 9-ply Cotton floss 1-ply #3 Pearl #4 Kreink braid 1-ply Caron Wildflowers 1-ply Caron Impressions	22-24
30-40	Embroidery floss	26-28
50-70	Silk Beading needle with broken tip	

Yarn Requirements for Bargello Patterns

Canvas	Thickness (in plies)	Needle Size
10	5	18
12	4	19-20
13	3	20-22
14	3	20-22
16	2	22
18	2	23-24
20-40	1	23

Chapter Four

Blocking and Finishing

You may think, after placing the final stitch in an exacting needlework project, your job is done. This is rarely true. With a little practice and patience, you can block and mount your own projects. Paying a professional is expensive, but do not be intimidated by the amounts charged by professionals. The process is truly simple, and almost anyone can master it.

Blocking

After you finish your project, whether you have stitched it using stretcher bars or in hand, it probably requires some blocking. Projects stitched in silk and rayon should not be immersed in water for blocking, since water can stain the yarns, or make them bleed.

A few tools are needed here. First, you need a large fiberboard, which you can purchase at your local lumberyard. This board measures four feet by eight feet, but do not fret. Cut it into various useful sizes—once you manage this, you will never have to repeat it. I recommend cutting a piece to two feet by two feet. This practical size holds many projects. For bell pulls, four feet by two feet is a good size.

Once you have cut the board to the size you need for the job, you need to cover it with white, 100 percent cotton fabric. This protects your needlepoint projects from snagging on the wood or being stained—do not skip this step. Heavyweight muslin is a good choice. Some people prefer gingham. Fabric with printed squares can be a practical choice—the squares function nicely as guidelines for squaring the project on the board. Of course, if you choose patterned gingham, then you must first be sure that you mount it perfectly straight on the board. As a simpler solution, I suggest you cover the board with plain white fabric and make lines later with an indelible marker. Your fabric should be one and a half times larger than the board. For example, if the board is two feet by two feet, then the fabric should be three feet by three feet. Lay the fabric on the floor, and then lay the board on top of it (see diagram).

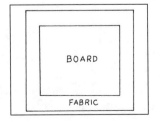

Fold the fabric over on two opposite sides to enclose the board.

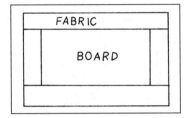

You may want to secure the fabric with pins, and repeat on the two other sides.

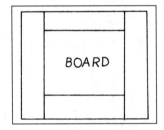

Your next step is to stitch the envelope around the board. To do so, use a large needle and long piece of string. Make zigzag stitches back and forth along two opposite sides of the fabric. Again, repeat the process with the other two sides. You may want to whip stitch the loose fabric on all four corners.

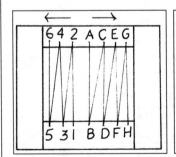
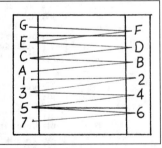

Stitch the fabric.

After you stitch the fabric, pour very hot water over the board. This shrinks the fabric, making the cover taut over the board. Any little ridges or tucks left on the fabric cover could catch under your needlepoint, distorting the grid. Once dry, your blocking board is ready for use. As I mentioned, at this point, you may want to make a grid of squares with indelible ink to help in blocking. One-inch squares are usually sufficient.

Marking a blocking board

Stretch project into shape   First four pins

Depending upon the stitches you used to make the project, you will want to block the needlepoint either face up or down. If the stitches are three-dimensional, as in "The Theater," you want to block the project face up. If blocking a flat stitched item such as Basketweave chair seats, your best choice would be face down. The idea is to block the project as flat as possible.

Begin with your blocking board and T pins. I recommend T-pins rather than wig pins, as T-pins are much stronger. In the middle of each side, pin the needlepoint on raw canvas to make the center of the motif taut. Then place eight pins, one on either side of each of the first, centered pins. If you are misting the project, continue misting and pinning, misting the project every five minutes until the last pins are at the four corners.

Blocking a three-dimensional project

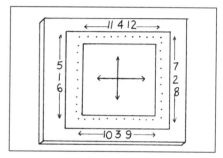

Order for pinning

Blocking a flat project

Check the accuracy of your blocking with a T-square or a ninety-degree triangle. Sometimes, the needlepoint is square on the sides but not in the middle of the motif. If this is the case, stick T-pins into the required areas to straighten the grid. Place the T-pins straight up and down into the canvas, perpendicular to the blocking board. After four to six hours of drying, remove the pins in the center of the canvas.

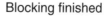

Mist with water

Blocking finished   Details

Some people prefer using bottled, distilled water in a mister, spraying the entire needlepoint project, and misting the project every five minutes. I prefer to immerse the entire piece in a tub of water and gently remove the excess water. The needlepoint is then ready to block. If the canvas has been distorted into a parallelogram, you may need to stretch it on the bias.

Allow the blocking board to lie flat for at least 24 hours, so that the yarn colors do not run down to one side. After this, you may want to stand the board on its side just to have it out of the way. Because sunlight is an enemy of needlepoint, do not be tempted to let it dry in the sun. This will fade the colors of your yarns much quicker than they would otherwise fade. After 24 hours, sometimes the canvas relaxes, and you have lumps and ridges. While this is not cause for panic, it is cause for starting over. The canvas was not stretched tightly enough, and it needs to be blocked again. Many people, in their first attempts at blocking their work, are afraid that the canvas will tear, and they fail to stretch the canvas enough. Unless the canvas you have purchased is quite cheap, it will hold up to many pounds of pressure.

When the project has dried completely, remove all the T-pins from the board. Now you have several options for finishing your project. You may want to mount it in a frame, make a pillow, create a bell pull or add it to another object.

If you are sure the needlepoint is square and clean, you can use the following, quick blocking method. Try a light steaming with your iron. For this job, you need a clean towel and a steam iron. Place the towel on the canvas, and lightly force the steam through the towel down into your project. Do not place the iron directly on your canvas. This crushes the texture of the stitches and could cause damage to the fibers.

There are a few things to keep in mind when blocking needlepoint projects. First, never block soiled needlepoint. If you do not clean soils first, they can be permanently embedded in the work during blocking, and you will never get the project clean.

If you painted your canvas before stitching, you had better hope you had first tested your paint for colorfastness. If you doubt the colorfastness of acrylic paints and markers, spray a layer of clear acrylic over them before stitching.

A round or curved piece should be blocked as though it were a square or rectangle.

If you do not have two inches of empty canvas on all sides, sew a strip of fabric close to the needlepoint, and T-pins can be placed in the fabric during blocking.

Always use rustproof T-pins for blocking.

Placing the pins too far apart can cause a scallop. Try not to place pins more than half an inch apart.

Never use staples when blocking. They cut canvas threads, weakening your canvas.

When blocking a large piece, such as a rug, where you have seamed the canvas together, you may have to steam press the seams to ensure the canvas lies flat. To do this, follow the process for steam blocking. Again, never place the iron directly on the needlepoint.

Never use soil resistant products on wool, silk or other animal fibers. These fibers need to breathe, or they will rot. Anti-stain products seal off the fibers.

Sometimes the canvas simply will not block back into its original position. A few things might have gone wrong to contribute to this obstacle. Perhaps too many fibers have been stuffed into the canvas. To correct this in the future, use fewer plies in the needle for that size canvas. Another problem may be that you used too large a needle for the grid. Try a smaller needle in the future.

If your motif includes stripes, take care to make sure you block them as straight as possible. Crooked lines make rags of heirloom embroidery.

When you feel the grid on the canvas is square, leave the area for a while and then return to see whether it is still straight. Without a doubt, you will think someone has sabotaged your work. Rest assured no one has played a cruel joke. What happens is, after working on the project for a while, your "brain" fixes it for your eyes, and tricks you into thinking your lines are straight. After a "mini-vacation," your eyes will see straight again, and you will once again clearly see the areas that need improvement.

The best rule to remember, in avoiding distortion, is to use stretcher bars and when possible, stitch Basketweave rather than Half Cross or Continental. An ounce of prevention…

Even the most seasoned stitchers sometimes let their tension vary—sometimes your mood is enough to influence the tension of your stitching. This can change the quality of the finished project. Try to find a comfortable position to sit in while you stitch, and stick to that position. Changes in your posture can affect the quality of your work. Also, try to make the thread rest straight and smooth on the canvas. Never tug the canvas or yarn. Sometimes, nothing you can do will block out tugging.

Mounting

You have surmounted the obstacle of blocking, and your project is ready for mounting. What to do? Well before you ever got to this point, you have determined just what purpose your project is intended to serve. If you have chosen to stitch a pillow, you have several options. If you have finished a picture project, you would show it to its best advantage by mounting it flat.

If you are making a pillow for your stitching, think of it as a frame of sorts for the picture that is your motif. A box with or without piping around the edges would be appropriate to "frame" the motif. A highly textured design without a definite motif may be best with knife edges on its side. To help blend the colors and fibers, perhaps tassels would finish the look.

One way to make a frame for the pillow is to have a single or double welt around the edges. Try pushing the welt corners in and fasten with covered buttons for a casual look, something that might be appropriate for a den or office. Try using covered buttons on top of a plaid, as was done in the tartan pillow pictured in color on page 139. The pillow is wool on 14/1 canvas. The buttons were stitched with cotton floss on 18/1 canvas. A professional upholsterer finished the covered buttons. Attach the buttons on an angle, since the differences in plaid would be noticeable if you were to try to match them.

If the needlepoint is round, a welt can still be used. Try making pleats around the project and pull the flaps open. Anchor the flaps down with a few quick stitches. For a softer look, try lace, perhaps accompanied with a ruffle of fabric.

Pillows

There is quite an array of materials from which to choose when it comes to stuffing pillows. You can buy a pre-made pillow form, or you can find polyester batting, wool, and feathers. Pre-made forms are usually square or round, in standard sizes, such as twelve inches by twelve inches and fourteen by fourteen. Make your needlepoint project the size of your intended pillow, plus two rows of Continental stitches on all four sides. Place the needlepoint and backing fabric right sides together. Stitch between the Continental and the motif on three sides, leaving the fourth side open. Insert the pillow form into the opening. Turn the seam allowance of the needlepoint and fabric into the pillow, and hand stitch the entire length.

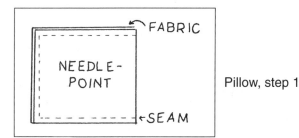

Pillow, step 1

Pre-made pillow forms, of course, offer the assurance that your pillows will always be smooth and straight, and their stuffing will not be lumpy. On the whole, they make it much easier to create a professional look.

Polyester batting is a loose fiber that can be shaped into any form. Some people make doll-shaped pillows, or form them after other objects. Round, cylinder, triangle and other shapes turn out best when they are stuffed with polyester fill. To use polyester, stitch between the Continental rows and the motif on all sides, leaving a gap large enough to turn the needlepoint and fabric inside out. After you turn the pillow, tuck the raw edges inside, and finish stitching the edge by hand.

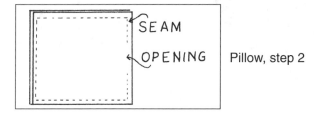

Pillow, step 2

Feather-stuffed pillows create a traditional, more formal look. Old, feather-stuffed bed pillows can be an inexpensive source for the material. You can also buy new feathers from an upholsterer. Do not stuff the feathers directly into the pillow; they must be encased in a fabric first, such as pillow ticking. If you cannot find pillow ticking, use another tightly woven fabric. Years ago, I made pillows for our living room, and in my ignorance, I stuffed the feathers directly into the pillows. This resulted in feathers on the floor, all over the couch, floating in the air and decorating everyone who used the pillows. The horny ends of the feathers poked through the fabric, creating renegades. If you use old bed pillows, beat the

feathers to one side of the rectangle casing. With your sewing machine, stitch the fabric along the entire case. Cut the excess fabric along the seam. If needed, repeat the process for your desired dimensions.

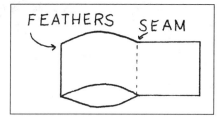

Pillow, step 3

Piping

Adding piping to the seams of knife edged pillows as well as boxed pillows creates a wonderful, finished look. You might consider piping as a frame for the needlepoint work. You may want to use a color in the stitching work, depending upon the effect you wish to achieve. If the stitching uses many colors, you might simply want to use the color of your backing fabric.

Add bias cording around your pillow by following these simple steps:

1. With a pencil, draw a line 1-1/2 inches from the edge of fabric that has been cut on the true bias. Repeat the marking process again, using the pencil mark to measure your next line.

2. Cut the strips on the marked lines.
3. To make the bias strip the correct length, it is necessary to join the ends. To do so, place the right sides of the fabric strips together, joining the ends of the strips.

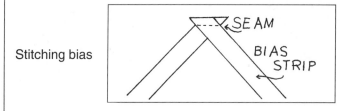

Stitching bias

4. Using a sewing machine, stitch 1/4 inch along the edge. Repeat until you have added enough strips for the entire length you need.

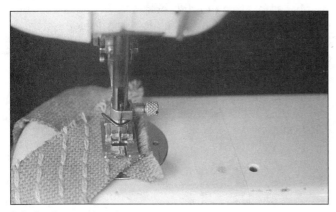

Stitch pieces together.

5. Press all seam allowances open.

6. Place cord inside the bias strip you have created. Roll the fabric around the cord and stitch, with a zipper foot on your sewing machine, along the length of the cord and tape.

7. The two extra rows of Continental you added to the stitching of your needlepoint serve as a seam allowance. Note the picture. The needle indicates the necessary placement of the machine stitching.

8. Pin the cording in the middle of one side on the needlepoint and stitch the bias cording down onto the project.

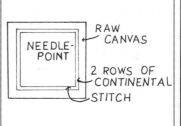 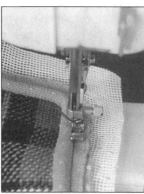

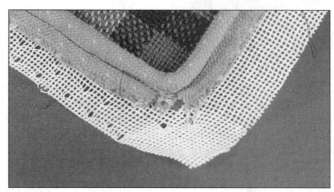

9. To miter the corners, you will need to have the sewing machine needle down into the needlepoint. Lift the presser foot up. With heavy sewing scissors, clip the bias strip at a 90-degree angle from the cording. Pivot your needlepoint and cording to stitch the next side.

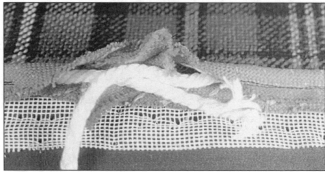

10. Continue stitching until you arrive at a point three inches from your starting point. It is imperative that you have enough piping and cord to overlap the ends.

11. Lay the ends of the cording together. Trim the cord so that you have a two-inch overlap.

12. Separate the four plies of the cording, and cut away two.

13. Repeat the same process on the other end of the cording.

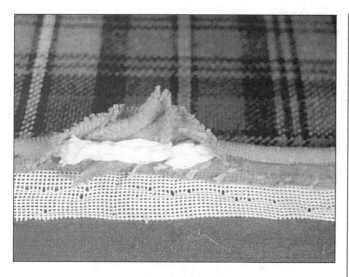

14. Twist the remaining ends together to make a single, complete cording, using two plies from each end.

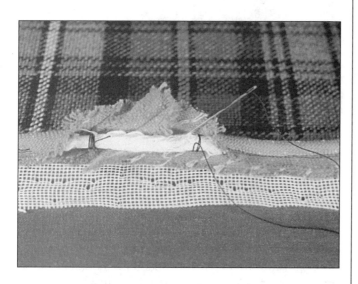

15. Stitch the ends to create a single, continuous piping.
16. Fold the bias fabric over the cord and stitch.

Finished piping

Corners

Whether you use a pre-made pillow form, loose batting or feathers, your pillow can have round or square corners. Not all designs are good candidates for round corners. Four-Way Bargello, plaids, square motifs and other designs that create exact rectangle patterns may not be appropriate on round-cornered pillows, as part of the motif may become lost. Take a look at the photos of pillows in the color section. If the box pillow with the diamond motif had rounded corners, it would appear awkward with the square background stitch.

The following diagram shows how to stitch square corners. Note the small stitches. They represent the Continental stitches for the seam allowance. The Cashmere stitches are the stitched motif. The long horizontal and vertical lines represent the placement of the machine stitching. A very sharp corner was achieved by stitching along the Continental rows.

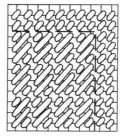

A good corner

A sharp corner

In the second diagram, you will notice the same set of stitches. This time, the corner has been stitched to make a soft curve. Imagine a nosegay of flowers on this pillow. The roundness of the flower petals and bending stems, combined with the soft edges of the pillow, create a relaxed feeling. Piping, cording and braids can all be used with curved and rounded corners.

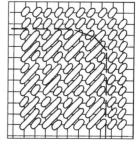

A curved corner

Cords

Often a project will look unfinished unless it has something at the knifed edge. This may be the situation for pillows or scissors charms. You can always buy cording, but it is also simple to make. It can add appeal to a project, especially in a color to set off the work. To tie in the color scheme with your needlepoint, you may wish to use one or more shades in the cording.

The number of plies to use to make the cording should be determined by the weight of the yarn used to stitch the project. For a project stitched in Persian yarn, I would recommend six or eight plies in the cording. The instructions show a project stitched in tapestry yarn, with four plies incorporated into the cording. The scissors charm used multiple plies in Marlitt rayon. Extra care was taken when working with the rayon, to avoid snagging the delicate fibers. Keep metallics in mind, too. I used metallic yarn, two-ply Kreinik Metallic #16 Braid, to finish the edges of "The Butterfly." For a softer effect, I twisted very little to coil the yarn.

To figure how much yarn you will need, measure the perimeter of the project. If your pillow is twelve inches by twelve inches, the total is 48 inches. Then, multiply this number by three, to equal in this case 144 inches. Add a couple of inches for waste, and you arrive at the length of yarn needed for each double ply. For example, if you are using tapestry yarn, and you want a four-ply cord, then you need two lengths of 152-inch yarn.

To make a cord, you will need the following:
Yarn
Hand Drill
Cup Hook
Scissors
A helpful friend

Follow these steps to create the cord:
1. Cut the length of yarn you need for the project, as figured above.
2. Have a friend hold the two ends while you loop the yarn on a cup hook.
3. Stand back at a distance from the hook, to tighten the yarn between you and your friend.
4. Twist the yarn with the hand drill. Continue twisting until the yarn starts to kink.

5. Give the friend your drill, taking care not to tangle the yarn. Hold the middle of the twisted yarn.
6. Slowly twist the middle in the direction the yarn wishes to go. Continue doing so until the entire length of the yarn has twisted around itself. Tie the ends together to ensure the yarn will not become untwisted. It is now ready to be sewn onto the needlepoint project.

Twist cord around itself

To attach the cord, make small whip stitches in a matching shade of thread, if you do not want the stitching to show. For a different effect, you might use a contrasting color for a couched look. Talon metal thread was used to couch the Kreinik, for the effect of invisible stitching.

When the "Scissors Charm" was created, all four sides were measured, and thirteen inches extra was included for the loop. An extra length was added for the tassel at the bottom corner. After I made the cord, I used small whip stitches to attach it to the charm, allowing extra cording at the bottom corner, where the cord started and stopped. Kreinik fine braid finished the tassel and the top of the charm. This finished the charm, and made the cording appear as a single, continuous line.

Braiding

Braiding can be used in much the same way as cording, to add a nice finish to a project. This was the approach I used to finish the edges of the mouse pad. Using J. L. Walsh, Inc. silk yarn, I made a simple braid. I could not get the length of yarn I needed to surround the whole piece, so I added two tassels at opposite corners, to cover the points where the yarns started and stopped. The braid was glued to the edge of the mouse pad. If you prefer, you can use needle and thread. Use your imagination for creating finishes for your own projects.

Tassels

Tassels can make a wonderful addition to a pillow. A tassel can add a casual or formal effect, depending on the tassel itself. You might choose silver or gold-toned metallic yarns to create a formal look, while cotton or wool would make a more casual statement. You may wish to combine two or more colors from the project in the tassel. Of course, you do not want to use too many colors in the tassel—this will only muddy the effect. Choose two or three colors that you wish to emphasize. If the colors of a room are also in the needlepoint, use these in the tassels to tie the pillow in with the décor.

Tassels

Adding a tassel presents you with almost limitless options. Any yarn can be adapted to the purpose, including cotton, wool, acrylic, metals and novelty yarns. Consider different sizes. Pearl cotton or embroidery floss could tie the tassel very nicely. Be creative with colors. Perhaps make the tassel in one shade, and tie it in another. Also, you may want to make webbing around the ball of the tassel. The picture shows a sampling of tassels.

On the gold and white pillow in the color section, wool fiber was used for the tassel and silver Japanese metal was webbed at the top. You might add some unique object to the tassel. For example, metal threads could be added to the outer edges. Perhaps braids would make a nice addition down the whipped area. Even small tassels on a larger tassel might be fun to add on the pillow. How about yarn in another color hitched at the whipped binding, or two or three tassels at each corner for a dramatic effect?

The size of the tassel changes the measure variances. For example, a four-inch tassel should have a ball with a one-inch diameter. A six-inch tassel might have a two-inch ball. A thinner tassel would have a smaller ball, while a thicker one would need a larger ball. Length and thickness of the yarn should be in proper proportion to one another—but, these are often matters of taste. Rug yarn would require a smaller number of wraps around the cardboard than would Persian. In the sample pictures, one skein of tapestry wool was used for one tassel. This means that 40 yards were used for each corner of the pillow. Allow for variances in using Persian and other yarns. My best advice is to experiment. It is the only way to truly discover what each tassel requires.

You can also find many ready-made tassels on the market, in natural, synthetic, and metallic yarns. They are available in many sizes and styles. Your local fabric or home décor shop ought to have many from which to choose. Look carefully, and you are almost sure to find something to accent your project—and braiding to match your tassels.

While they may seem complicated, tassels are relatively simple to construct.

To make a tassel, you will need the following materials and tools:

Yarn (of your own choosing, to match or accent your project)
Cardboard
Needle
Scissors

1. Cut a length of cardboard a little longer than the desired length of your tassel.

2. Wrap the yarn over the cardboard several times.

3. With a threaded needle, slip the yarn under the wraps and tie tightly. You may wish to make several knots to secure the yarn.

4. Cut the opposite end of the wraps and remove the cardboard.

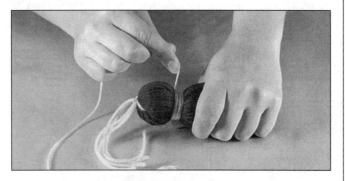

5. About one inch from the tied end, wrap another yarn around the tassel several times.

6. Cut the yarn and thread it onto your needle.

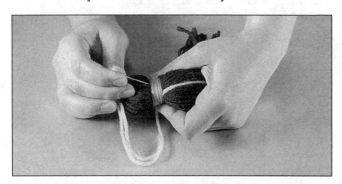

7. Insert the needle into the tassel so that the end runs under the wrapped yarn and down the tassel.

8. Trim the ends of the tassel so that they are square.

9. If you used embroidery floss or other multiple-ply yarn, separate the plies that hang below the ball of the tassel.

You have two options for attaching the tassel to your project. You can either attach it to the finished project, after it has been sewn and stuffed. Or you can attach the tassel as you sew the backing to the project.

For the first method, make the tassel and then sew it onto the corner of the pillow, sewing the ties into the pillow stuffing. The second approach offers a more professional appearance:

1. After your needlepoint has been blocked and cleaned, place the tassel on the project where you would like to attach it.

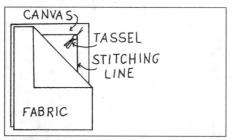

Place the tassel

2. Pin or stay stitch to anchor the tassel.

3. Pin the fabric and needlepoint sections right sides together.

4. Machine stitch along all four sides. Leave an area open for turning the pillow inside out. Start and finish in the middle of one side, not at a corner.

5. Finish as you would a knife-edged pillow.

Framing

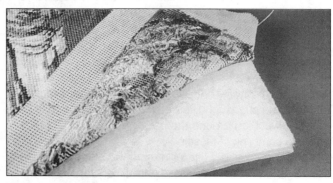

Batting for mounting

One of the most expensive and popular ways to finish needlepoint is to have it framed. Here, too, you have many options. You might choose a deep or shallow frame, wood or metal. There are countless styles available. You might hang a project with no frame at all, for a more contemporary look. To spare yourself cost and trouble, you can plan ahead. Before you even begin stitching, plan the size of your project, so that it fits into a pre-fabricated frame, and you do not have the bother of having a frame custom-made. You can also find pairs of molding strips, in lengths starting at a couple of inches and going up from there. These can accommodate almost any size picture you wish to stitch. Everything you need including instructions is packaged and ready to assemble. You can find these in art supply stores, hardware stores and needlework shops. Use care when you choose your frame—you do not want it to clash with, or overpower, the project that no doubt consumed many hours of your time. Err on the side of simplicity, if you must.

If you choose to first mount your needlepoint on stretcher bars, and then mount the whole lot in a frame, you want a frame with a deep enough back to fit the stretcher bars. It would be unsightly to have the bars sticking out of the back. To avoid potential problems such as this, purchase the bars first and then the frame.

The following directions show you how to mount your project on stretcher bars that are then inserted into a custom frame.

Stapled Method for Framing

The following items and materials are needed:
Frame (Purchased)
Measure
Ribbon
T-Square
Stretcher Bars
Needlepoint
Scissors
Stapler
Staples
Glue
Ruler
Wire
Hammer
Razor Blade

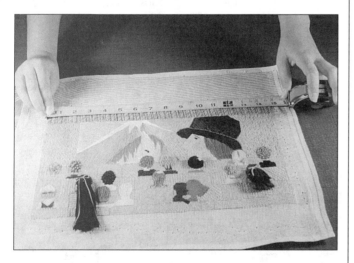

1. Measure the needlepoint project to determine the necessary size of the frame and stretcher bars.

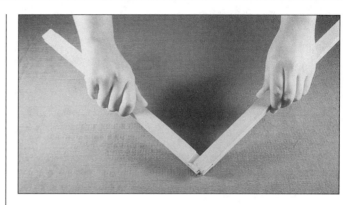

2. Piece the four sides of the stretcher bars together. You may need a hammer to tightly drive together the tongue and groove.

Tighten tongue and groove

3. Use a T-square to align all four corners.

4. Staple the corners to secure them.

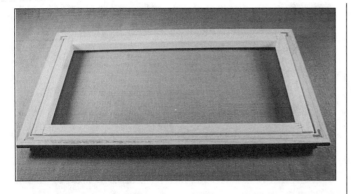

5. Check the stretcher bars against the frame to ensure correct size. The bars should be slightly smaller than the inside of the frame, to allow space for the canvas.

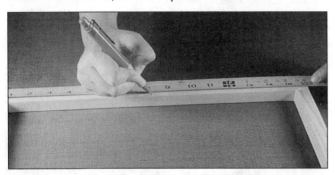

6. Find the middle of each edge of the needlepoint and stretcher bars. Mark a line for future reference.

7. Staple all four sides of the needlepoint at the middle of each edge on the bars, using the marks you made in step 6.

8. Staple again, on either side of each of the first four staples:

Staple placement

Continue to staple until you reach all four corners, where you should place the last four staples. Hint: Use the grid of the canvas to help align the project on your boards.

10. When the needlepoint is straight on the bars, tighten the staples using the hammer.

Mitering corners, step 1

11. To miter the corners, first, pull the point towards the center of the needlepoint and staple it. Then pull one side toward the middle and again secure with a staple. Repeat on the other side of corner. Do this on all corners. Trim any bulk. Do not be afraid to trim—your project will not come loose at this point. Bulk only detracts from the final appearance.

Mitering corners, step 2

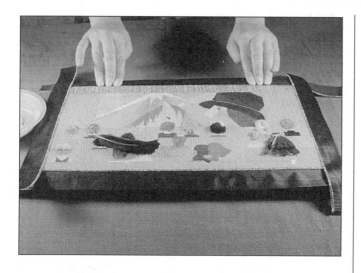

12. You may choose to use a matte board to finish the edges on the picture. In the example, a ribbon is used in place of the matte board. The ribbon is glued to all four edges, except for the corners, which need to be trimmed.

13. Mark the corners with a pencil, making a straight line at each point where the ribbon overlaps.

14. Cut the marked line through both ribbons, to make a neat miter.

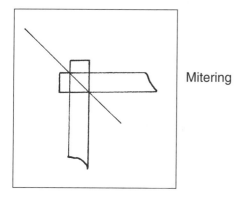

Mitering

15. Glue the corners down. Trim the bulk on each corner.

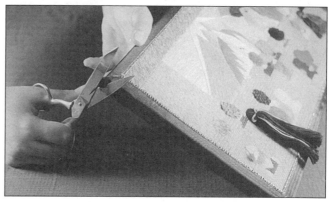

16. Insert the project into the frame and secure with staples.

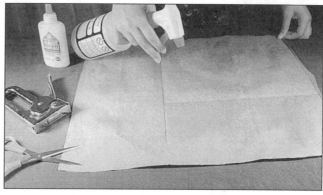

17. Place paper over the back for a neat look. Spritz and iron a paper bag to remove all wrinkles.

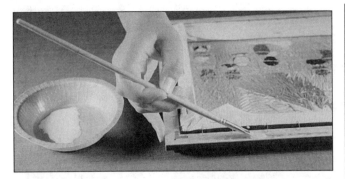

18. Run a line of glue on all four sides of the frame.
19. Place the paper on top and smooth the edges.

20. When dry, use the razor blade and trim the edges close to the frame.

21. Hammer a nail 2/3 up on the right and left on the underside of the frame, and then attach wire.
The picture is now ready for hanging.

Laced Method for Framing

You will need the following tools and materials:
Large Needle
Needlepoint
Paper
Clothespins
Frame
Scissors
Razor Blade
White Fabric
Heavy Thread
Masonite Board
Measure
Pencil
Glue

1. Measure the needlepoint to determine the size of the frame required.
2. Cut Masonite board to fit the frame, making it 1/8 inch smaller on all sides to allow for canvas folds.

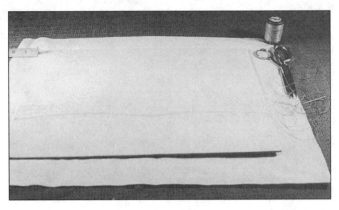

3. With scissors, cut white fabric four inches larger than the board. Place the board on top of the fabric and fold two opposite sides over the edges.

4. With a long piece of thread and a large needle, begin in the middle of one side, making zigzag stitches back and forth along the two sides of fabric.

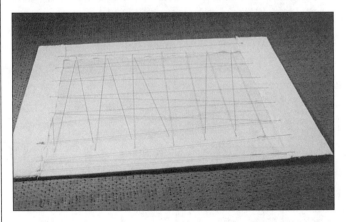

5. Repeat the stitches in the opposite direction.
6. Repeat steps 4 and 5 to finish the other two sides of fabric.

7. Whip stitch the four corners to secure.

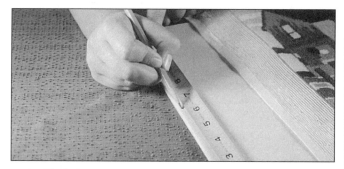

8. Find the middle on each side of the needlepoint and covered board. Mark a line for future reference.

9. Match the lines on the board and needlepoint to align the grid. Secure with clothespins.

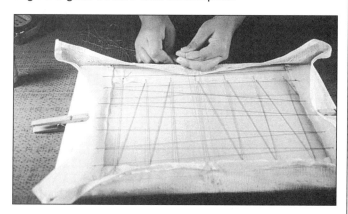

10. On the underside, repeat steps 4 and 5, catching the canvas to secure the needlepoint. To finish the back, follow the instructions for the Stapled Method, steps 16-21.

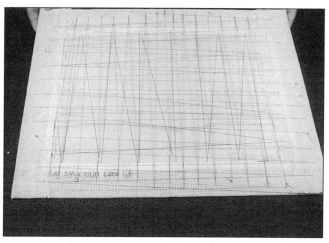

A laced canvas

Laced Method for Round Projects

The lacing method can also be used if the needlepoint and frame are round. The technique is different but with practice, your project will come out smooth and square.

To begin, you need the same tools as used in the lacing method for square projects. Your Masonite board should be 1/8 inch smaller on all sides, the same as before. Cover the board with white fabric. Then, with a small scrap of white fabric, cut a circle smaller than the size of the picture frame. The difference between the size of the circle and the frame depends upon the dimensions of the frame. If the project is very large, the fabric circle should be about two or three inches smaller. A very small project should have a fabric circle one inch smaller than the frame. Using the sewing machine, hem all around the fabric circle.

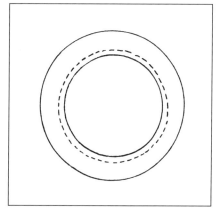

Hemming a circle

Place the needlepoint face down on a table and lay the Masonite board and fabric on top. Pin the north, south, east and west sides of canvas on the fabric circle.

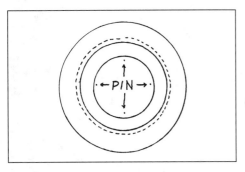

Circle in place

With heavy thread, lace the needlepoint to the fabric, just as in the previous method—only here, you stitch in a circle, rather than a straight line. Tie off the thread. Mount the project into the frame the same as the former procedure.

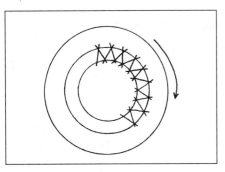

Zigzag into place

If a very small project is to be mounted in a frame two inches or smaller, omit the fabric circle and weave the thread between the Masonite board and canvas.

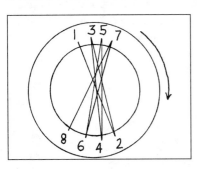

Zigzag for small circles

Mounting Without a Frame

To mount a project without a frame, you will need the following tools and materials:

3/4 inch Plywood
Staples
Staple Gun
Ribbon
Needlepoint
Saw
Measure
Pencil
Drill
Glue
Sandpaper

1. Measure the exact size of the needlepoint.
2. On the plywood, mark pencil lines to indicate the finished size of the needlepoint.
3. With a saw, cut the board along the pencil lines.
4. Sand any rough edges on the board.
5. Mark the center of the needlepoint on all sides. Do the same with the board, but make the pencil line on the edge of the board.

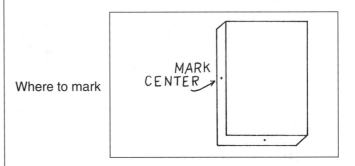

Where to mark

6. Align the marks on the needlepoint to the marks on the edge of the board.
7. At the center of each side, staple the needlepoint to the board. Make these first four staples in the center of each side.

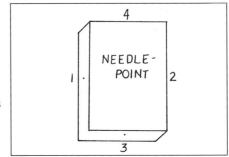

First four staples

8. Make the next set of staples next to the first four. Notice the diagram for proper placement.

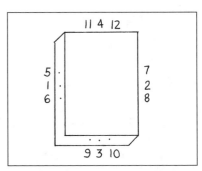

Second set of staples

9. Continue stapling until you reach the corners.

10. To reduce bulk, cut off the extra canvas at each corner.

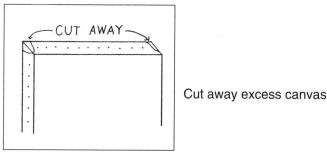

Cut away excess canvas

11. With glue, hide the edges of the board with ribbon. The "seam" will be on the bottom of the picture, where it will not be seen.

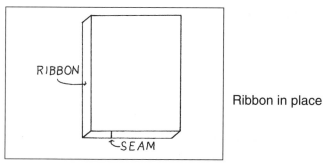

Ribbon in place

12. When the ribbon reaches around the board, cut it so that the ends touch each other. Do not overlap or tuck under.

13. With a small drill, make a hole in the upper half on the back of the board.

Your picture is now ready to hang.

Upholstered Seats

A drop-in seat is among the simplest upholstered pieces you can make. With a few basic instructions, anybody can master this project.

There are, of course, a few rules to remember. Because the needlepoint area will serve as a seat, you must choose stitches that hold up to a great deal of wear. Some examples of hard-wearing stitches are Basketweave, Chottie's Plaid and Florentine. For a further list, look at the Stitch Durability chart, page 145. Also, think ahead and plan your motif, so that it lies correctly on the seat of the chair. Check to make sure patterns run in the direction you want them to run. Sea Shell motifs are not comfortable to sit on, while rose petals invite you to settle down for hours.

Be generous with the blank canvas that you need for blocking and finishing. It is frustrating to work with one inch of canvas in blocking a large piece. If your chair seat is a rectangle, work the project and block as a square, and trim and fit the project later. If you are working your own pattern and not a pre-worked center, start in the middle of the motif and work your way out, to ensure that your motif is centered.

You do not want a bulky back. Make sure the yarn tails are anchored flat without bumps, or the finished seat will have lumps on the top where the stitches are thicker on the reverse side. A flat underside makes the needlepoint wear evenly with use. Remember that needlepoint is a thick upholstery fabric. Before attaching the seat to the frame, check to see whether the frame needs to be shaved down to accommodate the extra fibers.

Chapter Five

Projects to Stitch

Belts

With a project such as this, your possibilities are endless. They can be as unique as you and your family and friends. For fastening the ends, you can use double rings, eyelet and ribbon, buttons or pre-fabricated buckles. Buckles are available at fabric, yarn and notion stores. Shop around and see what is on the market. You may find a buckle with two hooks, which you can use interchangeably with many belts. Depending upon your waist and preference, make belts of very wide or narrow widths. You can create an entire wardrobe of colors, patterns and motifs.

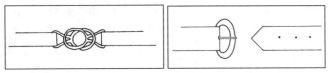

Purchased buckle   Buckle and eyelets

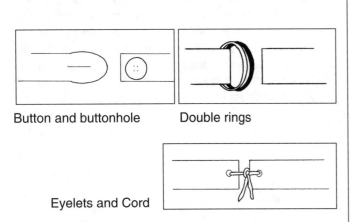

Button and buttonhole   Double rings

Eyelets and Cord

To create this project, you will need the following tools and materials:

5 skeins #444 Paternayan Persian yarn
(more may be required)
2 Rainbow Gallery plastic canvas metallic needlepoint yarn, gold
14/1 Interlock canvas
(size will depend upon the waist size)
#20 Tapestry needle
Sewing thread
Sewing needle
Hammer
Thin fabric or bias tape to match the project
Buckle and eyelets
Masking tape
Marking pen

1. Measure your waist to determine the length required for your canvas. If using a belt buckle and eyelets, allow extra length so that the belt can overlap. Also remember to add two inches on all four sides for blocking.

2. Bind all four sides of the canvas with masking tape.

3. Mark the canvas to indicate the exact size of the belt.

4. Stitch the entire belt in Eugene using two-ply Persian and one-ply metallic thread.

5. Block the needlepoint.

6. Cut the canvas half an inch from the stitches.

NEEDLEPOINT

7. Turn the raw edge over and hammer to flatten. Miter the corners.

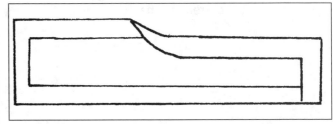

8. Using Herringbone stitches, baste the raw canvas onto the underside of the needlepoint. On all corners, whip stitch the mitered areas.

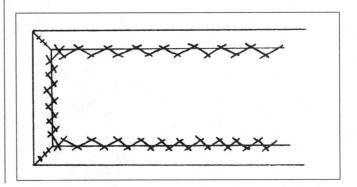

9. Whip stitch lining material or wide bias tape onto the back of the belt.

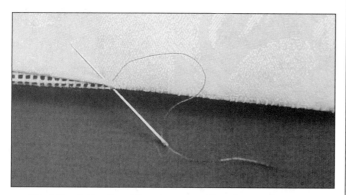

10. Attach the buckle, rings or other fasteners.

Upholster a Chair Seat

To create this project, you will need the following tools and materials:

Measuring tape
Staple gun
Staples
Scissors
Pencil
Hammer
Screw driver
Chair
Needlepoint

1. Measure the chair seat before stitching the needlepoint. Add 1" on all sides for turning under the seat. Allow 2" of bare canvas on all sides of the stitched motif.

2. Stitch the needlepoint to the size of the chair's upholstery plus one extra inch of area.

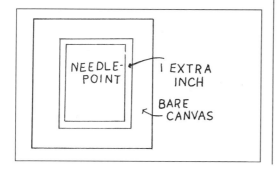

3. Block the project.

4. Remove the seat from the chair. If the upholstery fabric is bulky, remove it. If not, you can leave it.

5. Find the middle of each side of the needlepoint and the seat. Mark lines at these points.

6. Staple all four sides of the needlepoint to the middle of each side on the seat, using the marks from step 5.

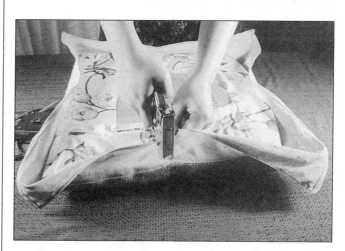

7. Insert staples on either side of each of the staples you have just placed. Be careful not to make ridges in the cushion. Take your time. If you must, remove the project and staple again to correct any errors.

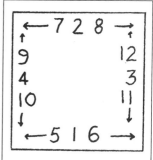

8. Hammer the staples down into the seat board.

9. Cut away the bulk at the four corners. Do not be afraid to cut. The needlepoint is securely attached to the chair seat.

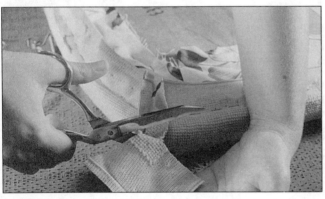

10. Staple the tip of the corner.

11. Secure one entire side of the corner, and then finish with the other side.

12. Attach the seat to the chair frame.

Mouse Pad

To complete this project, you will need the following tools and materials:
  13" by 12" 14/1 Interlock canvas
  J. L. Walsh silk #223 12 strands (blues and purples)
  J. L. Walsh silk #212 12 strands (blues and purples)
  J. L. Walsh silk/wool 12 strands (blues and purples)
  Fraze metal yarn
  Clear drying, flexible glue
  Scissors
  12" by 13" stretcher bars
  Thumbtacks
  Pencil
  Masking tape
  Fabric paint (if desired)

1. Measure the required amount of canvas by laying the mouse pad on the canvas.

2. Allowing two extra inches on all sides, cut the Interlock canvas.

3. Bind the raw edges with masking tape.

4. Attach the canvas to the stretcher bars using thumbtacks.

5. Lay the mouse pad on top of the canvas. Use a pencil to mark an outline around the pad.

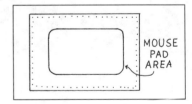

6. Compare the mouse pad and canvas and determine where any lettering and/or picture needs to be hidden on the pad.

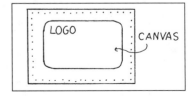

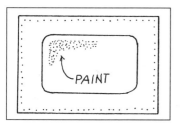

7. If you wish, paint the canvas before stitching.

8. When the paint is dry, stitch flowers using Detached Chain, Bullion Knot, French Knot, Leaf and other stitches to the areas you would like covered on the mouse pad. Cut Fraze into short bits and use as you would beads. Be sure you cover the areas of the mouse pad that need to be hidden.

9. Apply a generous layer of clear drying, flexible glue to the entire top of the mouse pad.

10. Using the pencil lines for reference, lay the needlepoint on top of the pad.

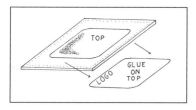

11. Let the project dry. It is best to lay the project face down, with books on top. To keep the stitches from flattening, prop the edges of the stretcher bars on a baking dish or a similar item.

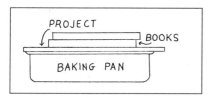

12. After the glue has set, remove the project from the stretcher bars. Trim the canvas close to the edge of the mouse pad.

13. Glue braiding on the sides to hide the raw edge of the pad. If you like, attach a tassel.

CD Player Pocket

For this project, you will need the following tools and materials:
12" by 12" Interlock canvas
5" by 6" Interlock canvas
4 #462 Golden Beige Paternayan Persian yarn
2 #492 Light Beige Paterayan Persian yarn
9 #R50 Red Paternayan Persian yarn
24 #050 Black Paternayan Persian yarn
1 #002HL Gold Kreinik Metallics #16 braid
1 Skein #869 Hazelnut Brown DMC embroidery floss
1 Skein Black DMC embroidery floss
1 Skein #326 Very Dark Rose DMC #5 Pearl
1 Skein #5270 Red Metal DMC floss
1 Skein #5282 Gold Metal DMC floss
230 Black seed beads
3" by 2" red felt
Gold glitter fabric paint
Red fabric paint
Black sewing thread
Paper scissors
Newspaper
#20 Tapestry needle
Beading needle
12" by 12" stretcher bars
1/2 yard fabric
1/4 yard lining
Scissors
Red sewing thread
3/4" square hook-and-loop fastener (such as Velcro®)
Hammer
Paintbrush

1. Using the diagram, mark your canvas as indicated.

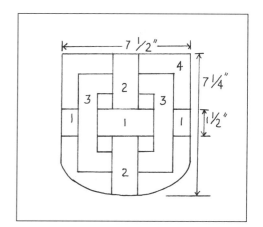

2. If you use stretcher bars, place the larger canvas on wooden bars.

3. Paint gold glitter paint in the areas where Web and Jus will be stitched. Red paint will be placed in the space for Emily.

4. Number one on the diagram indicates where Jus is inserted. Use one-ply Golden Beige #462 for the foundation. Two-ply DMC metal is used for Slashed Cross and three-ply DMC #869 embroidery floss is used for the Gobelin.

5. Number 2 on the diagram indicates Web stitches. Here, use two-ply Persian #492 for the long stitches and one-ply Kreinik #16 braid for the couching.

6. Number 3 on the diagram represents Emily. One-ply Persian #R50 is used for the foundation. Three-ply DMC Red Metal #5270 is used for the crosses. Stitch seed beads where the graph indicates French Knots.

7. Continental number 4, is stitched in all the black areas.

8. Make two rows of Tent stitches along the sides and bottom of the front using two-ply Red Persian yarn. Do not stitch along the top.

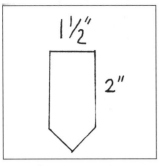

9. On the smaller canvas, mark the dimensions of your tab. Mount.

10. Web stitch is sewn onto the canvas, as it was in step 5.

11. Block canvases, if necessary.

12. Cut out the front, leaving a generous amount of canvas around the pocket. The extra canvas will be trimmed later.

13. Cut the lining fabric to the exact size of the needlepoint plus 5/8" seam allowance.

14. Cut the backing fabric into a rectangle the size of your needlepoint canvas.

15. Make the tassel. Wrap Red Pearl cotton around a 2-1/2" long piece of cardboard 20 times. Tie one end and cut the other. Wrap Black embroidery floss around the fringe three times, then Kreinik #16 braid five times. Repeat with Black embroidery floss and tie off.

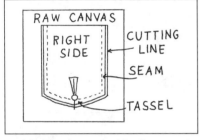

16. Pin the tassel in the exact center on the bottom of the front. Remember to pin the tassel up toward the stitching (see diagram).

17. Pin the needlepoint and the fabric, right sides together, with the needlepoint side up. With a sewing machine, make one continuous stitch along the sides and bottom, between the motif and Tent stitches. Do not use a serger for this seam.

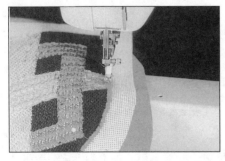

18. If necessary, stitch over the same line for reinforcement.

19. Trim the excess seam allowance to 3/8".

20. Clip the curves at a 90-degree angle from the sewing machine stitches.

21. Turn the project inside out, so that the right sides of the needlepoint and fabric are facing out.

22. Use a clean hammer to pound the seam flat. Do not iron the needlepoint for this step, or you will flatten the stitches and not the seam.

23. Turn the top down and hammer, as in step 21.

24. Trim away the bulk from the top of the pocket seam allowance.

25. Turn down the entire top of the pocket. Pin the back side in place. For the front, pin and hand stitch the top seam allowance to the back of the stitching.

26. Cut a 60 by 1-1/2" strip of fabric for the strap.

27. Making two 1/4" turns down the long sides, stitch the edges of the handle.

CD pocket

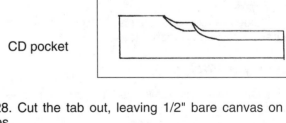

28. Cut the tab out, leaving 1/2" bare canvas on all sides.

29. Turn the bare canvas under the stitching on the sides and pointed end, and pound flat with a hammer. Do not turn the short, straight end.

30. Clip as needed and pin the bare canvas in place. Stitch Herringbone stitches to secure.

31. Cut red felt the exact size of the needlepoint. Pin the felt in place and stitch it onto the tab.

32. Stitch the fuzzy half of Velcro® square on the tab.

33. Pin the handle and flap on the back of the pocket at A and B (see diagram).

34. Machine stitch along the top back, making sure the handles and flap are secured.

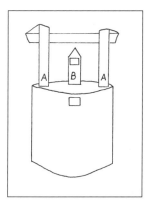

35. Machine stitch the hook side of the Velcro® to the top of the needlepoint.

36. Stitch the lining sides and bottom together. Clip as in step 12.

37. Place the lining inside the bag, making sure the wrong sides are together. Pin in place.

38. With needle and thread to match, stitch-in-the-ditch to attach the lining and needlepoint along the bottom and side seams.

39. Stitch the top of the bag to the lining.

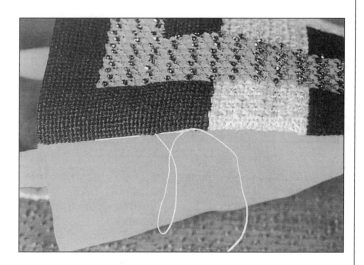

Switch Plate

This is a "just for fun" project that allows you to use your imagination and throw caution—and proper stitching techniques—to the wind. Choose a pattern of stitching that has very little yarn on the underside of the canvas, so that it lies flat. Stitches such as Half Cross, Tent, Chottie's Plaid and Reversible Alternating Tent are good choices. Avoid stitches that pile up, such as Zed, Pisces, Detached Chain and Cut Turkey. Couching should only be included with very thin yarns. On the underside, keep all yarn tails to a minimum. Chottie's Plaid was a good choice for the example. Tails were left untied in the margin.

When the project was finished, the tails were glued to the reverse side. As an alternative, you may want to glue the sides, and then cut the yarn tails without tying them. To allow the pattern to repeat itself more over the small area, 18/1 canvas was used. Because the project does not have finished edges, Interlock was used. Interlock canvas does not fray, as Mono does. Not rolling the raw canvas prevents bulk at the edges. Because this is a quick, fun project, I did not take all the necessary steps for creating heirloom-quality embroidery.

To complete the project, you will need the following tools and materials:
8" by 7" 18/1 Interlock canvas
1 Skein #369 Pistachio Green DMC embroidery floss
1 Skein #704 Chartreuse DMC embroidery floss
1 Skein #701 Christmas Green DMC embroidery floss
1 Skein #554 Light Violet DMC embroidery floss
1 Skein #552 Dark Violet DMC embroidery floss
Glue
Switch plate kit
#24 Tapestry needle
8" by 7" stretcher bars
Scissors
Thumbtacks
Masking tape
Screwdriver

1. Bind the raw edges of the canvas with masking tape.

2. Attach the canvas to stretcher bars using thumbtacks.

3. On the mounted canvas, draw a pattern using the switch plate as a template.

4. Use six plies in your needle. To make the Chottie's Plaid in the sample, stitch a row of 1 Christmas Green, 2 Chartreuse, 1 Pistachio, 1 Dark Violet, 1 Light Violet. Do not go over the lines, and do not stitch where the switch pokes through the plate. Do not worry about the screw holes.

5. If the canvas distorts, block it.

6. When the project is dry, remove it from the board. Turn the canvas face down on the mounting board and pin in place.

7. Apply a thin layer of flexible glue on the entire back of the needlepoint. Let dry.

8. Cut out the needlepoint along the exact line of your template.

9. Sandwich the needlepoint and plastic plate together. Mark where the screw holes should be made. Remove the canvas from the plate and cut holes where they are needed.

10. Sandwich the plastic plate and needlepoint again. Screw the plate on the wall.

Tapestry

To complete this project, you will need the following tools and materials:

14 Skeins #730 Nature Spun 100% wool knitting yarn

8 Ecru DMC #3 Pearl

3 Ecru DMC #5 Pearl

1 Ecru DMC #8 Pearl

4 #5283 DMC Silver Metal floss

1 #158 Baroque crochet cotton

4 Rainbow Gallery plastic canvas #10 metallic needlepoint yarn

3 Ecru DMC embroidery floss

1 Skein Ecru rug yarn or other heavy yarn

1 Skein Ecru rayon floss

3 feet by 6 feet 5/1 Penelope canvas

Masking tape

Large frame

#13 Tapestry needle

#18 Tapestry needle

#22 Tapestry needle

Sewing needle

White sewing thread

About 16 small pearls

4 Shi Sha mirrors

Found objects (brooches, earrings, buttons, charms, etc.)

Masking tape

Light (not black) marking pen

Hammer

Beeswax

White bias tape

1. With masking tape, bind the two cut ends of the canvas. The selvages need no binding.

2. Attach the canvas to the large frame.

3. Using a marking pen, draw long lines horizontal and perpendicular on the canvas. Each square should be 5" by 5", or 25 threads by 25 threads.

4. Follow the diagram and stitch list to apply the stitches to the canvas. Do not stitch Surrey or Binding at the sides and ends. These will be stitched later.

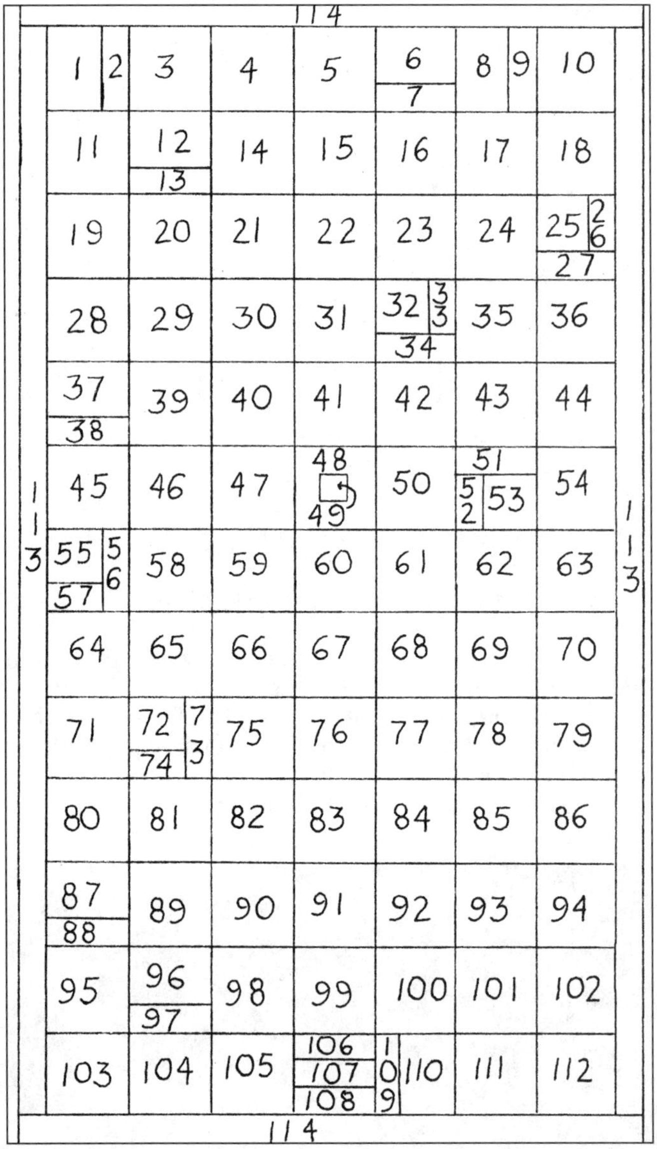

Diagram (grid labeled 114 top and bottom, 113 on left and right):

1 2	3	4	5	6 / 7	8 9	10
11	12 / 13	14	15	16	17	18
19	20	21	22	23	24	25 2 6 / 27
28	29	30	31	32 3 3 / 34	35	36
37 / 38	39	40	41	42	43	44
45	46	47	48 / 49	50	51 52 53	54
55 5 / 57 6	58	59	60	61	62	63
64	65	66	67	68	69	70
71	72 7 / 74 3	75	76	77	78	79
80	81	82	83	84	85	86
87 / 88	89	90	91	92	93	94
95	96 / 97	98	99	100	101	102
103	104	105	106 / 107 / 108 109	110	111	112

5. When finished stitching, remove the canvas from the frame.

6. On a flat surface, pound the bare canvas to the underside of the stitches with a hammer.

7. On both selvage edges, stitch Binding the entire length of the tapestry.

8. Pin the long selvage edges to the underside of the canvas, being sure no bare threads are exposed on the right side.

9. With a sewing thread and needle, Herringbone stitch the raw canvas to the back. Reinforce your thread with beeswax.

10. Stitch bias tape on the edges of the unfinished ends.

11. Pin the raw canvas to the backside of the tapestry. Be sure to expose one row of unworked thread on each end. Stitch Herringbone to attach the canvas.

12. Stitch Surrey along the entire two ends. Trim as needed.

Stitch List:

To stitch the following, note the numbers in parentheses, which indicate the total threads required to work the stitch. The first number refers to the horizontal stitches and the second number is for the vertical threads.

1. John: three-ply wool, one-ply DMC metal (22 by 25)
2. Plait: three-ply wool (3 by 25)
3. Large Moorish: three-ply wool, one-ply #5 Pearl (25 by 25)
4. Knotted III: three-ply wool, wooden bird sewn on (25 by 25)
5. Milanese: three-ply wool (25 by 25)
6. Oblong with Back: two-ply wool, one-ply Rainbow metal (25 by 20)
7. Darning (3-2 weaving): one-ply wool (25 by 5)
8. Diaper: three-ply wool (24 by 25)
9. Couching: three-ply wool, one-ply #8 Pearl (1 by 25)
10. Woven Flat (over 5 canvas threads): three-ply wool, two-ply DMC metal (25 by 25)
11. Reversed Eyelet: three-ply wool, two-ply Rainbow metal, one-ply #3 Pearl (25 by 25)
12. Eastern: Two-ply wool (25 by 22)
13. Sprat's Head with Couching: three-ply wool, one-ply wool with one-ply DMC metal (25 by 3)
14. Aubusson: four-ply wool for upright, three-ply wool for Continental (25 by 25)
15. Tied Cashmere: three-ply wool, one-ply #5 Pearl (25 by 25)
16. Framed Diagonal Scotch: three-ply wool, two-ply DMC metal with one-ply rayon floss (25 by 25)
17. Encroached Gobelin: three-ply wool, Buttons sewn on (25 by 25)
18. Diagonal Ray: three-ply wool (25 by 25)
19. Sturgeon Trail: three-ply wool (25 by 25)
20. Wicker: four-ply wool, brooch sewn on (25 by 25)
21. Kip: three-ply wool, two-ply Rainbow metal (25 by 25)
22. Stem: three-ply wool (25 by 25)
23. Staggered Cross: three-ply wool, three-ply #5 Pearl (25 by 25)
24. Mettler Variation: three-ply wool, two-ply DMC metal with one-ply rayon floss (25 by 25)
25. Alternating Scotch Variation: three-ply wool, three-ply #3 Pearl (21 by 24)
26. Herringbone Couching: four-ply wool, two-ply crochet cotton (4 by 25)
27. Bokhara Couching: one-ply rug yarn, one-ply DMC metal (21 by 1)
28. Hungarian Brick: four-ply wool (25 by 25)
29. Ashley: three-ply wool, two-ply crochet with one-ply DMC metal (25 by 25)
30. Framed Scotch: three-ply wool (25 by 25)
31. Criss Cross Hungarian: three-ply wool, two-ply #5 Pearl with one-ply DMC metal (25 by 25)

32. Algerian Eye Variation: three-ply wool, three-ply #3 Pearl (24 by 24)
33. French Knots: four-ply crochet cotton (1 by 24)
34. Bullion Knots: one-ply wool (25 by 1)
35. Continental With Shell III and Buttonhole Flowers: three-ply wool for Continental; for shell, two-ply #5 Pearl and six-ply embroidery floss; for Buttonhole Flowers, one-ply #5 Pearl (25 X 25)
36. Jus: three-ply wool, two-ply Rainbow metal (25 by 25)
37. Double Fishbone: three-ply wool, four-ply crochet cotton (25 by 24)
38. Rep: two-ply wool (25 by 1)
39. Horizontal Hungarian: four-ply wool (25 by 25)
40. Large Knitting: three-ply wool, antique brooch sewn on (25 by 25)
41. Cross: three-ply wool (25 by 25)
42. Horizontal Elongated Cashmere: three-ply wool (25 by 25)
43. Carl: four-ply wool, one-ply Rainbow metal (25 by 25)
44. Chop Sticks: three-ply wool (25 by 25)
45. Suzie's Garden: three-ply wool, four-ply #3 Pearl, two-ply Rainbow metal (25 by 25)
46. Narrow Oblong Cross: four-ply crochet cotton with two-ply DMC metal (25 by 25)
47. Ridges: three-ply wool (25 by 25)
48. Long Armed Cross: three-ply wool (over two threads in each direction)
49. Moon: three-ply wool, 36-ply embroidery floss in middle (21 by 21)
50. Paul and Lin Variation: three-ply wool, three-ply #3 Pearl (25 by 25)
51. Tuft: five-ply wool (25 by 1)
52. Ley's Trail: two-ply wool, one-ply #3 Pearl (1 by 24)
53. Starry Crosses: three-ply wool for crosses, four-ply crochet for eyelets (24 by 24)
54. Large Brick: three-ply wool (25 by 25)
55. Four-way Mosaic: three-ply wool (24 by 24)
56. Chain: one-ply wool (1 by 25)
57. Chain Couching: one-ply rug with two-ply DMC metal, two-ply rayon for couching (24 by 1)
58. Raymond: three-ply wool (25 by 25)
59. Jacquard: three-ply wool (25 by 25)
60. Knotted II: three-ply wool (25 by 25)
61. Janina: three-ply wool (25 by 25)
62. Large Checker (flat over 5 threads): three-ply wool (25 by 25)
63. Emily: three-ply wool, three-ply #3 Pearl, two-ply DMC metal with one-ply rug (25 by 25)
64. Mixed Milanese: three-ply wool (25 by 25)
65. Reverse Tent I: three-ply wool, brooch sewn on (25 by 25)
66. Parisian Cross: three-ply wool (25 by 25)
67. Two Sided Cross: three-ply wool, two-ply Rainbow metal (25 by 25)

68. Slanted Gobelin IV with Back: three-ply wool (25 by 25)

69. Fill In: three-ply wool, buttons sewn on (25 by 25)

70. Oriental III: three-ply wool, six-ply crochet cotton (25 by 25)

71. Small Checker: three-ply wool (25 by 25)

72. Norwich: three-ply wool (22 by 22)

73. Astrakhan Velvet (Over one Penelope thread): three-ply wool (3 by 25)

74. Running Cross: two-ply wool (22 by 3)

75. Slashed Oblong: three-ply wool (25 by 25)

76. Two Tone Sunburst with Continental Gone Wrong: four-ply wool with #3 Pearl for Sunburst, two-ply rug for French Knot, three-ply wool for Continental (25 by 25)

77. Saint George and Saint Andrew: three-ply wool (25 by 25)

78. Weaving: four-ply wool, one-ply wool (25 by 25)

79. Dana: three-ply wool, one-ply Rainbow metal (25 by 25)

80. Brighton: three-ply wool, two-ply cotton crochet with six-ply DMC metal (25 by 25)

81. Raymond Variation I: three-ply wool, one-ply Rainbow metal (25 by 25)

82. Rococo: two-ply wool (25 by 25)

83. Web: three-ply wool (25 by 25)

84. Frosty: three-ply wool for the foundation; one-ply wool for Cross with French Knot, Smyrna and Woven Cross I; two-ply wool for Cut Turkey, Petit Point, Reinforced Cross and Rep; three-ply for Alternating Tent, Breton, Back side of Basketweave, Closed Cat, Continental, Continental Gone Wrong, Cross, Dotted Scotch, Encroached Slanted Gobelin, Eyelet, French Knots, Horizontal Kalem, Large Eyelet, Medium Rice, Oblong Cross, Oblong with Back, Pyramid, Padded Upright Gobelin (over 1 thread), Raised Work, Ray, Reverse Tent I, Running Cross, Scotch, Slashed Oblong, Small Cross, Surrey and Woven Scotch; six-ply for Gobelin Droit (25 by 25)

85. Eugene: three-ply wool, two-ply Rainbow metal (25 by 25)

86. Indian Stripe: three-ply wool, buttons sewn on (25 by 25)

87. Oblique Slav: two-ply wool (25 by 24)

88. Round Braid: two-ply wool (25 by 1)

89. Doublet: three-ply wool, three-ply #3 Pearl, six-ply DMC metal (25 by 25)

90. Medium Rice Checker: three-ply wool (25 by 25)

91. Underside of Basketweave with Shi Sha: three-ply wool, two-ply #3 Pearl (25 by 25)

92. Boxed Step: three-ply wool (25 by 25)

93. Fishbone I: three-ply wool (25 by 25)

94. Rotating Flat: three-ply wool (you may want thicker) (25 by 25)

95. Edge: three-ply wool, two-ply #5 Pearl, one-ply Rainbow metal (25 by 25)

96. Half Eyelet: two-ply wool (25 by 24)

97. Feather Half Cross: two-ply wool (25 by 1)

98. Heavy Cross: three-ply wool (25 by 25)

99. Herringbone Done Diagonal: three-ply wool (25 by 25)

100. Knit One Pearl One: three-ply wool, one-ply wool (25 by 25)

101. Belly Feathers: three-ply wool, three-ply #3 Pearl, two-ply Rainbow metal (25 by 25)

102. Plait Gobelin: three-ply wool (25 by 25)

103. Half Framed Scotch (over 5 threads): three-ply wool, two-ply crochet cotton (25 by 25)

104. Fancy Cross: three-ply wool, one-ply Rainbow, two-ply #7 Pearl (25 by 25)

105. Staircase: three-ply wool, brooch sewn on (25 by 25)

106. Cashmere Checker: three-ply wool (25 by 3)

107. Staggering Crosses: three-ply wool (25 by 21)

108. Woven Cross I: one-ply wool (25 by 1)

109. Reinforced Cross: one-ply wool (1 by 25)

110. Ben: two-ply wool, one-ply wool (24 by 25)

111. Framed Scotch Variation: three-ply wool, small pearls sewn on (25 by 25)

112. Oatmeal: three-ply wool (25 by 25)

113. Binding: three-ply wool (1 by 325)

114. Surrey: three-ply wool (177 by 1)

Tote Bag

To stitch the tote bag, you will need the following items:
2 Skeins of three-ounce acrylic knitting yarn
4 Sheets 7/1 plastic canvas, 10-1/2" by 13-1/2" (71 by 91 threads)
#18 Tapestry needle
Paper scissors
1/2 yard lining fabric
Sewing thread
Sewing needle

Use one-ply knitting yarn for all the stitches listed in the instructions. The four sides, two handles and bottom all have one bare canvas thread on all four sides, so that the sides can be joined after they have been stitched.

1. With paper scissors, cut two pieces from a sheet of canvas to measure 71 by 26 threads. These are the smaller sides.

2. For the handles, cut from another sheet two pieces, each measuring 8 by 87 threads.

3. The bottom of the tote is 91 by 26 threads. Cut the bottom from the same sheet of canvas used in step 2. This should leave you with two remaining uncut canvases.

4. Find the exact middle of a large canvas sheet.

5. Following the graph and list of stitches, apply the stitches to the canvas.

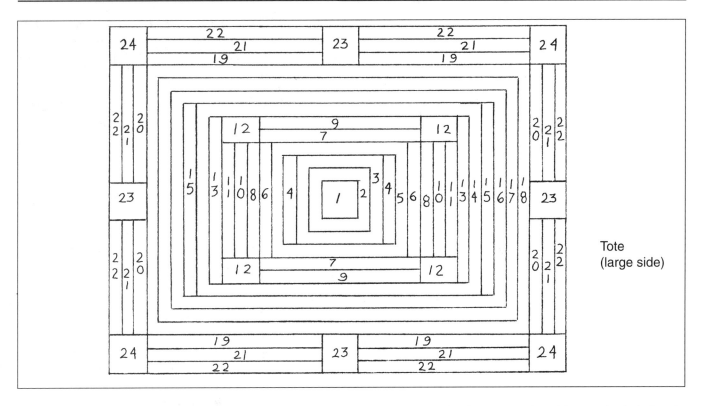

Tote
(large side)

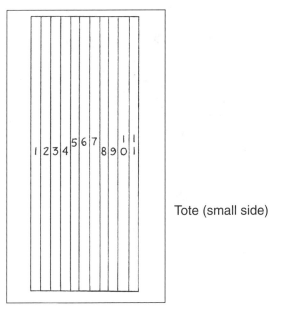

Tote (small side)

6. Repeat steps 4-6 on the other large canvas.

7. Follow the list and graph for the two smaller sides.

8. Stitch Medium Checker on the two long, narrow canvases.

9. Apply Continental stitch to the bottom.

10. Match a smaller side to a larger side, wrong sides of the canvas together.

11. Stitch Binding, beginning at the top and running the entire length of the corner.

12. Repeat this Binding stitch with the other three corners. Remember to alternate the large and small sides.

13. Match the bottom to the sides and stitch (again with Binding) around all four sides.

14. Bind stitch the sides of the handles.

15. Begin at the top corner of the tote bag with the Binding stitch. Work all the way around the top, matching and stitching the handles as you go.

16. Cut two pieces of fabric, one 14-3/4" by 11-3/4" and one 5-1/8" by 11-3/4".

17. Cut one piece of fabric, 5-1/8" by 14-3/4".

18. With right sides together, pin the fabric so that the 11-3/4" sides meet. Alternate the larger and smaller pieces of fabric as you pin.

19. Stitch the seams together, making a 5/8" seam allowance.

20. Pin the bottom of the lining to the sides, matching right sides of the fabric.

21. Stitch together.

22. Insert the lining into the tote bag and turn the excess fabric on the top edge under to match the Binding stitch. Whip stitch the circumference.

Stitch List:

Follow these directions to create the stitches as used in the project. On some stitches, note the numbers in parentheses. These numbers indicate the threads on the canvas required to work the stitch. The first number indicates the horizontal, while the second refers to the vertical threads.

Larger sides:

1. Continental with Bullion Knots: Continental (13 by 13), Bullion Knots worked in a circle

2. One Scotch, two Cashmere, one Pyramid (6 by 4), two Cashmere: Repeat to make a square.

3. Knotted II: 22 threads. Turn the canvas to its side and make another 22 Knotted II. Repeat to make a square.

4. Alternating Tent: 25 threads.

5. Two Color Herringbone: Cross 27 threads horizontally, and 31 threads vertically.

6. Continental Gone Wrong: 31 threads.

7. Two rows of Stem with Back: 35 threads (Note: Back stitch covers two threads, except in the middle, which covers three).

8. Two rows of Stem: 31 threads (Note: Back stitch covers two threads except in the middle, which covers three).

9. Chain: 35 threads.

10. Chain: 31 threads.

11. Woven Cross I: 31 threads (Note: The middle cross covers three threads).

12. Continental: (7 by 5).

13. Gobelin Droit with Chain Couching: Gobelin Droit covers four threads. Chain catches two Gobelins. One-ply yarn is inserted under the second and third holes in the canvas and is run under Gobelin Droit.

14. Two rows of Knitting I (59 by 43): Work the bottom row starting two threads past the Gobelin Droit. When you finish the end of the row, begin the right vertical row two threads over.

15. Cross II: Stitch eleven crosses; middle cross traverses three canvas threads.

16. French Knots (67 by 47)

17. Scotch with Continental: The horizontal row consists of eleven Scotch, Continental (7 by 3) and another eleven Scotch. The vertical row requires eight Scotch, Continental (3 by 5) and 8 Scotch.

18. Cross I: Stitch 75 horizontally and 55 vertically.

19. Reverse Eyelet (found at the bottom and top horizontal rows): Work the lower row in the graph. Do not work the bold stitches or the French Knots. Bottom horizontal 1 (1/4 eyelet), 4 (1/2 eyelet), 1 (1/4 eyelet), 7 bare threads, 1 (1/4 eyelet), 4 (1/2 eyelet), 1 (1/4 eyelet).

20. Reverse Eyelet (right and left perpendicular): 1 (1/4 eyelet), 3 (1/2 eyelet), space, 3 (1/2 eyelet), 1 (1/4 eyelet), 7 bare threads, 1 (1/4 eyelet), 3 (1/2 eyelet), space, 3 (1/2 eyelet), 1 (1/4 eyelet).

21. Long Armed Cross: Stitch horizontally across 34 threads, then leave seven bare threads, then stitch another 34 threads; vertically, stitch across 24 threads, leave seven bare, and stitch another 24 threads.

22. Saint George and Saint Andrew: Stitch horizontally across 34 threads, leave seven bare, and stitch another 34 threads; vertically, stitch across 24, leave seven bare, and then cross another 24 threads.

23. Houser with Continental: Continental (7 by 7)

24. Shi Sha Buttonhole Method with Continental: Stitch with embroidery floss. Continental (7x7). Stitch with acrylic.

Smaller sides:

1. Gobelin Droit with Chain Couching: Gobelin Droit covers four threads. Chain catches two Gobelins. Insert one-ply yarn under the second and third holes in the canvas and run the yarn under the Gobelin Droit.

2. Chain: One thread

3. Knotted II: Three threads

4. Cross I: One thread

5. Stem with Back: Four threads

6. Alternating Tent: Two threads

7. Triple Cross III: Four threads

8. French Knots: One thread

9. Knitting II: Two threads

10. Closed Cat: Two threads

11. Continental: One thread

Gold and White Pillow

To create this project, you will need the following tools and materials:

35 Strands #01 Paternayan Persian yarn
2 Skeins Ecru DMC embroidery floss
2 Skeins Ecru DMC #5 Pearl cotton
1 Skein #5283 DMC Silver Metal floss
1 Skein Japanese Metal #7
20 Clear seed beads
36 Pearl beads
10" by 10" 14/1 Interlock canvas
10" by 10" Stretcher bars
20 Tapestry needle
White sewing thread
Sewing needle
1/4 yard Velour fabric
Matching thread
Masking tape
Thumbtacks
Polyester fiber

1. Bind the edges of your canvas with masking tape.

2. Attach the canvas to the stretcher bars with thumbtacks.

3. Following the list of stitches and graph, apply the stitches to the canvas.

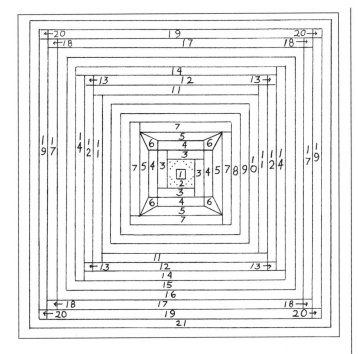

4. Remove from the stretcher bars and block if necessary.

5. Cut four trapezoids from the Velour fabric. The top measurement is 12-1/8" and the bottom is 6-3/8". Use a 5/8" seam allowance.

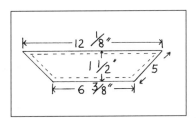

6. Cut a square measuring 12-1/8" by 12-1/8".

7. Matching right sides together, pin the small side of the trapezoid fabric to one edge of your needlepoint.

8. Stitch together with a machine, sewing a line between the zigzag and the Continental stitches.

9. Repeat step 8 on the remaining three edges of the needlepoint.

10. Match and miter the corners of the fabric and pin together. Hand stitch the corners with sewing thread.

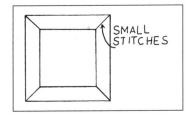

11. Match the square velour and needlepoint, right sides together. Pin and sew, leaving a slit.

12. Turn the pillow right side out.

13. Stuff with polyester filling and slip stitch the opening together.

14. Make and attach tassels.

Stitch List:

1. Pyramid: (6 by 6) Two-ply Persian.
2. Continental: Three rows in each direction, two-ply Persian.
3. Knitting III: Fourteen threads, rotate and repeat, DMC #5 Pearl.
4. Mosaic with Slashes: Eight Mosaics, skip the corner and repeat, two-ply Persian, Slashes require two-ply DMC Metal.
5. Darning Variation: One-ply Persian, crossing three threads.
6. Diagonal Leaf: Four-ply rayon.
7. Van Dyke: Cross 26 threads, turn and repeat, in two-ply Persian.
8. Alternating Tent with Couching: Two rows of Tent in one-ply #5 Pearl; for the Couching, one-ply Japanese #7.
9. Slashed Gobelin III: 36 threads, six-ply embroidery floss.
10. Cross II with Upright: Cross 42 threads, in two-ply Persian.
11. Closed Cat: Cross 46 threads, in one-ply Persian.
12. Gobelin Droit with Herringbone Couching: Cross 52 threads; Gobelin Droit requires two-ply Persian, Couching requires one-ply DMC metal.
13. Diagonal Butterfly: One-ply #5 Pearl.
14. Double Knot: Crosses 56 threads (with approximately 13 knots), using two-ply Persian.
15. Back: Two rows; first row crosses one thread, and all others cross four; in the second row all stitches cross four threads; two-ply Persian.
16. Cross II: Covers 64 threads, six-ply embroidery floss.
17. Framed Scotch: Sixteen Scotch stitches, each covering four threads, one-ply pearl #5.
18. Pearl Beads: Three rows of three in each corner
19. Zigzag Flat with Couching: Zigzag the first row over two, then three, then four, then three, then two; for the second row, cover four, then three, then two, then three, then four; use two-ply Persian. For Couching, use one-ply Japanese and one-ply embroidery floss.
20. Pyramid: (6 by 6) Two-ply Persian.
21. Continental: Two rows, two-ply Persian.

The Butterfly

To stitch the Butterfly, you will need the following tools and materials:
20" by 20" 14/1 Interlock canvas
12" by 12" 14/1 Interlock canvas
20" by 20" working stretcher bars
12" by 12" working stretcher bars
Masking tape
Tapestry needle

Sewing needle

Thumbtacks

15 Skeins #312 DMC Light Navy Blue embroidery floss

30 Skeins #334 DMC Medium Dark Baby Blue embroidery floss

8 Skeins #726 DMC Light Topaz embroidery floss

4 Skeins #780 DMC Dark Topaz embroidery floss

36 Skeins #869 Marlitt Brown rayon floss

2 Skeins #815 Anchor Pink rayon floss

4 Skeins #867 Anchor Yellow rayon floss

2 Skeins #838 Marlitt Blue rayon floss

3 Skeins #810 Anchor Kelly Green rayon floss

8 Skeins #1030 Anchor Willow Green rayon floss

5 Skeins #846 Marlitt Slate Gray Rayon Floss

1 Skein #801 Anchor Black rayon floss

1 Skein #818 DMC Baby Pink cotton #3 pearl

1 Skein #799 DMC Medium Delft Blue cotton #3 pearl

1 Skein #445 DMC Light Lemon cotton #3 pearl

1 Skein #5284 DMC Gold Metal floss

1 Skein #002HL Gold Kreinik Metallics medium #16 braid

1 Skein Gold Kreinik Japanese #7

Felt

Black leather or Ultrasuede

Brown leather or Ultrasuede

Matching brown sewing thread

Water soluble marking pen

15" by 15" stretcher bars for framing

15" by 15" frame

1. Bind all canvas edges with masking tape.

2. Use the marking pen to draw the foundation motif on the canvas. The circle should be 12" in diameter, and the large square should be 16" by 16". Flowers are about 2" wide by 3" tall.

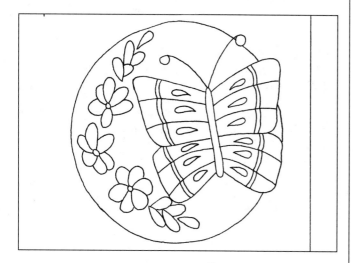

3. Use thumbtacks to mount the large piece of canvas on the stretcher bars.

4. Stitch the diamond motif with nine-ply embroidery floss, as indicated in the diagram.

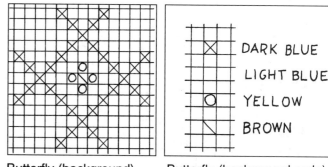

Butterfly (background)　　　　Butterfly (background code)

5. Stitch the flowers in Diagonal Mosaic with six-ply rayon floss.

6. Stitch the leaves in Mosaic with six-ply rayon floss.

7. Stitch the entire circle in Moorish II, with six-ply rayon floss.

8. Using two-ply Japanese metal and three-ply rayon floss, couch around the petals and leaves.

9. Make Bullion Knots in the center of each flower, using one-ply cotton Pearl.

10. Cut two 3/8" diameter circles from the felt.

11. Appliqué one circle at the tip of each antenna with sewing thread.

12. With one-ply #16 braid and one-ply DMC metal, couch along the side of the antenna, beginning in the middle of the felt circle, and working in a tight spiral. When the felt has been covered, continue couching toward the body of the butterfly. Repeat on the other side.

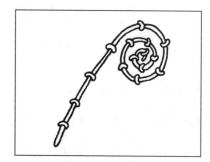

Butterfly (couching)

13. Remove the project from the working stretcher bars and mount onto bars that fit your frame (see the stapled method for framing projects, page 159).

14. Bind the edges of the smaller canvas with masking tape.

15. Mark all parts of the butterfly on the canvas.

16. Mount the project on working stretcher bars.

17. Cut twelve paisleys from the brown leather. Use matching thread to appliqué the leather onto the wings.

18. Using six-ply rayon, stitch the Willow Green on the wings of the butterfly. The right side is stitched in Diagonal Mosaic and the left is stitched in Reverse Diagonal Mosaic. Stitch as close to the appliquéd paisleys as possible. Do not stitch in the body area where the black leather will be attached.

19. Stitch the yellow areas on the wings in Continental using six-ply rayon.

20. Stitch Half Framed Scotch on the outside of each upper wing. Use six-ply rayon in Slate Gray, and use two-ply Black rayon for the framing.

21. For the lower wings, insert Diana in six-ply Gray rayon for the foundation and two-ply Black for the small, straight stitches.

22. Using one-ply Japanese metal and one-ply Black rayon, couch around each paisley.

23. Couch along the long lines on the wings in one-ply Kreinik metallic and one-ply black rayon. Start and stop at the edges of the wings and body. Do not couch into the area where black leather will be attached later.

24. Remove the canvas from your stretcher bars and cut out the butterfly, leaving 1/2" of bare canvas around the edges.

26. Use a hammer on a flat surface to pound the bare canvas to the underside of the stitches. Do not allow any bare canvas to show. Cut away any bulk in the body area, and do not turn canvas under in the area that will lie below the black leather.

27. With sewing thread and needle, use Herringbone stitches to attach the raw canvas to the back.

28. Use gray sewing threads to tack the sides of the upper and lower wings to the foundation canvas. Keep the tips of the wings free from the foundation, as the butterfly should bow on the foundation canvas. Take care not to snag the Moorish II stitches.

29. Tack the area to the canvas where the two sets of wings meet.

30. Cut a 40" piece of #16 braid, and make a two-ply cord (see Cords, page 156).

31. Use one-ply DMC metal to couch around the upper right wing, starting at the top of the body and working toward the middle. Repeat on the other side.

32. Make another cord, using a 30" length of #16 braid.

33. Couch around the lower right wing, beginning at the point where the two wings meet working towards the lower body. Repeat on the left side.

34. Cut the body from the black leather, and appliqué the body onto the butterfly.

35. Finish framing the foundation canvas.

Diamond Pillow

To create the diamond pillow, you will need the following tools and materials:

19" by 15" Interlock canvas
250 Strands #897 Lavender Paternayan Persian yarn
19" by 15" stretcher bars
#20 Tapestry needle
Masking tape
Thumbtacks
Marking pen
1 yard upholstery fabric
Sewing thread
Sewing needle
Cording
Fiber filling (for stuffing)

1. Bind all edges of the raw canvas with masking tape.

2. Mark the diamond motif on the canvas using a permanent marker. The diamond is 15" by 8-1/2", and the finished rectangle is 11" by 17".

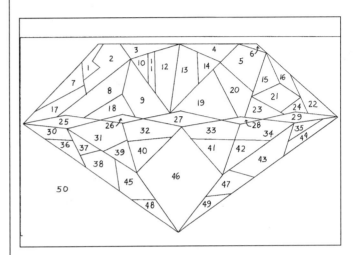

3. Use thumbtacks to attach the canvas to stretcher bars.

4. Follow the diagram and list of stitches to fill the canvas.

5. Stitch two rows of Tent on all four sides of the rectangle for finishing.

6. When finished, remove the canvas from the frame, and block the project, if needed.

7. Use 56" of upholstery fabric to create piping (see page 153), to fit around the project.

8. Pin the piping on the needlepoint and stitch together.

9. Cut a 12-1/4" by 18-1/4" rectangle of fabric.

10. Repeat step 8 and attach the piping to the rectangle of fabric.

11. Cut a 3-1/2" by 57-1/4" strip of fabric.

12. Stitch the two short ends together, using 5/8" seam allowance.

13. Pin the circle of fabric onto the piped needlepoint and stitch together.

14. Pin the other side of circle to the piped rectangle. Stitch together, leaving a small opening to turn the pillow right side out.

15. Turn and stuff with fiber filling.

16. Slip stitch the opening.

Stitch List:

1. Small Checker
2. Sturgeon Trail
3. OblongCross, workedhorizontally
4. Long Armed Cross
5. Double with CrossTied Gobelin
6. Surrey
7. Rep
8. Chevron
9. CrissCros Hungarian
10. Astrakhan Velvet
11. Chain
12. Staggering Flat
13. Interlocking Gobelin
14. Basketweave
15. Brick
16. Diagonal Mosaic
17. Scotch
18. Split Gobelin
19. Italian
20. Dillon
21. Double Knot
22. Woven Cross
23. Basketweave underside
24. Continental Gone Wrong
26. Continental
27. French Knots
28. Sprat
29. Plait
30. Mosaic
31. Triple Cross
32. Dutch
33. Gobelin Droit
34. Mosaic
35. Upright Cross
36. Darning
37. Horizontal Kalem
38. Framed Scotch
39. Bullion Knots
40. Cashmere
41. Diagonal Ray
42. Eugene
43. Milanese
44. Smyrna
45. Eye
46. Papermoon
47. Alternating Tent
48. Cross
49. Fishbone II
50. Flat, worked as a pattern (two-ply Persian)

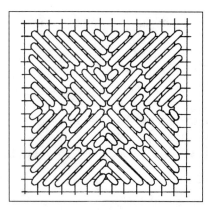

Diamond pillow (background)

Plaid Pillow

To create the plaid pillow, you will need the following tools and materials:

6 Strands #R10 Red Paternayan Persian yarn
40 Strands #733 Blue Paternayan Persian yarn
50 Strands #520 Green Paternayan Persian yarn
60 Strands #50 Black Paternayan Persian yarn
4 Strands #001 White Paternayan Persian yarn
1 Skein #701 Christmas Green DMC embroidery floss
1 Skein #666 Christmas Red DMC embroidery floss

1 Skein #334 Medium Dark Baby Blue DMC embroidery floss
1 Skein #310 Black DMC embroidery floss
1 Skein White DMC embroidery floss
15" by 15-1/2" 14/1 Interlock canvas
#20 Tapestry needle
6" by 6" 18/1 Interlock canvas
#24 Tapestry needle
Embroidery hoop
Masking tape
1/2 yard red velveteen
Red sewing thread
Marking pen
4 one-inch professional upholstery covered buttons

1. Bind all raw edges of the 14/1 canvas with masking tape.

2. Using Chottie's Plaid in two-ply Persian yarn, follow the count to stitch a 11" by 11-1/2" rectangle.

3. Stitch two rows of Continental on all four sides.

4. Block the needlepoint. It is imperative that plaid stripes be as straight as possible.

5. Bind all raw edges of the 18/1 canvas with masking tape.

6. Mark four 1-1/2" circles.

7. Stitch Chottie's Plaid in six-ply embroidery floss. It is best to stitch each button as though it were "placed" differently on the plaid.

8. Have an upholsterer finish the buttons for you.

9. Trim excess canvas on one of the 11" sides.

10. Cut a 1-1/2" by 12-1/2" rectangular strip of fabric.

11. Center the strip of fabric on the trimmed side of the needlepoint, matching right sides together.

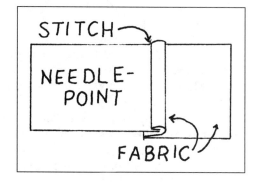

12. Stitch the pieces together by machine.

13. Turn the raw edge of the fabric under the needlepoint. Stitch-in-the-ditch.

14. Cut a rectangle of fabric measuring 6" by 12-1/2".

15. Lay the fabric right side up. Place the needlepoint overlapping the fabric to create a 5/8" seam allowance. Again, stitch-in-the-ditch.

16. Cut a rectangle to measure 17-1/2" by 12-1/2".

17. Pin the needlepoint and fabric together and stitch, leaving an opening for turning.

18. Turn the needlepoint right sides out.

19. Stitch the buttons on the needlepoint.

20. Stuff and slip stitch your opening.

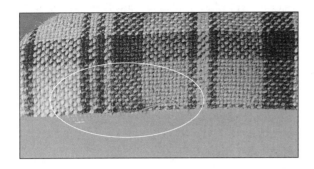

Use Chottie's Plaid with the following count:

2 Black	8 Black
3 Red	12 Green
2 Black	2 Black
12 Green	3 Red
8 Black	2 Black
2 Blue	12 Green
2 Black	8 Black
2 Blue	12 Blue
2 Black	2 Black
12 Blue	3 White
2 Black	2 Black
2 Blue	12 Blue
2 Black	8 Black
2 Blue	12 Green

For the buttons, use 18/1 interlock canvas with six-ply embroidery floss in needle

Scissors Charm

To create the scissors charm, you will need the following tools and materials:

2 Pieces 6" x 6" blue 18/1 Mono canvas
3 Skeins #840 Medium Brown Marlitt rayon
1 Skein #1140 Light Brown Marlitt rayon
1 Skein #812 Green Marlitt rayon
1 Skein #070 Green Kreinik fine braid (#8)
1 Skein #028 Gold Kreinik fine braid (#8)
2 Pieces of 6" by 6" White lining fabric
Fiber filling
#24 Tapestry needle
Masking tape

Note: Although the stitches on the canvas are straight, the seams lie on the true bias.

1. Bind all four edges of both canvas pieces with masking tape.
2. Find the exact middle of one canvas piece.
3. Using Kreinik #028 for the French Knot, #070 for the straight lines and Green Marlitt for the diagonal stitches, stitch Kathy.

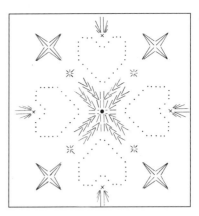

4. Using six-ply Marlitt Medium Brown, follow the count for the hearts.

5. Stitch the Tip of Leaf and Cross stitches that lie above the hearts. Use six-ply Marlitt Dark Brown for the Tip of Leaf and six-ply green for the Cross.
6. Make the Eyelet stitches in six-ply, Dark Brown yarn.
7. Diamond Eye I is stitched, following the first method, using Kreinik #070.
8. Lay the canvas pieces right sides together. Lay the fabric on each side of the two pieces of canvas. The fabric's right side should touch the canvas.
9. Stitch on the bias to make a 3" by 3" square. Leave one side open for turning.
10. Trim excess canvas, and turn the charm.
11. Stuff with filling. Turn the seam allowance in and stitch the charm closed.
12. Make a 16-ply cord using eight loops. See "Cords," page 156.
13. Attach the cord with slip stitches. To make the tassel and loop, whip one-ply Kreinik #070 around the cord.

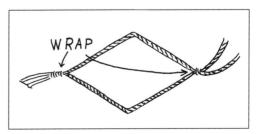

The Theater

To create this project, you will need the following tools and materials:

1 Strand #001 White Paternayan Persian yarn
1 Strand #050 Black Paternayan Persian yarn
2 Strands #104 Brown Paternayan Persian yarn
1 Strand #108 Green Black Paternayan Persian yarn
1 Strand #116 Dark Burnt Umber Paternayan Persian yarn
1 Strand #123 Light Burnt Umber Paternayan Persian yarn
22 Strands #126 Medium Light Burnt Umber
   Paternayan Persian yarn
34 Strands #132 Medium Uurnt Umber
   Paternayan Persian yarn
1 Strand #136 Beige Paternayan Persian yarn
2 Strands #138 Sun Tan Paternayan Persian yarn
1 Strand #140 Brown Paternayan Persian yarn
1 Strand #162 Dark Gray Paternayan Persian yarn
1 Strand #166 Light Gray Paternayan Persian yarn
1 Strand #210 Dark Rose Paternayan Persian yarn
1 Strand #234 Rose Paternayan Persian yarn
1 Strand #419 Saddle Brown Paternayan Persian yarn
20 Strands #445 Medium Ocher Paternayan Persian yarn
20 Strands #453 Light Ocher Paternayan Persian yarn
1 Strand #504 Dark Green Paternayan Persian yarn
1 Strand #528 Evergreen Paternayan Persian yarn
1 Strand #569 Green Paternayan Persian yarn
1 Strand #756 Light Blue Paternayan Persian yarn
1 Strand #783 Peacock Blue Paternayan Persian yarn
3 Strands #831 Light Pink Paternayan Persian yarn
1 Skein White DMC embroidery floss
1 Skein #310 Black DMC embroidery floss
1 Skein #319 Very Dark Pistachio Green
   DMC embroidery floss
1 Skein #322 Very Light navy Blue DMC embroidery floss
1 Skein #433 Medium Brown DMC embroidery floss
1 Skein #445 Light Lemon DMC embroidery floss
5 Skeins #471 VeryLlight avocado green
   DMC embroidery floss
3 Skeins #519 Medium sky Blue DMC embroidery floss
2 Skeins #543 Ultra very Light Beige Brown
   DMC embroidery floss
1 Skein #666 Christmas Red DMC embroidery floss
1 Skein #739 Ultra Very Light Tan DMC embroidery floss
1 Skeins #801 Coffee Brown DMC embroidery floss
1 Skein #826 Medium Blue DMC embroidery floss
1 Skein #898 Very Dark Coffee Brown
   DMC embroidery floss
2 Skeins #939 Very Dark Navy Blue DMC embroidery floss
2 Skeins #3033 Very Light Mocha Brown
   DMC embroidery floss
4 Skeins #3371 Black Brown DMC embroidery floss
2 Skeins #3829 Very Dark Old Gold DMC
   embroidery floss
1 Skein White DMC #3 Pearl Floss

1 Skein #311 Medium Navy Blue DMC #3 Pearl floss
1 Skein #310 Black DMC #5 PearlFloss
1 Skein #825 Dark Blue DMC #5 Pearl floss
1 Skein #995 Dark Electric Blue DMC #5 Pearl floss
1 Skein #996 Medium Electric Blue DMC #5 Pearl floss
18" White Mohair
1/4" Small chain
2 small silk flowers (plastic removed)
1/2" Fraze
6 blue seed beads
1 yellow seed bead
Pink felt
22" by 13" 14/1 Interlock canvas
22" by 13" working stretcher bars
10" by 10" 20/1 Mono canvas
16" by 9" stretcher bars for framing
16" by 9" frame
Marking pen
Masking tape
#20 Tapestry needle
6" Embroidery hoop

1. Draw the scene on the canvas with a marking pen.

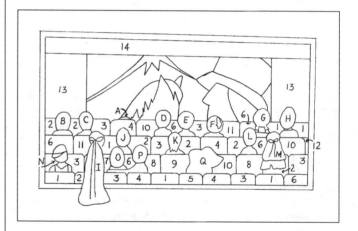

2. Bind all raw canvas edges with masking tape.

3. Attach the canvas to the stretcher bars to be worked.

4. Follow the diagram and the number sequence of the theater. Use one-ply #445 and #453 Persian yarn for the seats. Do not stitch any seats near the area where the silhouette will be placed.

5. Follow the diagram and the stitching list for the audience.

6. At number 13 in the diagram, stitch Darning in a downward direction in one-ply #132 Persian.

7. Stitch one-ply #739 embroidery floss randomly in the curtain area.

8. Repeat step 7 using #433 embroidery floss.

9. Using #216 and #132 Persian, stitch Beau Ridge for number 14 in the diagram.

10. On the screen, stitch the horse in Satin, using #3033 DMC for the body, and #3829 for the mane.

11. For the man on the screen, use the following colors: face, #543 DMC; hair, #801 DMC; hat, #939 DMC; brim, #322 DMC.

12. Also in Satin, stitch the man's eyes and the horse's eyes in black floss.

13. The mountain is #471 DMC, with white for snow.

14. To achieve a variegated look, #519 DMC was placed in direct sunlight for several days until the ends of the skein became sun bleached. Stitch Satin as usual.

15. Cover any raw edges of the Mono canvas with masking tape, and place the canvas in a hoop.

16. Stitch the silhouette, following the diagram.

17. Follow the instructions in Chapter 2 for attaching one canvas on another.

18. Stitch the seats that surround the silhouette.

19. Remove the canvas from the working stretcher bars and block as needed.

20. Frame the project as directed, using the stapled method, as found on page 159.

Stitch list for the Theater:

1. Basketweave
2. Mosaic
3. Encroached Gobelin
4. Reverse Tent
5. Basketweave, underside
6. Continental
7. Alternating Tent
8. Horizontal Kalem
9. Continental Gone Wrong
10. Diagonal Mosaic
11. Knitting I
12. Slanted Gobelin
13. Darning
14. Beau Ridges

Stitch list for the Audience:

A. Hair: Satin, two-ply #140 Persian

B. Hair: Satin, one-ply #162 and #166 Persian; Shirt: Continental, two-ply #756 Persian, Couching, one-ply #826 floss; Skin: Continental, two-ply #831 Persian

C. Hair: French Knots, two-ply #108 Persian, Chinese Loops, one-ply #108 and #162 Persian; Shirt: Continental, two-ply #528 Persian; Skin: Continental, two-ply #831 Persian

D. Hair: Satin, two-ply #104 Persian; Shirt: Continental, one-ply #311 #3 Pearl; Skin: Continental, two-ply #831 Persian

E. Hair: Bullion Knots, two-ply #132 Persian; Dress: Continental, two-ply #504 Persian; Chain attached

F. Hair: Cut Turkey, nine-ply #3371 floss; silk flowers attached; Dress: Continental, nine-ply #666 floss, two strands Fraze attached

G. Hair: Couching and loops, one-ply #138 Persian, Scalp: appliquéd circle of pink felt; Bows: one-ply #234 Persian; Dress: Continental, two-ply #831 Persian; Couching, one-ply #210 Persian; Skin: Continental, two-ply #831 Persian

H. Hair: French Knots, two-ply #116 and #123 Persian; Shirt: Continental, two-ply #050; Skin: Continental, two-ply #831 Persian

I. Hair: Loops (Diagrams 2 and 3) nine-ply #310 floss, Bow: one-ply #996 and #995 #3 pearl

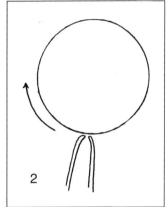 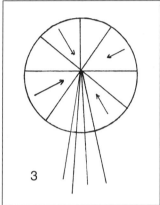

J. Hair: French Knots, one-ply #310 and #825 #5 Pearl; Shirt: Continental, one-ply white #3 Pearl

K. Skin on Head: Appliquéd small oval felt; Hair: Satin, one-ply #104 and #132 Persian; Shirt: Continental, one-ply #234 and #001

L. Hair: Satin with Bullion Knots, two-ply #136 Persian; Dress: Continental (brushed after stitching) one-ply white mohair; Skin: Continental, two-ply #831 Persian; six beads sewn at neck

M. Hair: Loops (Diagrams 2 and 4), nine-ply #3371 floss; Bow: one-ply #783 Persian

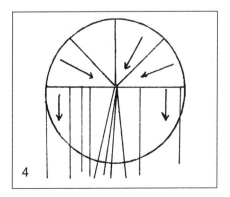

N. Hat: Spider Web (Diagram 5), six-ply #445 floss; Needle weaving (Diagram 6 and 7) six-ply #445 floss; yellow bead sewn on; Hair: Satin, two-ply #419 Persian; Skin, Continental, two-ply #831 Persian: Shirt: Needle weaving, six-ply #319 floss

O. Hair: Satin, two-ply #104 Persian; Dress: Continental, two-ply #569 Persian

P. Hair: Satin, two-ply #138 Persian; Shirt: Continental, two-ply #001 Persian

Q. Silhouette: Attached 20/1 canvas, Continental six-ply #3371 and #898 floss

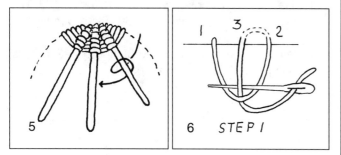

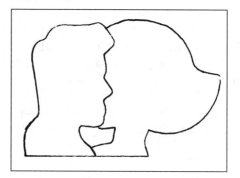

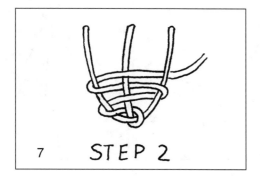

Chapter Six

Cleaning and Keeping Needle Art

Whether you are an old hand or a novice at stitching, at some point, your work will need to be cleaned. Everyday household dirt and wear are hard on embroidery—it is extremely important that you know how to best remove soils and stains. This chapter refers more to work that has been recently stitched—not family heirlooms or museum pieces, but new needlepoint used in daily living. Anyone who works with needlepoint will sooner or later have to deal with the issue of cleaning the needlework. Some surface dirt can be removed by vacuuming with a fine net on the nozzle. More deeply embedded dirt can be removed by applying a thin layer of magnesium carbonate over the work with a baby brush and lifting it off a few hours later. Take special care when trying to remove grease. It is very easy to cause permanent damage.

When you must remove a stain, first determine whether water will damage the work. If water has not removed all of the dirt, whatever remains could become deeply embedded, only to cause greater damage to the piece than if it were left alone. Never immerse metal threads. Silk, wool and cotton tested for color fastness can be immersed in water. To test colorfastness, wet a cotton ball with water and press it very firmly to the back of the needlepoint, to see whether the cotton picks up any of the colors of the yarn dyes. If color is present, you can be sure the colors in the piece will run. If you are not sure, do not wash the piece. Synthetic and silk yarns should not be steamed, since the heat can damage the fibers.

Always use soft water to wash needlepoint. A high calcium content can cause white materials to become gray. If available, rainwater gives good results. Soft soaps, such as Lissapol-9 and mild liquid detergents are good for needlepoint. Ivory makes a good, mild soap. Many museums wash their Oriental rugs with Ivory bar soap.

A recipe from 1880 for cleaning Berlin work called for 1/4 pound of soft soap and 1/2 pint of gin. It makes me wonder how the wool stood up. An old English method requires rubbing white bread on the needlepoint. Many products on the modern market claim to clean needlepoint satisfactorily. For the best results, make a small project and test it for yourself.

Between blocking and stitching, it is only recommended that a piece be cleaned if it is soiled (note precautions in Chapter 2 under Yarns, and Chapter 4 under Blocking). Oil from your hands and everyday dirt can be embedded into the fibers. Also, any chemicals you may have used in the stitching process could require removal. Years ago, I used break-away canvas to create Blackwork on a white fabric. After marking the canvas with a permanent marker, I also sprayed clear acrylic paint to ensure the marker would not run when the canvas was removed. After removing the canvas from the embroidery, I quickly mounted the fabric onto a set of stretcher bars and inserted it into a frame. A couple of years later, the acrylic paint caused the fabric to turn yellow. While the embroidery is still on the wall, the piece is ruined. All of this could have been avoided if I had washed the entire piece with soap.

Washing needlepoint rinses away some sizing. Sizing holds the canvas straight and stiff. Without it, the grid won't keep its shape after it has been blocked. Once the canvas has been stitched, and the sizing has been washed out, it cannot be replaced.

To wash needlepoint, add a pinch of salt and detergent to 96-degree water. Dip the piece up and down. The movement of water through the fibers cleans the needlepoint. If you must rub, do so on the back—not the front. Rubbing could fuzz the stitches. Rinse several times to remove all soap from the project. Roll the needlepoint in a large white towel to absorb the excess water. This step may need to be repeated. Block the work as needed, using rust-resistant T-pins. Place the piece in a warm place, so that it can dry quickly. Never place needlepoint in direct sunlight.

Items such as chair seats require special care. Try to avoid removing the needlepoint from the chair. After the cleaning and blocking processes have been completed, the shape of the embroidery could change. Also, when replaced on the seat frame, the creases would be different from before and the old, crushed stitches would look unsightly. If the embroidery is a few years old, do not expect the colors to look new. Colors fade with use, and chair seats can receive a good deal of use! To clean, try a dry cleaner spray. Follow the directions but do not saturate the needlepoint. Saturating the work means you have to block it again, and that is something you want to avoid.

If, after you have immersed a piece of needlework in water, you notice that dyes or inks have begun to run— do not panic. They can be removed. Soak the entire project in cold water for several hours—overnight, if you can. To remove the excess water from the canvas, hit the needlepoint against the side of a tub, or swing it in the air. Remove as much water as you can, using centrifugal force—much like the spin cycle in your washing machine. You may want to test it with a tissue to determine whether the colors are still running. If you notice a stain after it has dried, use 3% hydrogen peroxide—and use caution. If the stain persists, use lemon juice.

Three percent hydrogen peroxide is great for removing mildew, as is sodium perforate. Apply a small amount to the area and let it sit in the sun for a very short period, no more than one hour. After sunning the needlepoint, run cold water through the treated areas until the chemicals have been removed. Treating only the mildew is best. Never apply more hydrogen peroxide on the wool than necessary. Remember, too, that sunlight is hard on colors. When finished, rinse in clear water. If your needlework has any sort of odor after having been cleaned, allow it to air out a bit.

Oil-based stains are best removed with a dry-cleaning liquid. I really like a product called Energine. Dip a cotton ball into the Energine and push the cotton into the spot. Release. Continue dabbing until the oil has been removed. To prevent the stitches from fuzzing, do not rub in circles.

Rust can be removed with oxalic acid, a chemical used for developing photos. Apply the acid on the stain. Rinse several times in water to remove the acid from the fibers.

Before trying to remove a stain, first examine the spot. The appearance, odor and feel can help identify the problem. If the stain is red, chances are it is blood. A darker spot than the rest of the wool could be an oil-based stain. How the stain sits on the needlepoint also offers a clue as to its origin. Ink penetrates, while paint lies on the surface. Oil runs along the threads with the least twist. In needlepoint, oil runs in the direction of the stitches. Odors offer another clue. If you think the spot is oil-based, verify your hypothesis by the smell. The feel is just as important as the appearance and odor. Texture of a stain helps identify the problem. Egg can be recognized by its stiffness. Gum is sticky. Paint can be rough or smooth.

There are two major categories for stains, those removed with dry solvents and those removed with water solutions.

Water-removed stains include glue, egg and sugar. Dry solution stains are ink, gum and paint.

When you use water solutions to remove stains, keep in mind that lubrication is very important. Move the piece in the water to help remove dirt—this compares to the agitation of your washing machine. The water passing through the yarns and fibers flushes the soil particles out of the yarns. Yes, soap is needed, but the water itself is most important. Dirt does not dissolve, but lifts off the surface.

A couple of years ago, I had my living room chairs cleaned. The men who did the job wanted to clean my needlepoint dining room chairs. One man suggested I use a brush and rub the stitches clean. Wrong! A brush would only have made the Tent stitches fuzzy. Yes, the wool would be clean, but the chair seats would never be the same.

With care, your needlepoint work should rarely need much cleaning. While you are stitching a project, store it in a pillowcase when not stitching. If it is mounted on a floor frame, cover it with white fabric. Needlepoint should not be covered when mounted in a frame. Nevertheless, protect it from tobacco smoke, cooking fumes and odors in the air. When cleaning, vacuum your needlepoint every other month.

Try to discourage people from touching pictures and pillows. Yes, this is hard when people want to praise your work, but try to keep it to a minimum. Wash your hands before beginning to stitch. Your hands carry plenty of dirt. For items such as dining room chairs, any spills should be cleaned up as soon as possible. Do not use plastic covers for the chairs. Any condensation under the plastic could cause mildew or rot the wool. Do not use Scotchguard® or similar treatments on wool.

Rules for stain removal on needlework:

1. Treat the stain promptly. If possible, treat before the stain dries.

2. Before using the stain remover, test a sample. The seam allowance of a pillow or picture can come in handy in cases such as this.

3. If the entire piece needs to be cleaned, do not spot clean. This could leave a water ring.

4. When in doubt about what to use, apply only cold water. Let it dry before using another method.

5. Always work on the underside of the stain to avoid driving the problem completely through the work.

6. If you have a doubt about a method for stain removal, do not use it.

7. Test the effects of water or cleaning solutions before attempting the entire piece.

8. Chlorine bleach, dry bleach for colors or other bleaches should not be used. Never use these on wool or silk. They could cause yellowing or graying.

9. If you are using a commercial product, follow the directions carefully. Read the directions every time you use the product.

10. Woolite® contains bleach. While it is great for fine hand washables, it is not the right product for needlepoint.

Stains removed with solvents:

Dry Solvents	Water-based Solvents
Ball point pen	Animal products
Black carbon	Beer
Dry inks	Berry stains
Gum	Blood
Marking pens	Coffee
Nail polish	Cream
Oils	Egg
Paints	Fruit juices
Plastic-based adhesives	Gelatin
	Ice cream
	Leather dyes
	Liquor
	Milk
	Soft drinks
	Tea
	Tobacco
	Walnut stains
	Wet writing ink

Index of Stitches

CREATE SPECTACULAR PROJECTS WITH EASE

Twined Rag Rugs
Tradition in the Making
by Bobbie Irwin
Create wonderful, durable heirloom rugs, and benefit from increased dexterity and the rhythmic relaxation of twining. All you need is some inexpensive equipment, simple household tools, scrap fabric, and the easy-to-follow instructions in this book. The most intricate patterns are easy to learn. Patterns and instructions for nine samplers and ten full-size rugs are included.

Softcover • 8-1/4 x 10-7/8
128 pages • 100 illustrations
250 color photos
Item# WEAV • $19.95

Creating Texture with Textiles!
by Linda McGehee
Written for all levels of sewers, this user-friendly guide features step-by-step instructions to create spectacular one-of-a-kind designs on fabric with the use of any sewing machine. Techniques include piecing, spiraling, applique, piping, cording, embroidery, beading, among others.

Softcover • 8-1/4 x 10-7/8
128 pages • 20 illustrations
200 color photos
Item# TWT • $21.95

**Memory Crafting:
Beyond the Scrapbook**
130 Projects to Sew, Stitch & Craft
by Judi Kauffman
Noted crafter Judi Kauffman has created over 130 ways to preserve precious memories in displayable projects. From snow globes and paperweights to jewelry and pillows, each of these projects offers several options and simple techniques using popular techniques.

Softcover • 8-1/4 x 10-7/8
128 pages • 75 illustrations
100 color photos
Item# CMSC • $19.95

**Mary Mulari Appliques
With Style**
Designs & Techniques with Fresh Attitude
by Mary Mulari
Noted sewing teacher and author Mary Mulari presents basic how-to information, complete with step-by-step instructions and illustrations. Mary shares tips on choosing the right fabric, preparing your sewing machine, assembling and marking applique designs, as well as the basics of satin stitching.

Softcover • 8-1/4 x 10-7/8
144 pages • 200 illustrations
16-page color section
Item# MEAC • $15.95

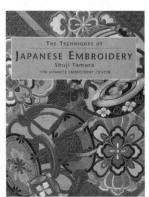

The Techniques of Japanese Embroidery
by Shuji Tamura
Create beautiful traditional Japanese embroideries using detailed illustrations and diagrams for more than 50 stitching techniques. Designs range from flowers, trees, and birds to more abstract works with information on how to create curves, angles, and texture. Metal threads are an integral part of the designs.

Softcover • 8-3/8 x 10-7/8
128 pages • 150 illustrations
90 color photos
Item# TJE • $23.95

Fabric Landscapes by Machine
*Decorative Stitching Styles
for Quilted Scenes*
by Linda Crone
Noted landscape stitcher Linda Crone guides you through the process with quick & easy instructions - basic supplies, decorative stitches and finishing touches. Stitch landscapes on garments, tote bags, purses, pillows, greeting cards, wall hangings, and picture frames. Patterns for sample scenes included.

Softcover • 8-1/4 x 10-7/8
128 pages
100 color photos
Item# LDMA • $19.95
